Blood on the Ve

Blood on the Veldt

The Anglo–Zulu War of 1879

ILLUSTRATED

James Grant

LEONAUR

Blood on the Veldt
The Anglo-Zulu War of 1879
by James Grant

ILLUSTRATED

FIRST EDITION

Leonaur is an imprint of Oakpast Ltd

Copyright in this form © 2020 Oakpast Ltd

ISBN: 978-1-78282-952-2 (hardcover)
ISBN: 978-1-78282-953-9 (softcover)

http://www.leonaur.com

Publisher's Notes

Contents

CHAPTER 1
Introductory

Before detailing the original cause of this, in many ways, disastrous strife, it may not be out of place to glance briefly at that which is but little known, namely, the past history of the Zulus, whose king was so lately resident among us—a people of whom we have heard much, and are likely to hear more; and who, it is not impossible, may eventually become a portion of Her Majesty's subjects in South Africa.

Zululand is the region north-east of Natal, extending to Delagoa Bay, and has an area of 10,000 square miles, with a black population of 150,000, the most warlike of all the Kaffir tribes. "Zulu," in the native language, is a word signifying "heaven," and was adopted by the tribe at the outset of its victorious career. Cetewayo, the late king, in his real character, almost rivalled his predecessor Dingaan, in cruelty, and Chaka, in military talent of its own kind.

About the year 1780 the Zulus were a race who found a meagre livelihood on the shores of the Mozambique Channel, and in the north and east of what is now known as Natal. Warlike by nature, athletic, tall and well-formed, they surpass most African tribes in ordinary intelligence, but are superstitious, savage and cruel; yet they readily enough permitted British subjects to settle in their domains near Port Natal, and even assisted them in cultivating the land. They have long known the use of iron, and how to point their deadly *assegais* with it, and also of firearms, which they obtained from American traders. Their chief articles of commerce are ivory, gold-dust, indigo, cotton and silk, pearls and corals, and British goods are chiefly required in barter.

Towards the close of the last century, we are told by Sir T. Shepstone (in his Cape of Good Hope Report), the two countries at present known as Zululand and Natal were thickly populated by many native tribes, closely located together, and intermarrying with each other, living in peace and amity, possessing flocks and herds, and cultivating the soil from which they drew sustenance. Each tribe had its own chief—a patriarch—possessing the powers of life and death.

The Zulus were then an inconsiderable tribe, occupying only a small portion of the country near the White Umvolosi River, and were tributary to the Umtitwa, a powerful tribe holding the country now called Zululand.

Jobe, chief of the Umtitwa, had two sons, and when old age came upon him, he made arrangements for the succession. To Tana, the elder, he assigned a royal *kraal* as a residence; but Tana, with his younger brother, Gondongwana, began to plot against the life of their father, who now resolved to put them to death. Tana was slain, but Gondongwana escaped, with a wound from a double-barbed *assegai*. It was dressed by his sister, who assisted him in his flight, and gave him a particular *kaross*, or mantle.

His personal history occasioned the great changes in the destiny of the immense native population occupying the country from the Zambesi to St John's River, and led to Natal becoming a British colony. His adventures, escapes, and perils, as he wandered about, would make a large volume. He eventually made himself chief of the Umtitwa power, and, in compliment to his wonderful history, he was designated Dingiswayo, or the Wanderer.

He no sooner found himself established as chief than he introduced the principles of military organisation which he had learned while wandering among the white men for some fifteen years. The chief of the then small Zulu tribe had an illegitimate son called Chaka, who was born in 1787, and was energetic and talented, but gave offence to the family of his father by the airs he assumed, and he was eventually compelled to enter one of Dingiswayo's regiments as a soldier, about 1805, and won a high reputation in tribal war.

After Chaka had been long enough in Dingiswayo's army to master the system introduced by that chief, his father died, and he became chief of the Zulus in 1810. His warriors in war fought with the heroism of desperation, well aware that after the fighting was over, they would all have to undergo the terrible ordeal of "The Coward's Bush." Then it was that Chaka was wont to review them on return from an expedition, and there it was that he dealt out praise or blame.

Drawing the regiments up in a huge semicircle, he made them march past in succession, and, as each passed a certain spot, the deadly order was issued, "Bring forth your cowards!"

Then all who had, or were supposed to have, failed in battle were brought forth, and put to death on the spot. He created an Imperial Guard of 15,000 warriors, who were ready at an hour's notice to march fifty miles, and "eat up" a town or tribe in two days. Having heard something of the Battle of Waterloo, he said to Mr. Nathaniel Isaacs, who visited him in 1825:

> Yes, there are only two chiefs in the world: my brother George, he is King of the Whites; and I, Chaka, am King of the Blacks. (*The Zulus and the British Frontiers.*)

By this time, in self-defence, the neighbouring tribes had been compelled to adopt the new military system, which so completely baffled ours at Isandhlwana and elsewhere, and many battles took place on every side, till eventually Chaka became—after killing the king who had shown him such hospitality, and exterminating half his people—sole and despotic monarch of what might be deemed a kingdom. As a sort of sacrifice to the manes of his mother, whom he conceived his father had ill-used, he had a massacre, which lasted a fortnight, and was witnessed by Isaacs, the Natal trader, who averred that 10,000 people perished. One of his palaces had its name changed to the "Place of Slaughter," to commemorate the fact of his there, putting to death a whole regiment of married soldiers, with their wives and children, because they had been defeated in battle.

Chaka, the uncle of Cetewayo, was now growing old, and his brother, Dingaan, put him to death in 1828, when he was in the act of giving an audience to an Amapondo deputation Dingaan, who succeeded, was only a modification of his brother, and, to avoid starvation and the other horrors of insecurity, some of the Amapondos and other tribes became Zulus, and Natal was transformed, from a peaceful and cultivated country, into a wilderness, in which the remnants of the denizens were always killing or being killed.

The arrival there of the emigrant Boers in 1837-8 introduced a new element into the politics of the country, and a fresh influence upon the Zulu population. When the Boers came, they found the subjects of Dingaan, King of the Zulus, occupying the whole of the upper part of the Tugela Valley, including the lower portion of the Mooi, Bushman's, and Buffalo Rivers, down to where Fort Buckingham stands now; while from that point to the sea the left bank only of the Tugela was occupied, because the inhabitants had been driven away by order of Dingaan, to prevent them from fraternising with the European settlers.

Dingaan, in heart as treacherous and savage as his predecessor, became incensed by the trespasses of the Dutch Boers upon what he deemed his territories, and began to scheme vengeance.

He invited M. Retief (whose family is still in Natal) the Dutch leader, with all his commando, to the number of sixty—all principal persons—to a dinner of friendship, to celebrate a treaty of alliance; and on pretext of Dingaan's anxiety that his white guests should take an active part in the festivities, they were requested *not* to bring their muskets; so the whole party—though previously warned by Thomas Halstead, an Englishman, of meditated treachery—went into the presence of the royal savage to return no more.

Sir William Harris, of the Bombay Engineers says:

During the interview, 3,000 Zulu warriors, standing up to dance, formed a ring round them, and for a time alternately retreated and advanced in the customary manner, until gradually pressing closer, they at length, upon a signal made by Dingaan, while the farmers were in the act of quaffing malt liquors, which had been liberally handed round, rushed with one accord upon their defenceless victims. The Dutchmen were dragged about half a mile across the river by the hair of the head, and their leader having been first ostentatiously butchered, the Zulus fell upon and despatched the rest—knocking out the brains of some with their war clubs, impaling and twisting the necks of others. Halstead, unable to quiet his own apprehensions, had concealed in his coat-sleeve an open clasp-knife, with which he stabbed two of the warriors who were preparing to seize him, and for this achievement, after having been made the spectator of the horrible massacre of all his hapless companions, he was skinned alive, and put to death by means of the most revolting and barbarous cruelties.

Encouraged by this, Dingaan resolved to cut off the British settlers, whose presence had been encouraged by Chaka, and he despatched an overwhelming force against them. The officer above quoted, in his *Expedition into Southern Africa*, says:

In the dead of the night of the 17th February, 10,000 savages dashed *pêle-mêle* into the sleeping camp, arousing its inmates with whoop and yell, and drove off 20,000 head of cattle, after butchering some six hundred souls, without reference to age or sex, barbarously cutting off the breasts of the women, and crowning the massacre by dashing out the brains of the helpless children against the wheels of the waggons.

Among all the Europeans now went forth the cry for revenge, and no white man disregarded it for hundreds of miles around. In April, 1838, impatient for action, 400 mounted Boers, under Piet Uys, marched upon Unkunkinglove, and found the whole Zulu Army drawn up on the heights for its defence, with two divisions advantageously posted in that form which proved fatal to our troops—a crescent—with a reserve in the rear.

Some of the horses took fright at the clatter of *assegais* on shields and the whoops and yells of the Zulus, and eventually the Boers were routed. The aged Piet Uys perished while endeavouring to save a comrade. His son, a boy of twelve years, fought bravely, and perished by his side, and both fell covered with wounds. On this same day the few Natal settlers who remained, under a Scotsman named Biggar, marched, 900 strong, to cooperate with the Boers, though only half that number had arms and ammunition, and while attacking a post on a bare bleak hill were suddenly surrounded by the Zulu Army 12,000 strong. The Natal men then threw themselves into a circle, the spearmen forming its outer face, the musketeers within, and after a bloody struggle of several hours' duration the Zulus broke in, two-thirds of the settlers were slain, Biggar and thirteen other leaders perishing among the number.

But Dingaan's career was drawing to a close, as half the Zulu tribe revolted against him under Panda, his brother, and joined the Dutch, against whom he prepared to take the field, with a large force, among which were a hundred warriors finely mounted and armed with muskets as well as *assegais*.

Leisurely gathering their forces together, under Andreas Pretorius, of Graaff Reinet, the Europeans prepared for vengeance and the demolition of the Zulu nation. He had 600 horse and four pieces of cannon, with which he encamped on the night of the 15th December, within a *laager* formed of waggons, and within a short distance of Unkunkinglove, and 10,000 warriors surrounded him before dawn. After a succession of terrible onsets, in which 5,000 natives perished, the Zulus were repulsed. They were mown down by the cannon and musketry of the Boers, and their power was effectually broken, while the casualties of the Dutch, as given by Sir William Harris, were only three farmers wounded, including Pretorius.

Dingaan set fire to his thatched capital and fled to the Amaswazi, a hostile native power in the north. They received him courteously, and then murdered him in the night. This expedition of Pretorius is still called by the Boers *Der Volks Raid*, as they deem it the Marathon or Bannockburn of Natal.

Panda was now proclaimed King of the Zulus in 1840, and at once assumed the government, if such it can be called, and for some years subsequently he had the good sense to prefer trading to fighting, and by the advice of the Colonial authorities relinquished many of the savage and despotic habits of his ancestors, and confirmed the territorial grant of Natal to the Boers.

A portion of the people who originally accompanied him into Cape Colony on his revolt, went back with him, but a large section, though they had fought on his side, and had contributed to his being made king, refused to do so, as they preferred the protection of the Boers to being any longer Zulu subjects.

They were about 100,000 in number—the aboriginal inhabitants of the country, embracing the first opportunity that offered itself to them of occupying their ancient homes without being subject to Zulu rule. The rapidity with which events succeeded each other prevented many from joining their respective tribes at the time, so that migration from the Zulu country of individuals and families connected with these tribes, was very considerable for several years after Panda became king.

He killed only as many of his people as was necessary to impose order among the rest, and, dying in 1872, was succeeded by his son Cetewayo, who was duly installed in power by Sir Theophilus—then Mr.— Shepstone, the Representative of the British Government, which now ordained that no Zulu should be put to death without a fair trial, and that the king's sanction should be obtained before the final sentence of the law was put in force.

But the son of Panda, while assenting, dissembled. He commenced to re-organise an army, which had become somewhat demoralised by the timid policy of his father. He collected all the old regiments and formed them into new ones, and strengthened the bonds of discipline, order, and duty among them. In a very short time that discipline, such as it was, and enforced by torture and death, became perfect, while its mobility remained as remarkable as ever. Such was the army of Cetewayo, in 1878. Captain Hallam Parr asks:

> Against whom was this formidable engine to be used? Was it for his amusement that Cetewayo had turned, like a savage Frederick the Great, his nation into soldiers? Was it necessary,

in order to resist the Swazis or keep down the Tongas, that he should keep up an army of 50,000 men, or had he been fired by ambition and bitten by the same lust of conquest as Chaka? I may venture to say that all South Africans and all those who have made the burning questions of South Africa their study, with very few exceptions, think the last explanation is the one which discovers the policy of the Zulu king.

Prior to entering on the story of the war it may not be out of place to give a description of the weapons with which this formidable army was equipped, the weapons our soldiers had to encounter.

The word *assegai*, as we have elsewhere shown, does not belong to the vernacular, but comes from the Moorish *sagaie*, a dart, and the Zulu name for the weapon is *umkonto*. The shaft—which has an average length of five feet, and is as thick as a slender walking-stick—is cut from the *assegai* tree, the fibre of which is not unlike mahogany. It is brittle, yet elastic, and gives the short spear that peculiar vibration on which much of its accuracy when launched depends.

If awkwardly thrown, the shaft on entering the ground is apt to break off above the blade, a circumstance which was turned to advantage by one celebrated Zulu chief.

SIR THEOPHILUS SHEPSTONE.

We are told that:

Before joining battle, he made his followers cut half-way through the staff just above its junction with the metal head. The consequence was that when the spear went home into a human body the shaft remained intact, but if it struck a shield, a tree, or the ground, it snapped, and became useless to the enemy.

The *assegai* heads are usually blade-shaped, but some are barbed—even double-barbed—while others are a mere spike. In the first form a ridge always runs along the centre of the metal, which is concave on one side and convex on the other, as the Zulu has an idea that from this peculiarity of shape, the blade will act as the feathers of an arrow do. The blades are made of soft iron, so that when blunted by use they may be sharpened more readily. The iron is fitted into the wood, not the wood upon the iron.

By making the tang of the blade red-hot, it can be forced into the thickest end of the shaft, which is then secured by a thong of wet hide, that contracts as it dries and becomes strong like a ferrule of steel.

There are two kinds of *assegais*; one for launching at a distance, the other, for stabbing—the invention of Chaka—has a blade that is long and straight. With this deadly weapon the Zulu kills alike his enemy and his game, and so sharp is it that he can shave his head with it. The warriors of Chaka carried very large shields, as those of Cetewayo did, but they had only one *assegai*, instead of the handful with which they were wont to go into action. Hence, they were trained to move more swiftly, to fight in compact masses, and to close with the enemy.

Hope of reward, with the certainty of what awaited them at "The Coward's Bush" in case of failure, made them quite invincible when opposed to neighbouring tribes; but with their conflicts with the Dutch Boers other conditions arose, and the old *assegais* and the old mode of fighting were resumed, and in his army Cetewayo reverted to the use of the stabbing *assegai*, and with it the use of the musket In defiance of the prohibitory laws concerning the importation of firearms into Southern Africa, as we have already stated, as many as 400,000 rifles, many of them breech-loaders, have passed into the hands of the natives.

Cetewayo is known to have acquired many thousand rifles through St Lucia and Delagoa Bays; some of them came from Genoa, and some from Birmingham, especially when affairs were looking black in Afghanistan, and we were on the verge of a war with Russia.

The war clubs used by the Zulus and other Kaffir tribes vary from

INTERIOR OF A ZULU KRAAL ON THE TUGELA RIVER.

fourteen inches to six feet in length, and are furnished with a knob—hence the name *knobkerie*. The shorter is hung at the girdle, and is used as a club at close quarters, or to be hurled after game, but the Zulus give a preference to the long-shafted weapon. They are usually made of acacia wood and some of the horn of the white rhinoceros.

The defensive weapon of the Zulu is a shield made of ox hide, oval in form, and quite impervious to the passage of an *assegai*. This completely covers him from head to foot. A central stick, long enough to project beyond each end, is within the shield, and forms the grasp for the left hand, while daubs of black, white, or red *denote* the particular "regiment" to which they belong. Married soldiers alone can wear the *isikokko*, or head ring (in which Cetewayo occasionally figured in England); they, too, carry white shields, while the unmarried carry black, when by valour in the field they have earned the right to bear one at all. A writer says:

> The shields are not the private property of the recipients, but of the king, who claims by right the hides of all the cattle in the military *kraals*. Each hide is supposed to furnish two shields—a large one for war and a smaller one for the chase. A number of men are constantly employed in converting hides into shields, and special store-huts are set aside for them when made.

Thus, as these were the king's property, it often happened that young warriors, whose addresses had been paid to the girls of a tribe with which they had been fighting, sent home their shields from the field of battle by their friends, and returned with their late foes to prosecute their love suits.

Prior to our war with him, Cetewayo showed much dexterity and some diplomacy in the way in which he played off the Boers of the Transvaal against the Natal Government; and the estimate formed of his character by Captain Parr, in his *Sketch*, is that he was an able, but unscrupulous and extremely ambitious savage, commanding n strong standing army of young warriors, all eager for battle, and whose presence and existence menaced with ruin the border farms and homesteads which were but within a short distance of his capital

Preluding the war with Cetewayo, were the first operations against his ally Sekukuni, during the February and October of 1878.

So far back as August, 1876, an unsuccessful attack had been made on his mountain fortress, of which detailed accounts are given in *The Transvaal of Today* by Mr. Aylward, who belonged to the Lydenberg corps of foreign volunteers, enrolled by the Dutch Republic, under Captain Van Schlieckmann, a gallant young Prussian officer of the highest connections and character, nephew of General Von Manteuffel. He was killed in a skirmish near Steelport, on which Aylward assumed the command of the small but well-equipped force, in which were many Britons, Germans, and Americans, who contrived to beleaguer Sekukuni till February, 1877, and compelled him to sue for peace, though they failed to storm his stronghold, and were repulsed with loss.

When the troops in South Africa were handed over by General Sir A. T. Cunynghame, to Lieutenant-General the Hon. F. A. Thesiger (afterwards Lord Chelmsford), at King William's Town, in British Kaffraria, on the 4th of March, 1878, they consisted only of the following:—

Two batteries of Royal Artillery; one company of Royal Engineers; the 24th, 88th and 90th Regiments in the Cape Colony; the 3rd Buffs and 80th in Natal; and the 13th Light Infantry in the Transvaal—in all about 5,000 men.

A wide-spread feeling of restlessness and hatred towards the white races had been for some time known to exist among the natives of South Africa, says the *Narrative of the Field Operations in the Zulu War* (a scarce work, prepared by the Intelligence Branch of the Quartermaster-General's Department, and one we may have frequently to refer to). And at the date when the war was ended by the death of Sandilli—as related in its place—disturbances claiming serious attention had occurred in remote districts; and while a war with the Zulus was deemed not improbable, hostilities were actually in progress in Griqualand West, in the country on the north-west of that territory, and in two districts of the Transvaal—one near Bloemhof, on the western side of the Transvaal, and containing considerable areas of pastoral and agricultural land, and the other near Lydenberg, known as Sekukuni's country.

The latter chief, who, with his tribe, was of Basuto descent, and was the most powerful one acknowledging the supremacy of King Cetewayo, after the attack by Aylward on his fortress, was left in undisputed possession of it on promising to pay a fine of cattle. At the date of these operations the boundaries of the Transvaal were very imperfectly defined, and while the Republican Government regarded the operations they had inaugurated, as "undertaken in self-defence against an insubordinate chief living far within the boundaries of the Republic," the view taken by our government was that Sekukuni was not a rebel against the Transvaal, inasmuch as his territory formed no part of that dominion, and that the war waged against him was an un-

17

justifiable aggression against an independent ruler; but when, in 1877, the Transvaal was annexed, Sekukuni's country was included, without any question, in the new territory added to the British possessions.

The fine of cattle remained unpaid to the new rulers, and though demanded, was not pressed.

In February, 1878, Sekukuni, as if to provoke hostilities, acting under the influence of Cetewayo, despatched a force, in conjunction with followers of his sister, Legolwana, to make a severe raid on a neighbouring chief, Pokwana, who was friendly to the British, and a sharp conflict ensued, the result of which was that the assailants were defeated.

Early in the next month, Sekukuni, on receiving a remonstrance from Captain Clarke, the British Commissioner for the district, being encouraged by the presence of fresh envoys from Cetewayo, replied that:

The British were afraid to fight—that the country was his, not theirs; that the white men must leave, and he was quite ready for war.

At this time the only force available for the maintenance of order was a slender body of Police and three companies of the first battalion of the 13th Regiment at Pretoria, from which they could not be spared, as their presence was requisite to hold in awe a portion of the Boer population, who bitterly resented the recent annexation. Under these circumstances Sir Theophilus Shepstone, the Administrator of the Transvaal, applied for additional troops to be sent to his assistance.

Consequently, three companies of the 90th Perthshire Light Infantry (now known as the Scottish Rifles) marched from Pietermaritzburg for Utrecht, while at the same time three companies of the 13th Somersetshire moved from the latter place to Standerton and Pretoria, while fifty local volunteers proceeded from thence to Fort Weeber, on the borders of the wild and mountainous district ruled by Sekukuni, and aided by a contingent furnished by Pokwana, attacked Masselaroon, the stronghold of his sister, Legolwana.

Like most of the Basuto towns, Masselaroon was quite capable of making a strong defence. Round a strong conical hill, the sides of which were well covered with thorn-bush, were clusters of native huts, built upon platforms levelled artificially. Each of these clusters was environed by a dense hedge of prickly pear, while the sides of the hill were scarped, and the approaches leading from one platform to another were strongly stockaded, and flanked by rifle-pits.

This fastness was of such strength that it could not be stormed easily, and as the native contingent was useless for such an attempt, the volunteers and police could only clear the northern end of the hill, and carry off some cattle; thus matters in the Transvaal remained still unsettled when, in April, two companies of the 13th Foot left Pretoria for Lydenberg, and another marched for Middleberg; but though Legolwana submitted, her brother Sekukuni remained in open revolt, and the small force opposed to him could only hold the fortified posts near the Lulu Mountains, among which his famous stronghold was situated; but these posts were insufficient to withstand the marauders of his tribe, who, in a combat on the Magnet heights, repulsed the volunteers, of whom sixteen were killed or wounded. They next assailed a detachment of the Diamond Fields Horse, consisting of eighty-three troopers, and carried off fifty two horses and all their cattle, and it soon became evident that the local forces were quite unable to cope with this revolted chief.

General Thesiger had now established his headquarters at Pietermaritzburg, and he resolved to increase the imperial troops in the Transvaal by one battalion of infantry. This officer—afterwards Lord Chelmsford, K.C.B., of whom we must often make mention—held the local rank of lieutenant-general, with the office of Lieutenant-Governor of the Cape of Good Hope.

He entered the army in 1844 as an officer of the Grenadier Guards, and served at Sebastopol and against the *sepoy* mutineers in Central India. In 1858 he was lieutenant-colonel of the 95th, or Derbyshire Regiment, and in 1867 accompanied Lord Napier of Magdala to Abyssinia as adjutant-general, in which capacity he was most favourably mentioned in the despatches to the War Office. From that time till 1876 he was adjutant-general in India, and had in every way the reputation of being an active and experienced soldier.

On the 13th of August he placed the command of all the troops in the Transvaal in the hands of Colonel Henry Rowlands, V.C. The 80th Regiment was now sent thither, and the force in Natal was further strengthened by the arrival of the 2nd battalion of the 24th Foot from the Cape, while the Frontier Light Horse, 200 strong, became also available for service in the Transvaal.

On the 28th the headquarter column of Colonel Rowlands' force marched from Pretoria into the long narrow valley of the Oliphant River, across which he moved on the 8th of September, and leaving a company of the 13th to occupy an entrenched camp, he reached the

Spekboom River, but not without various skirmishes with the enemy, who occupied the rugged hills on either side of his route.

On the 3rd of October he continued his advance from Fort Burgers to attack Sekukuni, at the head of 130 men of the 13th Foot, 338 of the Frontier Horse and Mounted Infantry, with two 7-pounder Krupp guns, that had formerly belonged to the Transvaal Republic. He marched up a valley and through a very rough country, and bivouacked near a dry water-course, where a little water was found for the men and horses by digging in the sand, and there he was attacked on three sides in the night, repulsing the enemy with loss.

The extreme dryness of the season, and the consequent want of water, so seriously affected his force, that Colonel Rowlands, on the 5th of October, ordered a retreat to Fort Burgers, and on arriving at the pools where the column had halted on the preceding day, the ground was found in possession of a strong force of the enemy. Unable, from the smallness of his force, to achieve anything. Colonel Rowlands continued his retreat for fifteen miles, and ultimately reached Fort Burgers, with his men, horses, and cattle utterly exhausted by trying marches under a burning sun and without water.

No further attempt was now made against the formidable Sekukuni, whose stronghold is described by Captain Lucas as a tremendous natural fortress, being a kind of "triangular enclosure of camelthorn hedges, backed with thick stone walls, and occupying a sort of platform at the head of a ravine between precipitous cliffs; the two paths or lanes of approach were barricaded with stone, and commanded on each side by a series of walled passages with many compartments, resembling pews along the aisles of a church."

On the 27th October Colonel Rowlands attacked a *kraal* belonging to one of Sekukuni's dependents, situated about five miles from the British camp, on the Spekboom River. The position was a strong one, as the rocks and caverns afforded a great amount of cover to the defenders. The force engaged consisted of three guns, 140 horse, 350 infantry, and 250 native troops. The place was stormed successfully; sixteen of the enemy were killed and many wounded, the loss on our side being eleven wounded.

Active operations in the Lydenberg district were now brought to a close, and all our troops were withdrawn to various garrisons in the Transvaal and to the frontiers of Zululand, where war was imminent; indeed. General Thesiger from the time of his arrival in Natal had been taught to regard it as a possible, if not probable, contingency.

CHAPTER 2

Sons of Sirayo: Cause of the War

The Zulu Army at this time consisted of about 40,000 men, in addition to which were two royal regiments, each having its own *kraal*, or headquarters. Five of these corps consisted of unmarried regiments, the others of single and married men. Each was divided into two wings, and each company had a captain and subaltern.

The Report of the Intelligence Department at the time says:

The Zulu Army as at present constituted, is drawn from the entire male population, as every male between the ages of sixteen and sixty-five is called upon to serve, without exemption. The military force consists of fourteen corps, or regiments, divided into wings, right and left, and the latter into companies. These, however, are not of equal strength, but vary immensely, even from ten to two hundred, according to the numerical strength of the corps to which they belong. In fact, the companies and regiments would be more correctly termed families, or clans, and each corps possesses its own military head-quarters, or *kraal*, with the following hierarchy: namely, one commanding officer, chief, or *induna-yesibaya*; one second in command, major, or *induna-yohlangoti*, who has charge of the left wing; two wing and company officers, according to the need of the battalion. As a rule, all these officers have command of men of the same age as themselves, and the method of recruiting is as follows:— At stated and periodical intervals, usually from two to five years, a general levy takes place, when all the youths who happen at the time to have attained the age of fifteen are formed into a regiment, and undergo a year's probation, during which time they are supposed to pass from boyhood to manhood. As the regiment becomes disciplined and seasoned, it receives large drafts from other corps, so that as the elders die out, young men come in to fill up the ranks. The entire Zulu Army consists of thirty-three regiments, married and unmarried No one in Zululand, male or female, is allowed to marry without the king's permission, and this is never granted till the men are forty years of age. They then have to shave the crown of the head, put a ring round it, and carry a white shield, in contradistinction to the unmarried regiments, who do not shave their heads, and carry coloured shields.

Many of these regiments are too young for active service, others are too old; consequently, it is estimated that about twenty-five regiments would be able to take the field, and these would perhaps muster 40,000. . . . We have heard a great deal about the drill of these, but their movements, so far as we can learn, are few and very simple, but very quickly performed in their own way. They form circles of regiments, in order to outflank the enemy. From this formation they break into columns of regiments, or companies, and from these into skirmishing order, with supports and reserves. The sole commissariat of the Zulu army consists of three or four days' grain, carried by the lads who follow each corps, and, if necessary, of a herd of cattle driven with the column.

Between the sable monarch at the head of this formidable organisation and the British Government, matters had been growing more and more perilous, till two conspicuous outrages in the early part of 1878 brought them to a crisis—these were what were called the affair of Sirayo and the Middle Drift difficulty.

Sirayo and his tribe had a quarrel with the Ischeni, a royal tribe; the king was appealed to, and in settling the dispute Sirayo lost all his cattle. Shortly after this, one of his wives fled with her lover into the land of Natal, accompanied by another wife. Nothing was done at the time, and all evidence proves that by *Kaffir* law:

A woman is not the slave of her husband. He has no property in her. He cannot, according to native law, kill, injure, or cruelly treat her. He cannot legally sell her, and, with the exception of paying cattle to her father as a dowry upon marriage, there is nothing to indicate that native law or custom treats the wife as a chattel.

Nevertheless, early one morning in August, 1878, the occupants of a police *kraal* in the Umsing division of the Klip River were roused by the shouts of an armed band, which surrounded their residence, and found themselves in the presence of 300 Zulus, led by two sons of the chief Sirayo. One said:

We intend no harm, provided we are not resisted; but we demand the persons of the two women, wives of our father Sirayo, who recently took refuge here, and if they are given up to us, we shall return at once.

22

The band was too strong to resist; the unfortunate women were surrendered, or rather, dragged out of the hut in which they were concealed. One of them was carried across the Buffalo in open daylight, and put to a barbarous death. The same night the incursion was renewed; the other woman was carried off and slain. It mattered not that they had committed an offence against Sirayo; they were found on British soil and under the protection of British law, and it seemed pretty plain now that Cetewayo meant to try conclusions with the British Government, for Sirayo was a favourite chief, and these young men were his favourite sons.

The surrender of them was demanded, and instead, Cetewayo sent £50. This sum was returned, and the offenders again demanded Cetewayo only shrugged his shoulders; and a plain intimation was sent that if the two lads were not given up by a certain date, war would be declared against him.

The defence made by the sons of Sirayo was:—

We did it; they were our father's wives: they forsook him, and deserved to be killed. Do not you Englishmen kill your wives, or your father's wives, if they run away?

COLONEL PEARSON.

23

Meanwhile the affair of the Middle Drift occurred. The government were constructing a road from Kranz Kop to the Tugela River, when Lieutenant Smith, the engineer, was attacked by the Zulus, and, with his men, stripped of clothing and severely maltreated. Reparation for this was also demanded by the government, which was quite aware of how Cetewayo had instigated Sekukuni.

Reparation was demanded in the form of 500 head of cattle; it was also required that the whole of Cetewayo's large army should be disbanded; that freedom of marriage should be allowed; that justice should be impartially administered: that missionaries should be allowed to return to Zululand; and that British Residents should be appointed for the settlement of disputes. It was further intimated to Cetewayo, that unless he complied with the terms on or before December the 31st, "then on January 1st, 1879, the British Army would commence the invasion of his land, and would enforce them at the point of the bayonet." But Cetewayo was unable even to sign his name, "and was as ignorant and savage as some of our Norman kings," and it was not thought likely he would submit.

During the whole of December Lord Chelmsford had worked arduously in the organisation of the troops under his command, which he formed in three columns, thus:—

No. 1 Column; Headquarters, Lower Tugela,
Colonel Charles Pearson, 3rd Buffs, commanding.

Naval Brigade.—170 seamen and marines of H.M.S. *Active*, with one Gatling and two 7-pounders, under Captain Campbell, R.N.

Royal Artillery.—Four guns, one Gatling, and rocket battery, under Lieut. W. N. Lloyd, R.A.

Infantry.—2nd battalion 3rd Buffs, under Lieut.-Col. Henry Parnell; and afterwards six companies of the 99th Regiment.

Mounted Infantry.—100 men, under Captain Piercy Barrow, 19th Hussars.

Volunteers.—Durban, Stanger, Victoria, and Alexandra Rifles, and Natal Hussars, 40 men per corps, all mounted.

Native Contingent—1,000 men, under Major Shapland Graves, 3rd Buffs.

No. 2 Column; Headquarters, Helpmakaar.
Colonel Richard Glyn, 24th Regiment, commanding.

Royal Artillery, N Battery, 5th Brigade, with two 7-gounders, under Major Harness, R.A.

GENERAL PLAN OF THE OPERATIONS IN ZULULAND, 1879.

Infantry.—Seven companies, 1st battalion 24th Regiment, and 2nd battalion 24th, under Lieut.-Col. Degacher.

Natal Mounted Police, under Major Dartnell.

Volunteers.—Natal Carbineers, Buffalo Border Guard, Newcastle Rifles, 40 men per corps, mounted.

Native Contingent—1,000 men, under Rupert Lonsdale, late 74th Highlanders.

No. 3 Column; Headquarters, Utrecht.

Colonel Evelyn Wood, V.C, C.B., 90th Regiment, commanding.

Royal Artillery, 11th Battery, 7th Brigade, with four 7-pounders and two rocket tubes, under Major E. Tremlett, R.A.

Infantry.—1st battalion 13th Regiment, and 90th Regiment Mounted Infantry.—100 men, under Major Russel, 12th Lancers.

Frontier Light Horse, 200 strong, under Major Redvers Buller, C.B., and the 60th Rifles.

Volunteers.—Kaffrarian Van-guard, Commandant Schermbrucker, 100 strong.

Native Contingent—The Swazis, 5,000 strong.

The Swazis came from the country north of the Zulus, and were their hereditary enemies.

The native levies raised by Lord Chelmsford, in addition to his European forces, amounted in all to 7,400. These were clothed with the conventional blanket of the country, in addition to a uniform costume, consisting of a corduroy tunic and breeches, with long boots of untanned leather and broad-leaved *sombrero* hat, and their leaders were generally officers who had retired from the British Army. Their arms were all serviceable rifles, of Sheffield and Birmingham make.

There was also a contingent of Boers, under Piet Uys, a splendid body of men, and all crack shots.

The known temper of Cetewayo rendered his acceptance of the ultimatum more than doubtful, and consequently it was necessary to make the most earnest preparations for that war which was sure to ensue; And for the contemplated offensive operations the transport question became, as usual, a serious difficulty.

A great number of ox and mule waggons were collected for the commissariat service of the three columns. The former were ponderous vehicles, capable of carrying 8,000 pounds' weight, and drawn by teams varying from eight to eighteen oxen. Thus, no less than 28,533 horses, mules, and oxen were at one time or other employed in transport

Colonel Pearson, commanding the right column, had served as adjutant of the 31st at the siege and fall of Sebastopol; Colonel Glyn, commanding the centre, was also a Crimean officer; and Colonel Evelyn Wood, commanding the left, was also an officer of very great experience. He entered the navy in 1852, and served in the Naval Brigade under Captain Peel; was severely wounded when carrying a scaling-ladder at the storming of the Redan, and was specially mentioned in the despatches of Lord Raglan. He served in the Indian campaign on the staff of Somerset's Brigade, and was present in many engagements, and won his V.C. in the jungles of Seronge, at the head of Beatson's Horse.

Redvers Buller, C.B., who had the Frontier Light Horse under him, had served with the 60th Rifles in the China campaign of 1860, and in the Red River Expedition, ten years subsequently.

It had been decided that the invasion of Zululand should be made by the simultaneous advance of the three columns by three different routes, while a fourth column, composed mainly of the native troops, under Colonel Durnford, R.E., should move forward at a later date, between the lines of the advance of the centre and right columns.

All these columns were complete in themselves. Communications were to be kept up on the flanks, thus giving cohesion with the effect of an advance in one extended line. The country in which these operations were to take place may be described as being over 15,000 square miles in extent. Its leading natural features are lofty open grassy downs, furrowed by deep water-courses, and broken by abrupt rocky eminences, the remainder being a line of low-lying alluvial country, varying from twenty to forty miles broad, and bordered by the sea. All the rivers are fordable when not at full flood. Wood and fuel are plentiful along the coast, but on the uplands, they are scarce and bad, consisting chiefly of brushwood growing on the mountain sides, and in the rugged *kloofs* and ravines.

The climate is warm, moist, and feverish, but dry and bracing in altitudes 3,000 feet above the level of the sea.

During the time allotted for the receipt of Cetewayo's reply, stores were collected at certain points near the frontier as rapidly as the difficulties of transport permitted. As there was no regular cavalry in South Africa, two squadrons of mounted infantry were, early in December, posted at various points along the frontier. These men were mounted on South African horses, and at first carried the regulation infantry rifle and bayonet, but were afterwards armed with Swinburn-Martini carbines and bowie-knives, which they could fix to the muzzles. The

2nd Squadron had also swords.

Cetewayo's term of grace had expired; the 11th of January, 1879, had come and gone, and no sign had come from him; but the *Natal Mercury* announced that he had shot all the inmates of three *kraals*, because they had bewitched the daughter of a chief.

On the following day the war had begun, and the Tugela was successfully crossed, the Zulus offering but slight resistance, and falling back into the interior as our troops advanced. The first to cross were the Naval Brigade of the right column (to details of which we shall first confine ourselves), the next were the Natal Mounted Volunteers, and then Colonel Pearson's infantry, who were ferried over in a *pont*, or flat-bottomed boat, 30 feet long, hauled across by oxen.

While a work called Fort Tenedos, with a large store-house, was being erected on the left bank of the Tugela, Colonel Pearson started with the first section of his column, leaving the others to follow, under Colonel Welman, of the 99th Regiment. He was accompanied by fifty store-waggons, and marching through an undulating and grassy country, free alike of bush and Zulus, he reached the Inyorie River, and encamped on its bank.

Colonel Welman came on next day with his command and eighty waggons.

The whole of Pearson's column now continued its march towards the Inyezane River, where there was open ground, and then, on the 22nd January—he halted for some hours to rest his cattle and breakfast his troops. A mountain ridge, known as Majia Hill, was now in front, and on it the dark figures of scouting Zulus were seen.

Colonel Pearson ordered the Natal Contingent to disperse them, which was accordingly done; but another dusky band showed themselves on a spur of the same hill, and in order to reach this spur it was necessary to cross a wooded ravine, with a marshy bottom, and when the company, under Captain Hart, emerged on the open ground beyond, a large body of Zulus appeared on the face of the hill, from which they opened a heavy fire at 400 yards' range.

They came on in the finest style, advancing rapidly over the slopes, skirmishing in extended order like regular troops, rushing from bush to rock in a steady, but stealthy manner, till within 150 yards of the outposts. Hart's men, being in the open, had to bear the brunt of all this, and almost at the same moment they had one officer, four non-commissioned officers, and four privates killed, as they failed to understand the order to "retire."

The foremost waggons had been parked for the halt when this heavy firing was heard in front, and Colonel Pearson, on learning that the enemy were there in force, advanced with two artillery guns, the Naval Brigade, and two companies of the Buffs, and took post on a knoll rising from a ridge, along which the road ascends to Etschowe. From thence he could see dense and sombre masses of the enemy working round his right flank towards the rear of his column, where the long string of waggons was now moving slowly up to park, and against these masses shells and rockets were now directed with terrible effect

Two companies of the Buffs and one of the Royal Engineers now darted out in skirmishing order, and, supported by some of the 99th Lanarkshire, ferreted the Zulus out of the jungly ground into the open, where they fell under the fire of Pearson's guns on the knoll, which hailed shot and shell among them.

Colonel Welman, of the 99th, now availed himself of this favourable time, when the Zulus were in a state of confusion, to send forward Captain Wynne and Major Barrow with some infantry. These, with, skirmishers and flankers on the left, and supported by two half companies of the Buffs and 99th, moved forward at a rapid pace.

The Zulus seemed bewildered by these movements, but not beaten, and Commander Campbell, with the Naval Brigade, seeing that they were making a flank movement to the left, at once obtained permission to drive them out of a *kraal* about 400 yards from the knoll Captain Hart, with his native levy, supported this movement, and possession was gained of some high ground to the left of the Etschowe road, and thus the flank movement—a favourite one in Zulu war—was effectually checked.

Colonel Pearson and Colonel Parnell, of the Buffs, had their horses shot under them, and several officers remarked that the fire of the Zulus, who were 5,000 strong, was particularly directed at all the leaders. Colonel Parnell, whose command had acted as a kind of reserve, now deployed at the double, and coming up on the right of the Naval Brigade, he swept, with the bayonet, the heights beyond the *kraal*, which a few minutes before had been crowded by warlike savages, who now fled in all directions, terrified by the death and destruction dealt among them by the rocket battery.

On the field 300 of them lay dead, and double that number of wounded were carried off by them into the bush. Pearson's whole loss was only 10 killed and 16 wounded.

After a halt the march was resumed for about four miles beyond

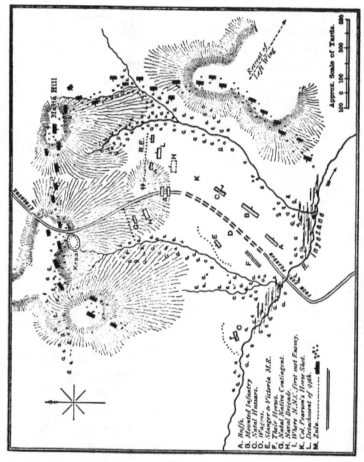

A. Buffs.
B. Mounted Infantry.
C. Natal Hussars.
D. Watsons.
E. Shepstone & Victoria M.R.
F. Their Horses.
G. Natal Native Contingent.
H. Naval Brigade.
I. Where N.N.C. first met Enemy.
K. Col. Pearson's Horse Shot.
L. Detachment of 99th.
M. Zulu.

PLAN OF THE FIGHT AT INYEZANE (JAN. 22, 1879).

the Inyezane River, to a ridge on which the column halted, and on the following day five companies of infantry were sent off to help Lieutenant-Colonel F.W. Ely, of the 99th, who, with three companies of the regiment, was toiling onward with a convoy of 70 waggons laden with stores and ammunition.

On the 23rd of January the column reached the old mission station at Etschowe. The deserted buildings were still in good repair, and as the position was a strong one, Colonel Pearson proceeded to make it more formidable as a depot for this line of invasion, especially as water was close to the new fort and well under its fire.

Here news reached the column of the terrible disaster at Isandhlwana, and, after taking council with his officers, Colonel Pearson resolved to remain where he was, confident that he could hold his ground for a couple of months at least. To save food he sent back the mounted men and Native Contingent, retaining 1,200 British troops, for whom he had 320 rounds per man in store.

CHAPTER 3

Disaster of Isandhlwana & Defence of Rorke's Drift

On the night of the 10th January, the 2nd, or centre, column, under Colonel Glyn, encamped on the right bank of the Buffalo River, at a place called Rorke's Drift. It must be borne in mind, amid these operations, that though cattle-tracks and footpaths traverse Zululand, no such thing as a regular road exists. The only wheeled transport which had ever entered these savage regions were the waggons of occasional traders or sportsmen, and the old grass-covered ruts left by these were the sole guide of our officers in selecting the line of advance.

After seeing the crossing of the Lower Tugela successfully achieved, though the current was deep, broad, and rapid, Lord Chelmsford, with an escort of Mounted Infantry and some Volunteers, started to communicate with Colonel Wood, whom he believed to have crossed the Blood River, and to be now approaching the left flank of the centre column, and, after a brief consultation with him, the general returned to his own camp at Rorke's Drift.

In the morning of the 12th January, at half-past three, a force under Colonel Glyn, consisting of four companies of the 24th Regiment, some of the Natal Native Contingent, and most of the mounted men, left the camp to reconnoitre the country of Sirayo, which lay to the eastward Lord Chelmsford and his staff accompanied this force, which after a five miles' march reached a ravine in the valley of the Bashee River, where a considerable number of cattle had been collected, and though they were unseen, being concealed in rocky *krantzes*, their lowing loaded the morning air.

A body of Zulus now appeared on the hills above, and against these the mounted men advanced, while the rest of the force pushed up the valley towards where the cattle were known to be, with orders to climb a hill on the left, work round to the right of the enemy's position, and attack and burn a *kraal* belonging to Sirayo's brother, whose surrender Government had required as one of the men who had violated British territory.

The moment the infantry got into motion, a sputtering fire was opened upon them from Zulus who were concealed behind boulders and bushes. The attack was led by the Native Contingent under Commandant Brown, the companies of the 24th acting as supports. The men of the former force dropped so fast that it required every effort of the white officers to get them to advance.

Gradually, however, they worked their way, planting in their bullets wherever a dark face or leg appeared, and when they had got within a short distance of the enemy's position, the men of the 24th made a rush at it.

Briskly fired the Zulus from their rocky hiding-places, and while one party of them made a resolute stand at a cattie *kraal*, another startled the troops by sending some huge boulders, which they had disengaged by levers, crashing down amongst them; but the enemy were driven up the hill, and put to flight in half an hour.

Meantime, the mounted men under Colonel Russell had quite a little engagement of their own, as they mounted the side of the hill and drove in the enemy, and by half-past nine a.m. the whole affair was over. Sirayo's *kraal*, which lay farther up the Bashee Valley, was burned later in the day, and about 1,000 cattle, sheep, and goats were captured. Of the Zulus 44 were killed or taken; our casualties were 14. Among the dead lay Sirayo's youngest son, and it was learned from a wounded prisoner that the chief himself, his eldest son, and other relatives, were not far off, at the head of a Zulu *Impi*. Sirayo's eldest wife and daughter, with a number of other women and children, were captured, but were sent back to their *kraals* by order of Lord Chelmsford.

On the 17th of January he rode out to the fatal Isandhlwana Hill, which, as fuel was easily obtainable there, he selected as the next halting-place of the centre column. The country, open and treeless, seemed quite deserted, and as no Zulus had been seen near Rorke's Drift, no earthworks to cover the crossing-place had been constructed there. At the camp on the Bashee River, however, a low wall or parapet was formed on the exposed faces.

LORD CHELMSFORD.

Leaving two companies of the 1st battalion 24th Regiment at Helpmakaar, and two of the 2nd battalion at Rorke's Drift, the column marched on the 20th January, and accompanied by 100 transport waggons, moved on to the hill of Isandhlwana, a name which (according to the Intelligence Report) signifies "The Little Hand," but which, with more probability, has been translated "The Lion Hill"

To the westward it is abrupt and precipitous, but slopes downward on the east to a water-course. At both ends are ridges or spurs that connect it with the smaller undulations, of which the more level part of the landscape consists. Over its western ridge passes the track from Rorke's Drift. On the immediate right was a *koppie*, or group of small hills, and others, covered with huge, grey boulders, were seen rising in succession away to the Buffalo River. To the left of the camp, at a mile's distance, a long ridge ran southward, and towards the east opened an extensive valley. On the extreme left of the camp, facing this ridge, were pitched the tents of the Natal Contingent Between these and the next two regiments, intervened a space of 300 yards. Occupying the centre were the British regular infantry, and just above them were the headquarters of Lord Chelmsford. On the right were the guns and mounted corps, lining the verge of the road.

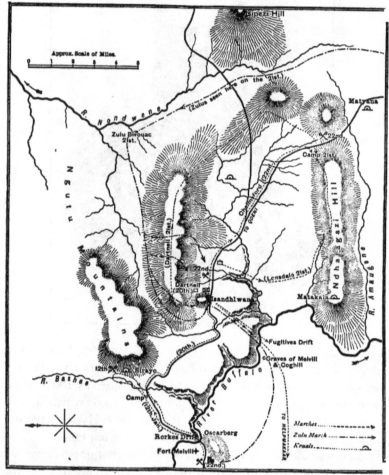

PLAN OF THE MARCHES NEAR ISANDHLWANA BETWEEN JAN. 12TH AND 22ND, 1879.

"The camp, therefore," says Major Ashe, "literally had its back to a wall"

34

The waggons of the column, on arriving in camp were formed up in rear of the ground occupied the corps to which they were attached, according to the Report of the Intelligence Department. As Zulus were reported to be in the vicinity on the night of the 20th, orders were issued for a reconnaissance to be made on the following day in the direction of a rocky fastness known as Matyana's stronghold, ten miles south-east of the camp, the circle of outposts from the centre of which extended about 2,500 yards by day, and about 1,400 yards by night, while the mounted vedettes were, of course, thrown still farther forward

At half-past four on the morning of the 21st, the Mounted Volunteers and Police, under Major Dartnell, proceeded to reconnoitre the higher ground, while two battalions of the Native Contingent, under Commandant Lonsdale, worked their way round the southern side of the Matakala Mountain, to examine the valleys below it.

The reconnoitring party bivouacked at some distance from the camp, from whence blankets and provisions were sent out to it on pack-horses in charge of mounted infantry, with whom Major Dartnell sent back a note, stating that there was a clear view over the hills to the eastward, and that the number of Zulus seen there about sunset was so great, that he did not deem the force with him and Lonsdale strong enough to attack, and requesting that three companies of the 24th might be sent out next morning.

A force was detailed to support him, and marched out of camp before daybreak. The men were in light marching order, without greatcoats or blankets, and each had one day's cooked rations with seventy rounds of ammunition. This force was accompanied by Lord Chelmsford and his staff. The author of the *Story of the Zulu Campaign* says:

At six a.m. on the 22nd, a company of the Natal Natives was ordered to scout towards the left, the enemy having appeared in that direction. Whilst these were away. Colonel Durnford arrived, about nine o'clock, with a rocket battery under Colonel Russell, R.A., 250 mounted natives and 250 native foot. News was brought in that the Zulus in very large numbers were driving the pickets before them. A later messenger—a native without uniform, supposed by some to be a Zulu purposely sent with false intelligence—brought the news that the Zulus had divided into three columns, one of which, it was supposed, was about to attack Colonel Durnford's baggage, still on the road from Rorke's Drift, the other to harass Lord Chelmsford and

Colonel Glyn's party in the rear, while the third was to hover round and watch the camp. Finally came the news, 'Zulus retiring in all directions.'

Colonel Durnford thereupon asked Colonel Pulleine to lend him a couple of the 24th companies, but he declined, saying his orders were to guard the camp, and he could not, under the circumstances, let them go without a positive command. Durnford then determined to go on with his own force, which he divided into three, one part being sent up the hill to the left (east), one to the left front, and a third to the rear, in the direction of Rorke's Drift, to act as escort for his baggage, which had not yet arrived. The rocket battery was with the party that proceeded to the front, under Colonel Durnford in person, to a distance of four or five miles from the camp, but being unable to keep pace with the mounted force, was soon left behind.

Weakened by these detached parties, the troops left in camp consisted of thirty mounted infantry for vedettes, about eighty mounted Volunteers and Police, two guns, and seventy men of the Royal Artillery, five companies of the 1st 24th, one company of the 2nd 24th, two companies of the Natal Contingent, and ten native pioneers.

The reconnoitring force was still far from Isandhlwana, and the Zulus in sight of it were seen to be retiring on what was afterwards found to be a preconceived plan; and prior to attacking a hilly position which they held, the general and his staff made a halt for breakfast At this period a messenger came from Colonel Pulleine that the enemy, 600 strong, had appeared on the left of the camp, and that he had sent out mounted men to patrol in that direction. Lord Chelmsford then ordered the Native Contingent to return at once to the hill of Isandhlwana.

Soon after, an encounter took place with the enemy in front; forty were killed and some taken prisoners. It was about noon now, and a suspicion that something was wrong at the camp first arose in the minds of the general's party.

One of the prisoners admitted that Cetewayo expected the muster of a large army—at least 25,000 men—that day, and even as he spoke the sound of heavy guns boomed through the sunny atmosphere.

"Do you hear that? There is fighting going on at the camp!" was now the cry.

And now a native on horseback came galloping down from a lofty ridge, to announce the startling intelligence that he could see the smoke of the firing enveloping the Isandhlwana Hill, and the flashing of the big guns there! (See *Smith-Dorrien, Isandhlwana to the Great War* by Horace Smith-Dorrien; Leonaur 2009.)

Lord Chelmsford and his staff galloped to the crest of the hill. Looking through their field-glasses in the direction of the camp, to them all seemed quiet then. The sun shone brightly on the white tents; no signs of firing were visible; bodies of men were seen moving about, but they were put down as those of our own troops.

Captain Lucas of the Cape Rifles, in his narrative, says:

> This was at a quarter before two o'clock, and not the faintest suspicion of any fatality seems to have crossed the minds of the general and his staff. It was not until a quarter to three that Lord Chelmsford turned his horse towards the camp.

When he, with Colonel Glyn's detachment, had come within four miles of it, they met with the Natal Native Contingent, which, on seeing that the camp had been attacked by an overwhelming force, had halted in a state of indecision and dismay. Half an hour afterwards a solitary horseman was seen approaching the general's somewhat bewildered party. He proved to be the gallant Commandant Lonsdale, who had ridden on in advance, and "the first words he uttered struck every one with consternation—'the camp is in possession of the enemy, sir!'"

Lonsdale had approached very near the camp when his attention was arrested by a bullet whistling past him. Looking up, he saw the Zulu who had just fired; at the same time, he saw what appeared to be groups of our soldiers in their red tunics bustling about the tents. He got within ten yards of the latter when he saw a Zulu come out of one with a blood-dripping *assegai* in his hand. He then perceived that the wearers of the red uniforms were all Zulus! He wheeled round his horse, and escaping a shower of bullets, galloped off to warn Lord Chelmsford of the dreadful trap into which he and all his party might have fallen. And now we must relate what occurred in absence of the general and main body of the column.

The body of troops despatched from the camp to the left, as reported by Colonel Pulleine to Lord Chelmsford, had become engaged with the enemy almost immediately; firing was heard all along the crest of the hill, and in about half an hour Colonel Durnford's mounted men reappeared, hotly pursued by the Zulus, who came over the crest in dark thousands, throwing out a dense cloud of skirmishers as they advanced, keeping up a desultory fire, and all in camp rushed to their arms. The *Daily News* says:

> The Zulu Army came on in regular battalions, eight deep, keeping up a steady fire, until well within *assegai* distance. They then ceased their fire, and hurled *assegais*. Our men kept up a very steady and telling fire, and great numbers of the enemy dropped, but without checking their progress. The places of the men who fell were constantly filled by comrades.

Prior to this the rocket battery had been overtaken, and its gunners, after a hand-to hand conflict, destroyed to a man, with Colonel Russell, but not before he had sent up three rockets as an alarm.

The cavalry on the left were now being driven vigorously back, and Captain W. Eccles Mostyn was ordered to advance with two companies of the devoted 24th to the eastern neck of the Isandhlwana Hill, where, at the distance of a mile and a half, the Zulus were pressing in great force along the north of it, to outflank the camp on the right, and with this wing of the enemy he became at once engaged

The remaining two companies of the 24th were sent to the left of the camp, and formed in skirmishing order near the Royal Artillery guns, which were already in action, and all men knew, as the horns of the Zulu army, advancing in a vast semicircle, closed on them, that they had to fight for bare existence now!

It was then half-past twelve p.m.

Lieutenant Pope's company of the 24th was thrown forward in extended order directly in front, near the waggon track, till his left files touched the right of those near the guns.

On this part of the field (says the Intelligence Report), owing to the Zulu advance being retarded by the mounted men, the pressure was as yet less severely felt than on the left, when the enemy, descending from the heights they had occupied, forced the defenders to fall back, and take up a fresh position, about 300 yards from the camp. This movement, while tending to unite the two portions of the force, had the effect of leaving the Native Contingent in a somewhat advanced position on the right of the companies of Younghusband, Mostyn and Cavaye at the salient of the defensive line, which now formed merely two continuous faces, one turned northward and the other eastward, and, so far as could be afterwards ascertained after all the dire slaughter and utter confusion that ensued, these troops were occupied with the enemy in their immediate front, till, at one p.m., they were found posted thus:—

On the left, and facing the north, were the companies of Younghusband, Mostyn and Cavaye in extended order, with two of the Native Contingent on Cavaye's right, and near them were the guns firing shot and shell eastward. To the right of the guns was one company of the 24th in extended order facing the east, and the remaining company of the 24th was stretched over the space between this point and that held by Lieutenant D'Aguilar Pope, which formed the right of the infantry line on the waggon track.

Beyond this, and at some distance in advance, was a force of mounted men, composed of those left behind in camp, and of those who had been in front with Colonel Durnford. The remainder of the Native Contingent was held as a kind of reserve in rear of the defensive line, all now hotly engaged, and was to have been employed to pursue the Zulus when recoiling from the attack which—following the experience of previous Kaffir wars—they were to be encouraged to make.

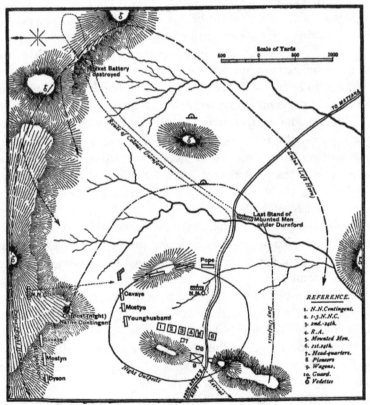

PLAN OF THE BATTLE OF ISANDHLWANA (JAN. 22, 1879).

The summit of the precipitous rock in front of which our troops were now fighting with desperation, is 4,522 feet above the level of the sea; but the camp upon its eastern slope was in no respect prepared for defence. The tents were all standing, just as they had been left when the troops under Chelmsford and Glyn marched out that mornings and their occupants were chiefly officers' servants, bandsmen, clerks, and other non-combatants, who, until they were attacked, were unconscious of danger.

Fifty waggons, which were to have gone back to the commissariat camp at Rorke's Drift, about six miles in the rear as the crow flies, had been drawn up the evening before in three lines on the neck between the track and the hill, and were still parked in the same position. All other waggons were in rear of the camps of the various corps to which they were attached. The oxen having been collected for safety when the Zulus first came in sight, were with these waggons, and many were regularly yoked in.

Meanwhile the Zulus had been steadily advancing eight deep as described, with their skirmishers in front, without check or halt, moving from the north-west in a deep formation of horseshoe shape, the left horn directed towards the British right, the right horn descending a scroggy and grassy valley at the back of the Isandhlwana Hill, while the force of the central mass was delivered directly at the open camp.

This was a little after one p.m., and then it was that our unfortunate soldiers were fully able to realise the strength of the enormous force that was advancing against them. Extended in a long thin line, covering 2,000 yards, they saw themselves opposed to a Zulu Army 14,000 strong, 10,000 of whom were hurling their strength against the camp, regardless of the heaviest losses.

By this time the foremost ranks of the Zulus were within 200 yards of the Native Contingent, which broke and fled, thus leaving a gap in the line, through which the Zulus poured like a living flood, and all in an instant became hopeless confusion, and before Mostyn's and Cavaye's companies of the 24th had time to form rallying squares, or even to fix their bayonets, they were slaughtered to a man. Captain Younghusband's company, which was on the extreme left, succeeded in retreating till a species of terrace or ledge on the southern face of the fatal hill was reached, from which spot they could see the Zulus using their stabbing *assegais* on all they overtook with fearful effect, their loud yells and demoniac shrieks loading the air, as the din of the musketry began to pass away.

The cannon had been firing case-shot latterly, but as the enemy closed in they were limbered up to retire; the limber gunners, unable to mount, ran after them towards the camp, but the Zulus who came up from the west were already there, and *assegaied* every man of them, save a sergeant and eight gunners in camp. Major Smith was slain in the act of spiking a gun, amid the most frightful *mêlée* and carnage, where horse and foot, Briton and Zulu, friend and foe, black and white, formed a dense, struggling, and fighting mass of apparently maddened men.

All who could escape endeavoured to make their way towards the Buffalo River, but that was impossible for even mounted men. The ground was rugged, intersected by water-courses, strewn with great boulders, over which the most active of the bare-footed Zulus, with foot-sole like a horse's hoof, could speed faster than a horse itself; and then in front rolled the river, swift and unfordable, and everywhere jagged with sharp rocks.

Those who reached the track that led to Rorke's Drift—the only hoped for shelter—found it to be completely blocked by the enemy. Most of the fugitives were entirely ignorant of the country through which they sought to make their way, and numbers were overtaken and slain by the swift Zulus. The route taken by the majority of the fugitives was along a deep water-course and thence to a point on the Buffalo, four miles distant from the camp. So hot, however, was the pursuit that no dismounted European succeeded in traversing even half of that distance, and of the horsemen who reached the river, many were shot or drowned in attempting to cross, more were slain on its banks, and only a few weak, thirsty, worn, and wounded creatures succeeded in reaching Helpmakaar.

Colonel Pulleine, of the 24th, on perceiving that all was lost and that the camp was in the hands of this terrible enemy, called to Lieutenant Melvill, and said:—

"You, as senior lieutenant, will take the colours and make the best of your way from here!"

He then shook Melvill's hand, and exclaimed, while seeming quite cool and collected—"Men of the 24th, here we are, and here we stand to fight it out to the end!" and there he perished with his gallant fellows of the old Warwickshire.

Lord Chelmsford's written orders to him were afterwards found on the field

Colonel Durnford, R.E., who, on his return to camp, had re-

ISANDHLWANA: THE DASH WITH THE COLOURS.

mained near the mounted men, would seem to have determined at first to form those under his command more compactly, and ordered the "retire "to be sounded, just before the Zulu rush had penetrated the line of defence, and as their right horn was closing in. At a stone *koppie*, or isolated rock, the colonel, with a party of mounted volunteers, 24th men, and others who had rallied round their commanding officer, Henry Pulleine, held their ground gallantly together, though attacked on all sides; but when the last cartridge was expended, the end could not be long delayed

LIEUTENANT MELVILL.

Melvill was adjutant of the 1st battalion, and rode off with the colours, accompanied by Lieutenant Neville Coghill, of the same corps, and Private Williams. These fugitives were closely pursued, according to Captain Hallam Parr, and held on together, with difficulty, till they reached the Buffalo, where Williams was swept away by the current and drowned Melvill's horse was shot in the stream, and the colours slipped from his grasp.

Lieutenant Coghill reached the Natal side in safety, but on seeing Melvill clinging to a rock, while seeking vainly to recover the lost colours, he forgot all thought of self-preservation, and bravely rode back to his comrade's assistance, and his horse was also shot. They both reached the Natal bank and tried to struggle on, but in vain.

Colonel Glyn in his despatch says:

The Zulus opened a heavy fire on our people, directing it more especially on Lieutenant Melvill, who wore a red patrol jacket.

43

LIEUTENANT COGHILL

Captain Parr says:

There are, not many hundred yards from the river's side, two boulders, within six feet of each other, near the rocky path. At these boulders they made their last stand, and fought until overwhelmed. Here we found them lying side by side, and buried them on the spot, where they fought and fell so gallantly. There is no need to remind Englishmen of their conduct. While we remember the Zulu War it will not be forgotten. They did not die in vain; ten days after they fell the colours were found in the rocky bed of the Buffalo.

Melvill, however, was a Scotsman, and Coghill was Irish, and the heir of a baronetcy as the son of Sir J. Jocelyn Coghill, of Drumcondra, in the county of Dublin. Melvill's watch was found to have stopped at ten minutes past two p.m.

The Queen's colour was subsequently found, as stated by Major Black of the 24th, and was afterwards presented to Her Majesty at Osborne, when she tied a wreath of *immortelles* to the staff head in memory of the two young officers who perished in defence of it. The colours of the 2nd battalion of the 24th had been left in the guard tent when the regiment marched out of camp, and were never seen again. The regimental colour of the 1st 24th was at Helpmakaar in comparative safety.

Of the awful scene in camp no white man saw the end! Of the conflict in and around the camp but little information exists. After the defensive line was broken, for a brief period men fought hand-to-hand in and among the tents. The only companies which appear to have made an organised resistance were Captain Younghusband's and the other two on his right, which made a wild and desperate attempt to rally. On the terrace below the Isandhlwana Hill he fought with his men till their ammunition was expended; now no more could be procured, as the waggons were in possession of the Zulus, and they all died where they stood.

This was about two p.m.

The Zulus themselves afterwards described how our brave young officers called on their men and encouraged them, and how often they charged through the little square (presumably of Younghusband's company), till, after their heavy losses, they became reluctant to attack it They told how the red soldiers taunted them to come on, and how, when ammunition fell short, they remained just beyond the bayonet blades, on which they often tossed the bodies of their own dead, and launched in their *assegais*, and then, rushing on, ended the one-sided conflict "Ah! those red soldiers at Isandhlwana," many Zulus said, "how few they were, and how they fought! They fell like stones—each man in his place." (*Sketches of the Kaffir and Zulu Wars.*)

We are told that one tall man, a corporal of the 24th, slew four Zulus with his bayonet, which stuck for a moment in the throat of his last opponent, and then he was *assegaied*. The only blue-jacket in camp, a man of H.M.S. *Active*, was seen, with his back against a waggon wheel, keeping a crowd of Zulus at bay with his cutlass, till one crept behind and stabbed him to death between the spokes. A Natal Volunteer, who had been sick in hospital, was found dead with his back against a boulder near the hospital tent, with about a hundred fired cartridges about him, his revolver empty, and a bowie-knife crusted with blood in his hand.

A resident in Durban wrote to a friend in England:

You will have seen of our great disaster at Isandhlwana, only a short distance from our border, where every man was butchered, those wounded tortured, and the sick in hospital and the dead horribly mutilated. The latter is not said much of in the papers, but the men who returned with the general saw enough of it—one poor little drummer boy held up on a bayonet. . . . But it is evident that our general was out-generalled by the Zulus, from not having sufficient cavalry scouts to ascertain where the mass of the enemy was. (*Daily News.*)

The description of the stand made by the last man, as given in the *Natal Times*, is full of pathos. He struggled up the steep hill in rear of the camp, till he reached a small cave or crevice in the rocks, into which he crept, and with his bayonet and rifle kept off the enemy. The ground in front of this cave fell abruptly down, and the Zulus, taking advantage of the rocks and stones scattered about, endeavoured, two or three at a time, to approach and shoot him.

The soldier, however, was very wary, and invariably shot down every Zulu as he appeared. He did not blaze hurriedly, but quietly dropped the cartridges into the breech-block of his rifle, took deliberate aim, and killed a man at every shot. At last the Zulus became desperate, and, bringing up a number of their best shots, poured in a concentrated volley and killed him.

This had lasted far into the afternoon, when the shadows were long on the hills, probably about five p.m.

A Zulu narrative of the conflict, as taken down from the lips of Methlagazulu, son of Sirayo, when a prisoner in Pietermaritzburg Gaol in the subsequent September, is not without interest, and is corroborative of what we have related. He stated:

We were fired on, first by the mounted men, who checked our advance for some little time. About the same time the other regiments became engaged with soldiers who were in skirmishing order. When we pressed on, the mounted men retired to the *donga*, where they stopped us twice. We lost heavily from their fire. My regiment (the Ngobamakozi) suffered most. When we saw that we could not drive them out of the *donga*, we extended our horn to the bottom of it, the lower part crossing and advancing on the camp in a semicircle. When the mounted men saw this, they came out of the *donga*, and galloped to the camp.

Our horn suffered a great deal both from the mounted men and a cross-fire from the soldiers, as we were advancing to the camp, the Nonkenke and Nodwengo regiments forming the left horn (a mistake for the right), circled round the mountain to stop the road, the main body closing in on the camp. I then heard a bugle-call, and saw the soldiers massing together. All this time the mounted men kept up a steady fire, and kept going farther into camp. The soldiers when they got together fired at a fearful rate, but all of a sudden stopped, then they divided, and some commenced running. We didn't take any notice of those running away, thinking the end of our horn would catch them, but pressed on those who remained.

They got into and under waggons and fired, but we killed them all in that part of the camp. (Those who ran took the direction of the Buffalo River, some throwing their rifles away, and others firing as they ran). When we closed in, we came on a mixed party of mounted and infantry men, who had evidently been stopped by the end of our horn. They numbered about a hundred. They made a desperate resistance, some firing and others using swords. I repeatedly heard the word 'Fire!' given by someone; but we proved too many for them, and killed them all where they stood

When all was over, I had a look at these men, and saw an officer with his arm in a sling, and with a big moustache, surrounded by *carbineers* and other men that I didn't know. We ransacked the camp, and took away everything we could find; we broke up the ammunition boxes and took out all the cartridges. We practised a great deal at our *kraals* with the rifles and ammunition. Lots of us had the same sort of rifle that the soldiers used, having bought them in our country, but some who did not know how to use it had to be shown by those who did.

This son of Sirayo has been described as a perfectly trained Zulu warrior, without an ounce of superfluous flesh on his lithe and muscular limbs, an exquisitely modelled figure, but with an eye the expression of which made the beholders shudder. One wrote:

> You can imagine, the tiger-like spring of such an enemy; the fierce gleam of the eyes as the deadly *assegai* plunges into the victim's heart, and the quiver of the muscles as the longer-handled weapon is hurled forward with unerring aim.

He was named Methlagazulu, signifying "the eyes of the Zulu nation," because his father's *kraal* looked towards that part of the British territory on which Cetewayo had so long kept a close watch.

The Zulu reserve, consisting of some 4,000 men, took no part in the action, but simply drove off the captured cattle, waggons, and plunder. When these were moved off, they took most of their dead with them in the waggons, piled on the debris of flour, sugar, tea, biscuits. When the ground was first seen after the disaster numbers of horses lay dead, shot in every position, besides mutilated oxen, mules stabbed

47

and gashed, while thick among them, scattered in gory clumps, lay the bodies of our soldiers, with only their boots or shirts or perhaps a pair of trousers to indicate to what branch of the service they belonged. In many cases they lay with sixty or seventy empty cartridges beside them, showing the desperation with which, they fought and died.

On that miserable day there perished of our troops on and around the hill of Isandhlwana twenty-six imperial officers and 806 non-commissioned officers and men, while the loss of the colonial forces was not less terrible, and included twenty-four officers. Five entire companies of the 1st 24th fell, with ninety men of the 2nd battalion. The loss in *matériel* was put down at 102 waggons, 1,400 oxen, two 7-pounder guns, 400 rounds of shot and shell, 800 Martini-Henry rifles, 250,000 rounds of ball cartridge, £60,000 worth of commissariat supplies, a rocket trough, a number of tents, and, for some time, the colours of the 24th Foot.

On the same afternoon about 250 men of the 13th Light Infantry and 24th, who had been on the march upward from Pietermaritzburg, left Helpmakaar for Rorke's Drift. *En route* they met some of the fugitives from the camp, who informed them of the great disaster there, on which they went back at once to reinforce the infantry posted at Helpmakaar.

And now to return to Lord Chelmsford. After meeting Commandant Lonsdale with his appalling intelligence, he sent an order for Colonel Glyn's troops at their bivouac to march instantly on Isandhlwana. He formed the native battalion which accompanied him in line, with a few mounted men on the flanks, and in this order marched forward for about two miles. He then halted it behind a ridge, which concealed it from those who might be in the camp, and sent forward the mounted infantry to reconnoitre. They returned with intelligence that the Zulus in many thousands were in full possession of the camp.

It was four p.m. when the order reached Colonel Glyn, who came up with Lord Chelmsford at ten minutes past six. The column was formed, the mounted men were sent in front, the guns were in the centre with three companies of the 2nd battalion 24th on either side of them, the advance was resumed, and by seven, when the sun set, the camp could be seen about two miles distant. Several tents had disappeared. The daylight faded rapidly out, and about a quarter to eight, when the column was within half a mile of the lion-shaped mountain, darkness completely enveloped the camp, with all its ghastly objects. Merely the black outline of the adjacent hills was visible, and on the

RORKE'S DRIFT BEFORE THE ATTACK.

crests of those to the northward, the equally black figures of the Zulus could be seen against the sky, and the last glow of the day that had gone.

The column was now halted, and a fire of shrapnel shell was directed by the artillery against the neck south of the Isandhlwana Hill, over which the road passes to Rorke's Drift. To this no reply was made, so the column advanced to within 300 yards of it, and opened with shell again, while three companies of the 2nd 24th, under Major Black, went forward with orders to seize the *koppie* to the south of it. This was done without opposition, and then the troops marched into the camp, which they found silent, and deserted by all save the dead Chelmsford's shattered force had marched thirty miles, and had not tasted food for forty-eight hours. Their pouches were not well filled now, and had they been resolutely attacked by the Zulus they must have shared the fate of those they saw stretched around them, and among whom they bivouacked

At four a.m. on the following morning the column started for Rorke's Drift (*i.e.,* ford), on a sad retreat; but there the first glad tidings they heard, were of the glorious defence made by Chard and Bromhead, two young subalterns, with a handful of men, at the *drift*

At Isandhlwana the Zulu Army was commanded by a skilful chief named Tshingwayo, who seems to have fought though the state of the moon was considered unpropitious, and the savage ceremonies which usually preceded an action had not been performed.

The successful defence of the commissariat camp came about thus.

When the centre column advanced on the 20th of January, one company of the 2nd 24th, under Lieutenant Gonville Bromhead, had, with a small party of the Natal Native Contingent, been left to guard the *ponts*, some sick men, and stores at Rorke's Drift. This officer was only twenty-three years of age, and was the youngest son of Sir Edmond de Gonville Bromhead, Bart, of Thurlby Hall, Lincolnshire, and had already served with his regiment in India. And with him was associated in the defence Lieutenant J. R. Merriot Chard of the Royal Engineers, who had previously served at Bermuda, and had been ten years in the service.

On a rocky terrace on the Natal side of the Buffalo, about a mile from the crossing-place, stood two stone buildings, with roofs of thatch, belonging to the Swedish mission station. Close to these the company of the 24th had encamped. The eastern edifice, formerly a church, was now filled with stores, while the other, which had been the dwelling of the missionary in that savage solitude, had been formed into a little

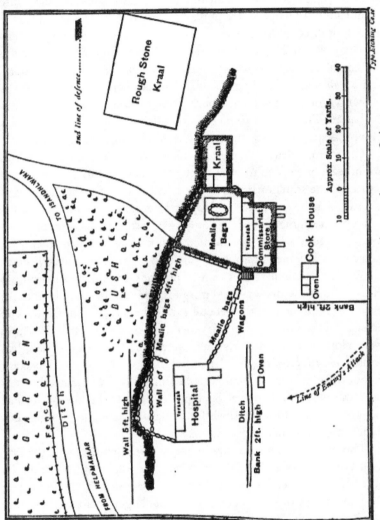

PLAN OF THE DEFENCES AT RORKE'S DRIFT (JAN. 22, 1879).

military hospital

The nearest troops to this sequestered post—a post in the silence and solitude of an unknown wild—were two companies of the 1st 24th at Helpmakaar, ten miles distant, and Major Spalding, who was in charge of the line of communications, had ridden over to that place to bring up one of these companies, leaving, for the time, the entire command of the *drift* on Lieutenant Chard, R.E.

About three in the afternoon of the 22nd, as this officer was watching the *ponts* on the river, there came galloping up from the direction of Isandhlwana, on horses flecked with foam, Lieutenant Adendorff, and a *carbineer*, with tidings of what had befallen the camp. The carbineer was despatched on the spur to Helpmakaar, while the two officers hastened to the post to prepare for a defence, that would doubtless prove a desperate one, as the enemy were known to be advancing.

Chard immediately drew in his small garrison, and, in concert with Bromhead, proceeded to have the tents struck, and to loop-hole and barricade the storehouse and hospital, and to connect the defences of the two, which were thirty yards apart, by mealie sacks and bags of Indian corn, forming part of the commissariat stores, and with these and a few waggons a *laager* was formed in hot haste. The *pont* guard was called in, and all men fit for duty were told off to their respective posts.

While these preparations were in progress, an officer of Durnford's Horse came in with about 100 troopers, and was asked by Lieutenant Chard to send them out as vedettes, and when pressed, to fall back in defence of the post. At 4.30 this officer returned to say that the Zulus were close at hand; that his men were already terror-stricken, had refused to obey orders, and had basely galloped off to Helpmakaar. About the same time, Captain Stephenson and his detachment of natives also drew off. It was at once perceived that the line of defence was too extended for the small force that remained, so an inner entrenchment was built of biscuit boxes.

The little garrison was now reduced to the company of the 2nd 24th, consisting of about eighty bayonets, the total number within the post being 139 men, of whom thirty-five were sick in the hospital

The parapet of biscuit boxes across the larger enclosure, was only two boxes in height, and it had barely been completed, at 4.30 p.m., when the sound of firing was heard, and some 600 of the enemy came in sight round a hill to the south, and advanced at a swift run against the post, and notwithstanding a tremendous cross fire, came within fifty yards of the southern wall; where, availing themselves of the cover afforded by the cookhouse and ovens, they kept up a heavy fire in return.

Meanwhile their main body moved to the left, round the building used as a hospital, and made a rush at the north-west wall and the breast-work of mealie bags; but after a short and desperate struggle, they were driven back with heavy loss to the adjacent bush. The mass of the Zulus who were still coming on lined a ledge of rocks near the post, and filled some caves overlooking it, about a hundred yards distant, from which they kept up a continual fire; while others, advancing somewhat more to the left, occupied the garden, the hollow road, and bush in great strength.

Taking advantage of the latter, which the garrison had not had time to destroy, they advanced close to the wall, and held one side of it, while our soldiers held the other, and then a series of desperate assaults were made, and repelled splendidly with the bayonet; and there Corporal Schiess of the Natal Native Contingent, was conspicuous for his bravery.

The fire of the enemy from the rocks and caves was badly directed, but it took the post so completely in reverse, that about six p.m., Chard and Bromhead drew their men behind the entrenchment of biscuit boxes.

Lieutenant Chard says in his report:

LIEUTENANT BROMHEAD.

All this time, the enemy had been attempting to force the hospital, and shortly after, set fire to its roof. The garrison of the hospital defended it room by room, bringing forth all the sick who could be moved before they retired; Privates Williams, Hook, R. Jones, and W. Jones, 24th Regiment, being the last men to leave, holding the doorway with the bayonet, their own ammunition being expended. From the want of interior communication and the burning of the house, it was impossible to save all. With most heartfelt sorrow I regret that we could not save these poor fellows from their terrible fate.

Five unfortunate sick soldiers were thus burned to death. One sick soldier had a narrow escape. He succeeded in getting away from the hospital, and hid in the bush all night exposed to a cross fire.

Two heaps of mealie bags were now converted into a species of redoubt, Commissary Dunne, a gallant Irish officer, working hard at it and exposing himself freely, though a man of great stature, and thus a second line of fire was obtained all round. The hospital was a sheet of fire; the darkness had fallen, and the little post was completely surrounded on every side, and the defenders after repulsing many attempts to storm it, and doing so with the greatest gallantry, were forced to retire to the centre, and then to the inner wall of a rough

LIEUTENANT CHARD.

54

stone *kraal* on the east, and that place they retained throughout

Privates John Williams, Henry Hook, William Jones, and Robert Jones, with Corporal William Allan and Private Frederick Hitch, all of the 24th, received the V.C. for their valiant defence of the hospital.

The Zulus were now 3,000 strong. Six times they got inside the barricades, and six times they were hurled back by the bayonet and clubbed rifle ere they retired to the *kraal*. Throughout the entire night the desperate struggle went on, and assault after assault was made and repulsed. Our soldiers fired with the greatest deliberation and coolness, not wasting a single shot, and aiming by the light of the burning hospital as long as it lasted.

At four o'clock on the morning of the 23rd, the firing of the Zulus ceased; they began to draw off defeated and disheartened, and by daybreak had passed out of sight over the hills to the south-west Lieutenants Chard and Bromhead then patrolled the vicinity, collected all the arms of the dead Zulus, and proceeded to strengthen their miserable defences in case the attack might be renewed, and just as they were removing the thatch, about seven in the morning, a large body of them were seen on the hills again.

Lieutenant Chard had contrived, by means of a friendly *Kaffir*, to despatch a note to the officer commanding at Helpmakaar for aid; but about eight p.m. the column under Lord Chelmsford came in sight, to the joy of the defenders of Rorke's Drift, who were thus saved from another attack and from too probable extermination, as the enemy retired immediately.

It would seem that Major Spalding, who had started on the previous day to Helpmakaar, was returning in the evening towards Rorke's Drift, with the two companies of the 1st 24th Regiment, under Major Upcher. Riding on in advance of these, Major Spalding arrived about sunset, within three miles of the environed post, when the Zulus opposed his progress, and he saw the mission house on fire; and probably believing all to be lost, he ordered the two companies back to Helpmakaar. When Chelmsford's column reached Rorke's Drift, his famished men were supplied with food, and measures were taken to improve the defences of the post; but, the disaster at Isandhlwana had deprived the centre column of its whole transport, and rendered the troops composing it incapable of making any offensive movement, as the officers and men found themselves with nothing but what they stood in.

The number of British defending Rorke's Drift, was eight officers and 131 non-commissioned officers and men; of these fifteen were killed and twelve wounded, two mortally. The attacking Zulus consisted of the Undi and Udkloko regiments, 4,000 strong, and of these 370 lay dead around the post. How many were wounded was never known. Lieutenants Chard and Bromhead received the thanks of both Houses of Parliament, were promoted to the rank of majors, and each received the Victoria Cross.

The Court of Inquiry which was held to sift the causes leading to the disaster at Isandhlwana, lies somewhat apart from our purpose.

Lord Chelmsford wrote urgently home for reinforcements—three British infantry regiments at least, two of cavalry, and one company of Engineers. He stated:

> The cavalry must be prepared to act as mounted infantry, and should have their swords fastened to their saddles, and their carbines slung, muzzle downwards, by a strap across the shoulders. The swords should be, if possible, somewhat shorter than the present regulation pattern. At least 100 artillerymen, with farrier, shoeing smith and collar maker, must be sent, out at once to replace the casualties in Lieutenant-Colonel Harness's battery. A dozen farriers or good shoeing smiths are urgently required for the several columns, and two additional veterinary surgeons for depot duty would be very valuable.

Singular to say, the home authorities failed to comply with these requests.

Before referring to the operations of Colonel Wood's column and the blockade of Etschowe, we shall close the story of Isandhlwana by that of the interment of the dead, which did not take place till the month of June, five months after the action.

The party detailed for this mournful service consisted of thirty dragoons under Captain Willan, K.D.G., and Lieutenant Taffe of the 16th Lancers; fifty dismounted dragoons under Lieutenant Burney of the 1st Royal Dragoons; sixty of Major Dartnell's Mounted Police; 140 of the 2nd battalion of the 24th under Captain Williams; 100 of Tataloka's Mounted Natives, and 1,000 native levies, the whole under the command of Brevet Lieutenant-Colonel Black of the 24th Regiment

Two mule waggons accompanied him, carrying picks, shovels, and reserve ammunition. When the party came to the hill where their gallant comrades were lying, great difficulty was experienced in finding the bodies, as the grass had grown so high that in many places it overtopped the heads of the searchers. Letters, papers, and photographs of loved ones far away at home were mixed up with brushes, boots, and saddlery of every kind, cut to pieces. According to an eye-witness:

> The stench from the carcases of the horses, mules, oxen, and the remains of the poor fellows who had fallen, was fearful . . . Birds of prey did not appear to have been at their horrid work, but there were undeniable traces of them outside (the camp) and along the way the fugitives took. One of the first things picked up was a sling of the colours of the 24th. Many of the recovered letters and photographs were very little the worse for exposure. Some regimental books were found, together with a considerable amount of money, cheques, and other property.

A strange and terrible calm seemed to reign in this solitude of death and nature. Grass had grown luxuriantly about the waggons, sprouting from the seed that had dropped from the loads, falling on soil fertilised by the blood of the gallant fallen. The skeletons of some rattled at the touch. In one place lay a body with a bayonet thrust to the socket between the jaws, transfixing the head a foot into the ground. Another body lay under a waggon covered by a tarpaulin, as if the wounded man had gone to sleep as his life-blood ebbed away.

In one spot over fifty bodies, including those of three officers, were found, and close by another group of about seventy, and considering that they had been exposed to the weather for five months they were in a singular state of preservation. Among those recognised were Captain Wardell, Lieutenants Anstey and Dyer, and Paymaster White, all of the 24th Regiment

To the left of these lay a group of the Natal Carbineers, with the body of Colonel Durnford covered with stones. Captain Gillmore, in his *Ride through Hostile Africa*, says:

> Peace to his ashes! for a braver soldier never drew a sabre or bestrode a charger, and I have a right to know, as I was acquainted with him from childhood.

He was known by his long moustache, his mess-jacket, and two finger-rings. Elsewhere lay twenty of the Natal Police, who were buried by their comrades. About 200 bodies were interred on the first day. The greater part of them were found lying on their backs, with outstretched arms. This was accounted for, as the Zulus always disembowel the fallen.

A second visit was paid to continue this grim task. On the right of the hill was found a very large group of slain around the body of an officer, in a position which they had evidently held till the last man perished. There, too, lay the body of a Zulu chief, covered by shields and stones. Many bodies were buried by the fugitives' path, where they lay in small groups. Near a tree, nine were found beside a waggon, the horses of which were *assegaied* in the traces. Here lay the bandmaster of the 24th; in a pocket were his watch, two rings, and his will, dated a day before his death.

Rider and horse, officer and private, boy and man, their grim and parchment-looking skins half-eaten by the carrion birds and half covering the bleaching bones, gave to the scene a terrible and weird significance which can never be forgotten.

In two days 500 were buried, but many must have escaped observation. Several evidences were found of the ferocity of the hand-to-hand struggle. In one place lay a 24th man, with a Zulu in front of him. He had a knife buried to the haft in his back, showing that he had been assailed behind after killing his enemy. Close by was a *carbineer* lying above a Zulu; he, too, had been stabbed in the back.

Had the 24th been allowed sooner to perform this duty, for which the survivors volunteered again and again, the work would have been more satisfactorily done, and many relics recovered that would have been precious to friends at home.

Amongst other mementoes, there was found—as was stated in an advertisement issued in July from the United Service Club, Edinburgh—close to the remains of an officer, a mourning-ring set with seven rosette diamonds, inscribed "In memoriam," with a date and initials.

CHAPTER 4

The Blockade of Etschowe

The left, or No. 3, column, under Colonel Evelyn Wood, whose name has now become a "household word," was encamped on the 10th January at Bembas Kop (which literally means an isolated hill), on the Blood River.

On the afternoon of that day he marched with two Royal Horse Artillery guns, six companies of the 90th, or Perthshire Light Infantry, six of the 13th Light Infantry, the greater part of Wood's Irregulars, and the Frontier Light Horse, and moved down the left bank of the stream.

Great were the difficulties of this march, as, in addition to those caused by marshy ground, it was necessary to cross tributaries which flow down from the Halatu and Icanda Mountains to the Blood River, through solitudes long tenanted only by the Kaffir crane, the wild duck, and snipe. To render the deep beds of these streams passable by guns and waggons, the banks had to be cut down, but by six in the evening the troops halted after a nine miles' march.

On the following day, at two in the morning, Colonel Wood marched with a slender flying column composed of the Frontier Horse, the two guns, forty-eight infantry marksmen in mule waggons, and 600 irregulars, leaving the remainder of his force to follow in support at nine miles' distance, under Colonel Philip E. Victor Gilbert, 13th Foot, an officer who served at the Battle of the Tchernaya, and fall of Sebastopol, and in the Indian campaigns of 1857-8.

Through darkness and fog from the marshlands, Colonel Wood pushed briskly on, guided by that gallant old Dutch farmer, Piet Uys, till he came within twelve miles of Rorke's Drift, where he had the interview with Lord Chelmsford already referred to, and from whom he learned that the central column had, without opposition, crossed the Buffalo River. On the morning of the 13th, after reaching Umoolooni, he was again on Bembas Kop, with the country around it impassable in consequence of the heavy rains to which his troops were exposed. His object was to cover Utrecht.

Amid all these movements, though Colonel Wood captured large quantities of cattle, no encounter took place with Zulus, yet they were present in arms and in large numbers, as they seemed to be without def-

SIR EVELYN WOOD.

59

inite orders from Cetewayo as to how they were to receive the British.

Wood remained for five days on Bembas Kop, making reconnaissances with his mounted troops, and on the 18th of January he advanced to the Inseyene (or Sandy River), a distance of ten miles, and had a slight skirmish with the enemy on the banks of the White Umvolosi River.

The two following days saw him moving along the stream, till he encamped near the *kraal* of Tinta, a chief who submitted, and, under a guard composed of a company of the Perthshire, was sent towards Utrecht On the 20th the Light Horse made a reconnaissance to the summit of the Zungen range—lofty, flat-topped mountains—but were met by the Zulus in such strength that they were compelled to fall back; and next day the construction of a stone *laager* fort was begun on the bank of the Umvolosi, where the stores were deposited, in charge of a company of the 90th, while at midnight on the 21st the column moved on a patrol towards the Zungen range of mountains. When there was no rain these night marches were not unpleasant

The Zungen range is the name given to the western portion of some hills which extend from east to west for the distance of twenty miles. The central of these is named the Inhlobane Mountain, which was yet to figure prominently in the annals of the Zulu War, and the eastern is the Ityenka.

Forming his column into three sections to scour these mountains, two reached their summit unopposed, driving back some bands of Zulus and capturing their cattle; but when the eastern extremity was reached, some of the enemy, estimated at 4,000 men, were seen at drill on the slope of the Inhlobane Mountain.

> Their evolutions, which were plainly visible by the aid of a glass, were executed with ease and precision; a circle, a triangle, and a hollow square, with a partition across it, being formed rapidly by movements of companies.

On the morning of the 24th January, Colonel Wood advanced again, and dispersed a body of Zulus on the north side of the mountain. During the brief engagement he received tidings of the startling disaster at Isandhlwana, and he immediately decided to withdraw to his old position on the White Umvolosi, and on the 25th his column reached Fort Tinta.

We must now recur to the movements of Colonel Pearson's column, which reached Etschowe on the 23rd of January, and where he lost no time in turning the old Norwegian mission-station into a fort, to be defended at all hazards and against all comers.

It occupied a very commanding position, being nearly on the summit of the Tyoe Mountains, more than 2,000 feet above the level of the sea, in a district wonderful for its natural beauty. Away to the north, through green grassy plains, rolled the blue and winding Umtalazi River, and beyond it rose pastoral undulations, devoid of bush, but dotted here and there by dwarf-trees and date-palms.

On the south lay a hilly and open country, bounded by the Umkukusi Mountains; on the westward lay the Hintza Forest, a great primeval wood, into the pillared stems and leafy gloom of which even the African sun seldom penetrated. To the east there stretched to the coast of Port Durnford some forty miles of undulating country, and away to the south-east there started up an abrupt eminence of rock, 600 feet higher than the old mission station.

The latter consisted of three brick structures thatched with straw, for which Colonel Pearson substituted less inflammable materials. These were utilised as military stores; and the church, also built of sun-dried brick and roofed with galvanised iron, was turned into a hospital, while its tower was selected as a look-out place, and proved of great service when signalling was resorted to.

While the troops were working hard engrafting a fort upon these edifices, and were ignorant of what had befallen the centre column at Isandhlwana, on the 28th of January Colonel Pearson received the following message from Lord Chelmsford:—

Pietermaritzburg, 27th January, 1879.
Consider all my instructions as cancelled, and act in whatever manner you think most desirable in the interests of the force under your command. Should you consider the garrison of Etschowe as too far advanced to be fed with safety, you can withdraw it. Hold, however, if possible, the posts on the Zulu side of the Lower Tugela. You must be prepared to have the whole Zulu force down upon you. Do away with tents, and let the men take shelter under the waggons, which will then be in a position for defence, and hold so many more supplies.

Though it was impossible from this brief memorandum to realise the extent or nature of the recent calamity, still it was sufficiently apparent to Colonel Pearson that the situation had somehow changed. A council of war was held, and it was decided by a small majority not to retreat to the Tugela.

Colonel Pearson, at an early period, began to experience the inconveniences of a blockade; his communications were cut off, and it was found that out of twelve messengers belonging to his Native Contingent, whom he had sent with despatches during the first week of February, only one arrived at his destination, all the others having been killed on the way.

Though he selected Etschowe as a depot, in consequence of the edifices which already existed there, it was not without disadvantages as a permanent fort. On three sides it was commanded at a short range, and some dangerous ravines, filled with sheltering timber, through which the foe could creep unseen, lay close to it. Plenty of good water was at hand; but there was not, as yet, a large stock of provisions in store, and a convoy, which was on its way with more, might be cut off.

While, therefore, it was determined that Etschowe should be held and fortified as strongly as possible, it was also decided to reduce the number to be fed by sending back all the mounted men and nearly the whole of the Native Contingent, consisting of two battalions, to Fort Tenedos, so called from H.M.'s ship of that name.

In its construction the fort was a six-angled work, about sixty yards wide, with a ditch eighteen feet deep, and twelve yards broad. The

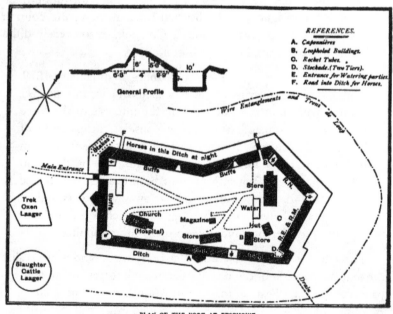

PLAN OF THE FORT AT ETSCHOWE.

Cape Argus says:

At the bottom it was profusely studded with *assegai* heads, to the number of several thousands, and the fore-ground was mined with dynamite. The parapets, carefully rivetted, were proof not only against musketry fire, but even field artillery, of which the enemy knew not the use.

Two well-built curtain walls ran out from its southern angles, enclosing a fine *kraal* for cattle and horses; and at its end was constructed an irregular redoubt, with a deep ditch and thick mud walls, defended by gigantic spiky thorns laid along the parapet. Day by day the troops, when not on other duty, were employed in felling trees to form abattis, hewing out gabions, cutting loopholes, filling sand-bags, and contriving every species of entanglement. Each face of the fort was cleared up to 800 yards, shelter trenches were dug for the first line of defence, and the ranges were carefully marked for the artillery and musketry fire. Every man had his proper place assigned him, and was in it on three minutes' notice.

At night outlying pickets, to the number of 300 men (chiefly natives), with five European officers, were thrown out to a distance of nearly five miles, as stated by the Cape Argus—a distance which seems somewhat great.

The convoy of supplies, escorted by three companies of the 99th Regiment, two of the 3rd Buffs, and two of the Native Contingent, the whole under Colonel Winchelsea Ely, with seventy-two waggons (six more were abandoned by the way), came safely into the fort, and on the 30th of January, in obedience to Lord Chelmsford's instructions, the garrison, instead of occupying tents without the defences, took shelter at night beneath the waggons ranged alongside the parapets within. The total strength of Pearson's force on that day consisted of 1,292 white and 65 black combatants, with 47 white and 290 black non-combatants. Colonel Pearson applied to Lord Chelmsford for seven more companies after be heard of Isandhlwana; but the general deemed it unadvisable to send them, and again suggested a withdrawal to the Lower Tugela.

Much more correspondence ensued to the same effect, and Colonel Pearson began to think of making a midnight march rearward; but by that time, about the 11th February, the Zulus were showing themselves in considerable strength near the fort, hovering in a menacing manner, without attacking it, and not even availing themselves of the eminences referred to, from which they might have harassed the garrison with their musketry.

The old Kentish Buffs were told off to the two northern faces. At the west angle was one gun, with a detachment of Artillery, and in the east salient were two guns, with a stronger party. The rocket-tubes were in charge of some marines. A company of Buffs held the gateway, with the loopholed church tower to retreat into. The south face was held by the 99th Lanarkshire with a Gatling gun, and for three miles along the Tugela torpedoes had been sunk in its bed by the bluejackets.

CETEWAYO, KING OF THE ZULUS.

The two line regiments had their bands with them, and these played daily, to cheer the men.

Lieutenant Henry Rowden, of the 99th Regiment, commander of the Mounted Scouts, had, by the end of February, explored all the country in the direction of the Isangweni military *kraal*, about three miles from Etschowe, and reported that upwards of 1,500 men were collecting. It belonged to the Isangu married regiment, men whose average age was fifty-four years, and stood on tableland, with forests running parallel on each side of it. Not far from it was a fortified *kraal* belonging to Dabulamanzi, a brother of Cetewayo, and Colonel Pearson was determined to attack and destroy both these places on the first possible opportunity.

At times it looked now as if the war were about to dwindle into mere bush-fighting, or into isolated and desultory attacks on, and by, the enemy, with the probability that the latter, if worsted, would retire into their rocky fastnesses and fever-infected swamps, where we should scarcely dare to follow them with impunity.

On the 1st of March we find the Special Border Agent, Mr. J. Eustace Fanin, writing thus to the Colonial Secretary:—

As regards Inyezane, Cetewayo contends that Colonel Pearson provoked the attack made on him by burning *kraals* and committing other acts of hostility along the line of march. He now asks that both sides should put aside their arms and resume negotiations, with a view to a permanent settlement of all questions between himself and the government. The king also states that he would have sent a message some time since, but was afraid, because when he sent eight messengers to the Lower Tugela they were detained; and he now begs that they may be sent back. I only asked the Entumeni men one question—*viz.*, whether the Zulu Army was assembled. They say it is not; the men are all in their *kraals*.

When the 2nd of March came, the latest news which the isolated garrison of Pearson had received was on the 8th of February, and they were in utter ignorance of the progress of the war and the fate of their comrades elsewhere; but on the former date there was great excitement among them, when a singularly bright light was suddenly visible in the direction of the Tugela, and which, though at first supposed to be a burning *kraal*, proved to be a flashing signal

For a time nothing could be read or understood till the following day, when the message was discovered to be:—

> Look out for 1,000 men on the 13th. Sally out when you see me to—

Nothing more could be made out till the 5th, when the light flashed again, and the message was read thus:—

> From Colonel Low, R. A., to Colonel Pearson. About 13th instant, by general's orders, I advance to support you with 1,000 men, besides natives, as far as Inyezane. Be prepared to sally out to meet me with your surplus garrison there by signal I may come by Dunn's Road. Make answer by flag on church.

Tantalising clouds enveloped the sky for the next few days, thus rendering communication by flashing impossible; but a few days after, a runner from Etschowe informed the signallers that their messages were understood.

Great efforts were made by Colonel Pearson to reply by signals, but owing to want of proper appliances, his first efforts were unsuccessful A fire-balloon made of tracing-paper was tried, and also a screen, 15 feet by 12 feet, set up on the sky-line, but both these proved failures. Captain McGregor then tried to direct the sun's rays by a small mirror to that point near the Tugela from whence the flashing came, and flashes were produced by covering and uncovering the mirror.

With an eye to relief or escape, in the beginning of March a route was surveyed by the Engineer officers from the fort to a point on the path that led to the Lower Tugela. As it ran through a district fairly open, by its use a long detour with guns and waggons would be rendered unnecessary. It was three miles in length, and working parties were daily employed on it, cutting down the steep banks of the watercourses and into the sides of the hills; and though often fired at by the Zulus, still the work progressed

A message now came that the relief was postponed till the 1st of April, when the entire garrison would be enabled to fall back, and consequently the ordered march to Inyezane on the 13th did not take place. By this time sickness was extending in the fort. There were twenty-five men on the list, and two deaths had occurred—those of Captain Herbert J. Williams, of the Buffs (formerly of the 4th, or King's Own), and Mr. Coker, a midshipman, who was a great favourite with all—a spirited lad, who fought his Gatling gun with great gallantry at the combat of Inyezane—and they were buried with military honours just outside the fort.

Though on the 15th of March large numbers of the enemy were seen moving past Etschowe in the direction of Inyezane, Colonel Pearson, to vary the monotony of life in the garrison, and especially as provisions were running short—the whole of the slaughter oxen having been consumed, and the troops being now supplied from the lean and sinewy carcases of the draught bullocks—resolved on making two raids in succession, and these were carried out with great spirit

The fortified *kraal* of Dabulamanzi was the most important point of these attacks. For the expedition the forces detailed were 100 bayonets of the Buffs and Lanarkshire Regiment, twenty-five of the Naval Brigade, with their Gatling gun, and a body of mounted Scouts, under Lieutenant Rowden, of the last-named corps.

Moving out of the fort at five in the morning, they descended the steep slopes that led to the river, and along a valley that narrowed as they proceeded. In some places their path was flooded by perilous *spruits*, or feeders, of the main stream; but Rowden's Scouts knew every portion of the country well, though the track was often hidden by sharp thorns and shaggy bush.

In some places bluffs overhead looked down on the party, and were explored by the Scouts, lest they might be manned by the enemy. Sunset found the expedition at a considerable distance from Etschowe, and a halt was made at a point where there were grass and water for the night, during which no one slept:

> As they had several alarms, and it became evident, from certain indications known to the experienced in Zulu warfare, that they were being reconnoitred by the enemy, though in all probability not in sufficient force to deliver an attack.

As it was quite possible that messengers might be despatched to adjacent military *kraals*, and a force brought that might exterminate them all in five minutes, an officer and two men made a reconnaissance in the dark round the bivouac, and discovered some caves that had evidently been recently occupied, amid a savage waste, strewn with enormous boulders of stone.

From them a path led to a piece of table-land some 50 yards in diameter, on a solid *kop*, or rock, 200 feet above where the three explorers stood, and by the weird gleams of the moon they were able to see that it was a point which twenty resolute men might hold against an army, and there too was a cave, affording additional protection. As these three adventurous men were returning to the bivouac, they were startled to see the dark outlines of several figures moving silently in the adjacent bush, and on these tidings every man stood to his arms.

The grey of the early dawn enabled them to see the enemy hovering in large bodies on the opposite ridges, and evidently puzzled by the movements of this handful of white men, the more so as one of Rowden's Scouts tied a handkerchief to an overhanging branch before leaving the *kop*, thus giving them the idea that a detachment occupied it, and that it was a signal, they knew not for what

However, the error served the troops admirably, and they were enabled to reach the summit of the *kop* (which means literally a *head*), and to get up their Gatling gun too. The horses could not ascend, but were knee-haltered in an excellent position half-way up; and when by sunrise the country was swept by field-glasses, the *kraals* of Dabulamanzi and his neighbour Ungakamatue were both visible.

Armed bodies of Zulus were seen departing in all directions, as if on errands of importance, and, aware of their superhuman activity, it was concluded that forces would soon arrive, and all retreat to Etschowe be cut off. To be besieged on the *kop* without provisions would ensure capture by starvation, so it was evident that it must be quitted at once.

As the *kraal* of Dabulamanzi was only a mile distant, as the road by which they had come was certain to be ambushed, and as one of the Scouts knew another path, it was boldly resolved to return by it, with what spoil they could collect in making a raid on the *kraal*.

Some of the soldiers cut long canes, fastened them between ledges of the rock, and fixed some coloured clothes thereto, leading watchers to believe there was a garrison still on the *kop*, which was quitted silently and swiftly through some dense bush on the reverse side, and down a deep and gloomy *kloof* almost closed in by hills 600 feet in height. They reached the vicinity of the *kraal*, but not before the enemy had opened fire on them at 700 yards from various points, which would have been most destructive had they been armed with rifles instead of old muskets.

By sound of bugle the skirmishers of the Buffs were closed in on the fifty men of the Lanarkshire, who formed the reserve, and both advanced through the *kloof* at a double, preceded by the mounted men; the *kraal* was swept from end to end, and set in flames, thus destroying all the stores of grain, while men, women, and cattle fled in all directions. Two large packages of mealies were brought off, but the

68

force was too slender to pursue the flying cattle, and the journey back to Etschowe became imperative.

The raiders had not proceeded above ten miles on their return, when they found, to their dismay, that their line of retreat had been discovered, and that they had dark ravines and woody *krantzes*, that might be full of men, to traverse.

As the party pushed swiftly on into the shadow of a dense forest, they lost sight of the pursuing Zulus, who eventually, in about an hour, to the number of 2,000, gained upon them quickly, and inspired by rage, were seen brandishing their *assegais* and waving their shields above their heads.

Evening was at hand, a mist was rising, and another hour would see these few Britons under the guns of Etschowe, but when within three miles of the latter, the rear-guard, consisting of a few men, were attracted by dark objects moving among some rocks on their left rear.

So fitful was the view obtained, however, that the men were unable to ascertain whether they were Zulus or some of the larger species of baboon, which often come out of their holes and caves to look at any human creature passing by. A steady watch was, however, maintained, and before many minutes they could plainly see that a large body of the enemy had—by the most tremendous pedestrian feat—succeeded in getting almost on a level with them, in a position to assail them in flank.

Soon this was done by a sharp volley, poured in at fifty paces' distance. Ten mounted men—only ten—all crack shots, now endeavoured to cover the flank, and did so with success. Galloping to a commanding position 500 yards from the Zulus, they dismounted, and opened a fire every shot of which told with such deadly effect that the Zulus fell back, as if waiting for their main body; and as the mist rose, they were seen carrying off their killed and wounded on the branches of trees freshly torn down. A running fire was kept up till the fort was reached, but this had no effect upon the pursued, whose fire in return decimated the foe, and eventually they drew off, just as the sun went down behind the mountains.

Though less protracted. Colonel Pearson's next expedition proved a more successful one. He learned from trustworthy sources that a body of Zulus was escorting a convoy of cattle for the royal *kraal* at Ulundi, and that its leader, having some contempt for the weakness of the Etschowe garrison, had only some 450 men to form the escort, which Pearson also understood to be not more than seven miles from the fort, and not far from the Inyezane River. For this expedition there were detailed only twenty blue-jackets, with the small engineer force, forty of the 3rd Buffs, twenty of the Lanarkshire, and the mounted Scouts of Rowden.

No Gatling was to accompany, as the utmost celerity of movement was required, and if the expedition did not succeed in its first dash, an immediate retreat upon the guns was to be made.

They marched from the fort in the dark, at half-past three in the morning of the 21st March, and reached the Inyezane River, which flows, 200 yards broad and 25 feet deep, for miles between mountains, the lower slopes of which are covered with splendid timber; above these start out bluffs and precipices more than 1,000 feet in height. The immediate banks of the stream are fringed luxuriantly with bamboo reeds, usually 12 feet in height, between which the tracks of the huge hippopotami are traceable at all times.

About eight a.m. a herd of cattle was sighted at grass, and by rapidly skirting the base of a hill, the little party cut in between it and a body of Zulus, who had bivouacked in front of some caves, and were busy cooking at fires lit in the open. The scouts, who had seen all this—themselves unseen—from the summit of a bluff, came sweeping down at a canter, and fell furiously upon the Zulus, to cover the retreat of the infantry, who captured thirty-five fine fat cattle.

A desultory fire was now opened from the hillsides by the enemy, whose numbers seemed to increase mysteriously on all hands, and in a short time it got within range of the rear-guard, wounding three; but by noon the whole party was safe in the fort, where the cattle were a welcome sight to the half-starved soldiers.

On the day before this last raid, a runner arrived from the Tugela with despatches, in which Colonel Pearson was distinctly informed that the column to relieve him would start on the 29th of March. During the previous fortnight the road we have referred to had been steadily in progress, and by the 21st was nearly complete.

It was asserted in the *Cape Argus* about this time that Cetewayo had prohibited the attack of fortified posts, that in the case of Colonel Pearson's garrison at Etschowe, it was his intention to starve out the garrison, by preventing all communication with the colony, that for this purpose a large force had been posted along the line of route, that two recent attempts to get through parties of the natives had been frustrated, and that a convoy of any length required a stronger escort than Lord Chelmsford had at his command. The *Argus* adds:

By making a detour of a few miles, it is stated that the whole of the bush and 'ugly' country could be avoided by a force marching without waggons. Possibly the men sent back will retire along this road, all the available cavalry being sent out from Fort Tenedos to its assistance. With fewer mouths to feed, Pearson may succeed in holding out until reinforcements arrive, and the offensive can be resumed all along the line. As regards the various fortified posts from Maritzburg to Rorke's Drift, the border patrols, consisting of police, volunteers, and natives, report the Zulus in force near the river every other day, but no attempt at passage has been made by any large bodies of the enemy. Small marauding detachments of twenty or thirty men frequently make their way across, and it is believed that the Zulus living near the river continue to fraternise with the natives upon this side, to whom the government, apparently, dares give no order to retire to some assigned distance inland.

Colonel Pearson, anticipating now the termination of the blockade, made preparations for the removal of the waggons which had been used as traverses within the fort, and under which his officers and men had slept in their great-coats and blankets.

Lord Chelmsford signalled on the 29th that a force 500 strong was to make a sally from Etschowe, and act in concert with the relieving column, in case the latter should be involved in a conflict. On the last day of March and the first of April the mounted men of the column were discerned by the field-glass at a great distance, and afterwards the *laager* formed by the main body in the valley of the Inyezane

A force was detailed to sally out, as ordered, and the night of anxiety wore on; the moon disappeared, and dawn broke in the east over the hill-tops, but before the detachment could sally out on the morning of the 2nd, the relieving column was seen to be hotly engaged.

Ghingilovo, the scene of this encounter, was in a direct line, and only a few miles distant from the fort, but the nature of the country between the battlefield and Etschowe was so rough and impracticable that it could only be reached by a great detour, to accomplish which four hours would have been requisite, and as useful co-operation was impossible, no sally was made from the anxious little garrison in Etschowe, whose situation would soon become perilous indeed if Lord Chelmsford was defeated.

71

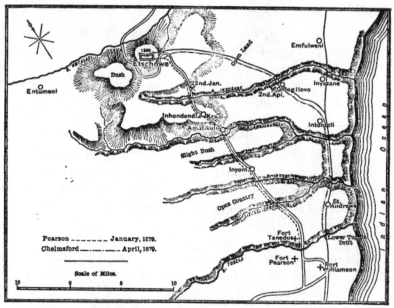

CHAPTER 5
The Laager at Ghingilovo

Fort Tenedos, the base from which Lord Chelmsford proposed moving to succour isolated Etschowe, was distant thirty miles from the latter, even by the road which had been discovered, and almost made by the garrison of that place, and in wet, stormy weather the encumbrances of transport made the march no easy matter.

The vanguard of the leading division, under Colonel Low, R.A., was composed of blue-jackets and marines, drawn from H.M.'s ships *Shah* and *Tenedos*, of twenty-six and twelve guns respectively—640 altogether, with two Gatlings, the Argyleshire Highlanders, 900 strong, the Lanarkshire Regiment, 400 strong, 180 Kentish Buffs, 350 mounted men, white and native, and a local contingent: in all, 350 horse and 3,720 infantry.

The second division, under Lieutenant-Colonel W. L. Pemberton, 60th Rifles, was composed of a Naval Brigade from the *Boadicea*, of sixteen guns, 200 strong, with one Gatling, the 37th Hampshire Regiment, a battalion of the 60th Rifles, making together 1,800 bayonets, with some 9-pounders and rocket-tubes. The commander of this division served throughout the Indian Mutiny, and had his left hand shattered by a bullet at Cawnpore.

The convoy numbered 113 waggons, 50 light and strong two-wheeled Scotch carts, and 56 pack mules. Each waggon had a team of 20 oxen. Every man carried in his spare and expansion pouches 200 rounds of ball ammunition. The convoy marched in the most compact order, flanked and escorted by Commandant Nettleton's Native Contingent, 887 strong, on the right, and Captain Barton's on the left.

The disastrous affair of Isandhlwana had greatly shaken the confidence of the native levies, and it was only after very considerable trouble, and by making it clearly understood that all deserters would be shot, that their obedience was secured.

The rain had fallen heavily, and the Tugela, at the point where the column crossed it, was 600 yards broad. The route adopted was different from that by which Colonel Pearson had marched in January: it passed through a more open country, was nearer the sea-coast, and, for the passage of horse, foot, and convoy, was safer, as it gave the Zulus few opportunities for ambush or surprise, and thus the column had achieved nearly half the distance to be traversed before any real difficulties began.

On its reaching the Amatikulu and Inyoni Rivers, an entrenched camp was formed, the waggons being drawn up in a square, with a

FORT PEARSON, ON THE LOWER TUGELA RIVER.

shelter trench twenty yards distant outside. Between this and the wag-gons and Scotch carts the troops bivouacked, as all tents had been left behind. The oxen were sent out and fed the moment the bugles sounded a "halt," and were thereafter taken within the enclosure for the night. Strict silence was enjoined

The Amatikulu River was crossed on the 31st of March, and at noon on the following day the column occupied an eminence a mile distant from the Inyezane River, where another waggon *laager*, of 130 yards each face, was formed. Close by it flowed the Ghingilovo stream, through long, feathery, and waving grass; but as the district was free from bush, it could afford no shelter to the enemy.

We have referred to the system of signalling that was adopted by this column and those on the church tower at Etschowe; and, indiffer-ent though it was. Colonel Pearson contrived to let Lord Chelmsford know that his last raid had been a successful one, that some cattle had been captured, and that the road he had cut through the bush south-wards would shorten the advance by five miles; also, that he was under no apprehension of starvation or assault for a few days yet; but should the column be delayed, he resolved to make a resolute sortie for life and liberty.

This message was written out, and read to the troops, who received it with three hearty cheers. The 57th Regiment, the "Old Die-Hards" of Peninsular fame, which had recently arrived from Ceylon, suffered in a greater degree from wet and cold than the troops that had come from home.

On the 1st of April large bodies of Zulus were visible in the dis-tance, and during the following night many signal-fires were seen blazing redly on the northern hills, plainly indicating that a great force was mustering in the vicinity, but the night passed without *alerte* or alarm. The rain fell heavily, wetting all to the skin; the weird moon shone in fitful gleams between black and flying clouds, and no sound was heard near the camp but the howl of the jackal and the scream of the expectant wild bird

On the 2nd, at dawn, the mounted men cantered out to reconnoi-tre, while the infantry unpiled and stood to arms within the trenches.

No one knew precisely where the Zulus were, as Captain H. S. Barrow, of the 19th Hussars, had reconnoitred on the 1st for eight miles to the northeast without seeing any trace of them; yet an attack might take place at any moment, and Lord Chelmsford pointed out to the various officers the important points of danger and defence in his *laager*, which overlooked the remains of the old *kraal* of Ghingilovo.

In front of the *laager*, behind a trench and an abattis, were posted the 60th Rifles, in their dark-green tunics; the blue-jackets of the *Shah*, with their "bull-dogs," as they playfully termed their destructive Gatling guns, held the right angle of the entrenchment.

Next them was a detachment of the 57th, and at the second corner were placed two Royal Artillery 7-pounders; the rear face was held by the Argyleshire Highlanders; at the next angle were two more Gatlings, under Lieutenant Cane, of the *Shah*, with that ship's rocket battery; and, prolonging the defences, were posted two more companies of Highlanders, three of the 3rd Buffs, and then the Lanarkshire Regiment. About six in the evening a general hum of intense satisfaction rose from the *laager*, when Zulus were seen advancing in skirmishing order, with dense masses in support, some miles distant from the right front.

On the opposite bank of the Inyezane two columns appeared, and these, after passing the stream at different points, rapidly deployed outwards, assuming a loose formation that enabled them to take advantage of any cover afforded by the ground, which in some places was studded with patches of bush, and in others was open but swampy.

Advancing from near a ruined mission station, the right of these two columns attacked the front or north face, held by the Highlanders. Through long grass, the skirmishers of the Unembomanabo and Unemsilya regiments came on, in somewhat close, rather than fully extended, order, flanked, as usual, by encircling horns, composed of the Nodwengo and Nonkenke regiments, yelling, and brandishing their shields and weapons.

Somapo commanded the whole, with Dabulamanzi as his second.

The men of the 60th, in their dark-green uniforms, as they lay flat behind a shallow breastwork, were scarcely seen by the advancing enemy, at whom they could take deadly aim with rifles rested firmly on the bank of earth.

In savage pride the Zulus came on, 10,000 strong.

Their white and coloured shields, the crests of leopard and feathers, and the wild ox-tails dangling from their necks, gave them a terribly unearthly appearance. Every ten or fifteen yards their first line would halt, and shot would be fired, and then, with a hideous yell, they would again rush on with a sort of measured dance, while a humming and buzzing sound in time

75

to their movement was kept up.

When they were within 300 yards of the *laager* a sheet of flame seemed to garland it. It became, as it were, zoned with fire, as the breech-loaders and deadly Gatling guns opened at once together, and in heaps the Zulus of the first line fell dead or howling and writhing on the earth, while the rest reeled and wavered, as they seemed to realise that this conflict was one in which their favourite weapon, the *assegai*, would prove useless, yet they struggled to within twenty yards of the shelter-trenches.

Fearless and desperate in the fierce longing to deal death among their enemies, the sight of the falling only seemed to inspire the main body to fresh exertion. They dashed through their line of wavering skirmishers, thrusting some aside and hurling others to the ground in their fury to close in and grapple with the defenders of the *laager*. For twenty minutes a shower of lead and iron was poured upon these naked masses, the places of the fallen being taken by others coming on, as columns in succession deployed in excellent order from the rear, reinforcing and feeding the first line, halting to fire, advancing, and re-loading. Beaten back twenty times, these brave fellows rushed forward twenty times with greater fury than ever.

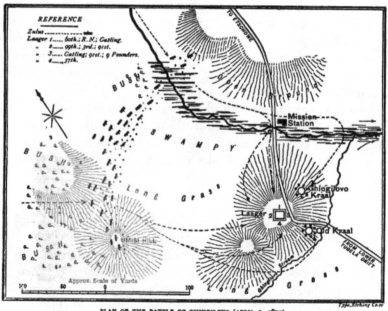

PLAN OF THE BATTLE OF GHINGILOVO (APRIL 2, 1879).

Their attack on the face held by the 60th was completely and sig-nally repulsed, and Lord Chelmsford rode along the line compliment-ing the Rifles on their behaviour.

About half-past six o'clock a sudden and well-executed change of front to the right without confusion or hesitation, was made by the Zulus, whose masses now hurled their strength on the face of the *laager* held by the 57th and Argyleshire Highlanders. If their courage seemed greater here their welcome was quite as hot. Major Ashe says:

> The 91st had not so many good marksmen in their regiment as the colonel could have wished, as many of his best shots were taken to supply Indian reliefs, but even the youngest soldiers seemed to gain skill and inspiration from what they had seen performed by the 60th.

Close and deadly was the fire poured in by the Highlanders and their comrades of the West Middlesex; but the fierce yells of the Zulus had ceased now, and their masses struggled onward in "the mute val-our of despair," and sure and terrible would the work of extermina-tion have been had they once succeeded in breaking into the *laager*.

Four times they flung themselves against it, but were hurled back by the dreadful fire that smote them, and at one time—about seven o'clock—it seemed as if they were upon the verge of achieving an entrance, for, to make sure of their work, many of them were seen kneeling in the open and firing from behind bleeding piles of their own dead to pick off the defenders of the breastworks.

But now, over the heads of the latter, a new line of fire was opened by the Native Contingent, who had climbed into the empty waggons, and reinforced the defence where it was needed most. Upon the left face of the *laager* the Zulus now made their last, their despairing and supreme effort, led by Dabulamanzi in person. They rushed to within twelve feet of the men's rifles, and several chiefs seized the heated barrels with the left hand, and with the right stabbed wildly with the *assegai* broken or shortened for attack at close quarters; yet, de-spite all their furious efforts and fearless courage, they never succeeded in achieving a hand-to-hand conflict, in which their numbers must eventually have borne our people down.

It is recorded that the various ranges of our rifles were distinctly traceable, by the lines or swathes of dead black bodies, with white shields, that lay at 100, 200, and 300 yards, in rear of each other.

At last they gave way, and began to retire in confusion. On the first

77

signs of wavering in their ranks Captain Barrow's mounted men filed out of the *laager*, formed squadron, and fell furiously sword in hand upon their right flank. A few shots were fired as Barrow's men advanced, and then the Zulus fled with the speed of horses, with Barrow and his troopers in close pursuit. The sword-blades of the latter were seen flashing and whirling in the morning sun, as cuts were given to the right or left, and point to the front, till the weapons were literally dripping to the hilt in the red work of slaughter.

The loss of the Zulus was 1,200 men; of the British, only 9 killed and 52 wounded. Among the latter young Lieutenant Johnson of the Lanarkshire, was hit early in the conflict Colonel H. H. Crealock, CB., the Military Secretary, and Captain W. C. F. Molyneux of the 22nd Foot, Lord Chelmsford's *aide-de-camp*, had their horses shot under them; and Colonel F. Vernon Northey of the 60th, was badly wounded, but never left his men till he fainted from loss of blood.

At the close of the action, however, and when he was roused from his state of insensibility by the ringing cheers of the British, which proclaimed the flight of the enemy, he suddenly raised himself on one hand from under the waggon where he was lying, and joined in the shouts of the men, thus bursting the bandaged wound and causing violent haemorrhage to recommence. This gallant and valued officer subsequently died, on the afternoon of the 6th, having lingered in considerable pain for four days.

He had served in the Oude campaign with the 60th Rifles, including the capture of Fort Mittowlie, and the action of Biswah.

Such was the result of the attack on Ghingilovo Laager, which lasted about an hour and a half.

About 800 Zulus were buried on the field, and 300 rifles, discarded in their flight, were subsequently gleaned. It was soon discovered that another great column of some 10,000 men had been despatched against us, on the day after Somapo had marched from the royal *kraal* at Ulundi, but, fortunately, it failed to effect a junction with his force.

Congratulations from Etschowe having been received and acknowledged by signal, the victorious troops passed the remainder of the day at Ghingilovo, when Lord Chelmsford had the *laager* reduced in size, but made stronger, as he had resolved to leave a part of his force there, while he pushed on to Etschowe, fifteen miles distant, with a flying column.

Leaving portions of the Buffs and 99th, with a party of the Shah's men to garrison Ghingilovo, under the command of Brevet Major Walker of the 99th, he marched for Etschowe with the 57th, 60th Rifles, and Argyleshire Highlanders, escorting 58 Scotch carts laden with stores, and preceded by mounted infantry under Captain Barrow, and some volunteers and scouts under John Dunn, who had been a resident in Zululand for many years before the war broke out. His great knowledge of the country proved invaluable during the campaign, and at its close he was appointed chief of one of the districts into which Zululand was partitioned.

The route chosen led up the right bank of the Inyezane, as far as the fort near which Pearson had fought on the 22nd of the preceding month. From thence to the ranges near Majia Hill a track was followed, and on all sides were seen skins, furs, feathers, shields, *assegais*, and rifles, cast away by the fugitives from Ghingilovo, but no dead bodies. Several small streams were forded, and extra grog was served out on these occasions, but as no vestige of the Zulu Army could be seen, the bugles sounded "halt" for breakfast, and the "prepare to dismount," and "off saddle" for Barrow's men, and fires were lit to cook the coffee.

The future progress of the column was much delayed by the natural difficulties of the road, after recent rains.

As Etschowe was reached, so says a correspondent, the order of march up the ridge became straggling, and as the sun was setting the fort was neared. It was a time of intense interest to all, when the camp which had been so long; isolated was approached; and with what emotions of joy must the holders of it have beheld the convoy coming! During their many weeks of imprisonment they had often cheered themselves by singing in hearty chorus

Hold the fort! a convoy's coming,
Work lads with a will!
Flash the signal back to Hopton,
We are jolly still.

The 60th, under Pemberton, pushed on in advance with the general, who all at once shouted, "Here's Pearson!" as that gallant fellow, on a grey charger, dashed round a hill, with his staff, and at the head of 500 men.

"How are you?" asked Chelmsford, as they cordially grasped each other's hand, and rode on towards the fort. The cords of discipline were relaxed, and the soldiers raised three of those ringing cheers that come from British throats alone, and the enthusiasm increased when the 91st marched in with all their pipes playing.

By six p.m. Barrow's men were at the fort, where the column arrived about midnight; and thus the relief of Etschowe was fully effected. During the ten weeks' blockade, four officers and twenty-seven soldiers had died, and at this date the number of sick amounted to about 120.

As the attack we recorded as having been made upon Dabulamanzi's *kraal*, did not include the private residence of that formidable personage, Lord Chelmsford had barely arrived at Etschowe than he resolved to have another raid in that quarter, and with Barrow's Mounted Infantry, to attack the chief *kraal*, which stood near the Entumeni Hill, some eight miles distant

Accordingly, on the 4th April, at eight in the morning, Barrow's men got under arms; their costume was a Norfolk jacket, now pretty well stained and patched, and high untanned boots. Accompanied by the general, Colonel Crealock, with his wound still open, Dunn, and some officers, as spectators, the indefatigable captain set out, his whole force, in saddle and on foot, amounting to only 225 men, who moved from the fort in sections of fours.

A four-mile progress over fragrant and elastic turf brought them in sight of the *kraal*, though little of it could be seen, since, instead of being built, as such places usually are, on some precipitous rock, it stood amid cosy, gentle, and grassy undulations, and its precise locality was at first known when some Zulus were seen running, as only these people can run, and driving cattle before them.

Detaching portions of his men right and left, as scouting flankers. Captain Barrow, of the 19th Hussars, who, as one of those officers "specially employed," held the local rank of major, led the direct way to the *kraal* at a canter; and the place was surrounded without a shot being fired as yet Lieutenant Rawlins and a few men were now ordered to search, and set it on fire at once, provided there were no women or children in it, and as none were there, it was set in flames at several points.

While this was in progress, a musket-shot came from a spot near it, and a small group of Zulus, led by Dabulamanzi in person (as John Dunn, who knew him, affirmed after looking through his field-glass), were seen aiming with deliberation about 1,200 yards off. A few shots were exchanged, and the *kraal* was left sheeted in flames, and hidden

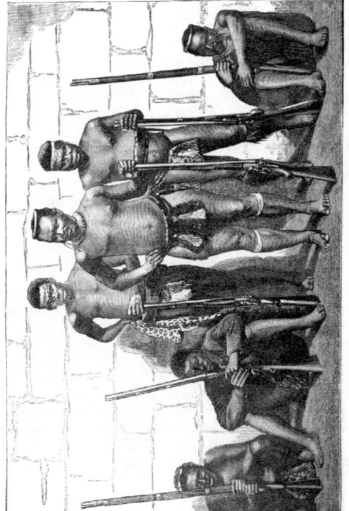

DABULAMANZI, ONE OF THE ZULU LEADERS AT ISANDHLWANA AND GHINGILOVO.

among volumes of dense white smoke.

On the 5th April, having destroyed as much of the laboriously-constructed works at Etschowe as time would permit, the column, with that of Pearson, began the return march to Ghingilovo, five miles distant from which Lord Chelmsford halted and encamped, but not without a small disaster occurring. A young sentry of the Argyleshire Regiment, imagining that he saw Zulus in the darkness, fired without challenging, as he ought first to have done.

The picket to which he belonged fell back; John Dunn's men, who were out scouting, now also fell back, and, in doing so, stumbled against a picket of the 60th, composed of young men, who recklessly opened fire at once, in defiance of all their officer could do to prevent them; and thus one of their own number was killed and four wounded, with nine of the luckless scouts.

After reaching Ghingilovo Lord Chelmsford issued orders with reference to guarding and strengthening the camp there, and departed on the following day, *en route* for Durban, to organise new plans for an immediate advance, prior to detailing which we must refer to some of the important operations of the left column again after the 24th of January, and during the spring months of the year.

CHAPTER 6

Storming the Inhlobane Mountain

When tidings of the disaster at Isandhlwana reached Brigadier Wood, then with the left column at the Zungi Mountain, he fell back on Fort Tinta, where he halted on the 25th January, and by the 31st had reached the banks of the White Umvolosi. On the same day he marched to Kambula Hill, where water was plentiful, wood easily obtainable, and where, accordingly, he formed an entrenched camp.

En route he had obtained full particulars concerning the Maglusini or Baglusini *kraal*, which he knew to be a muster place, and where were large quantities of Indian corn and other stores for the use of the Zulu armies, and towards which great droves of cattle had been seen driven.

Unless he proceeded with caution, and without ostentation, it appeared obvious to Colonel Wood, that the destruction of these magazines could be achieved only with a severe loss of men. He thus resolved to secure the same result by means of a raid of cavalry, composed of the dashing Frontier Horse, under Colonel Redvers Buller, and the Dutch *burgher* force, or troop of Piet Uys, 140 strong.

At four in the morning of the 1st February these troops left Kambula, and marched on the Maglusini *kraal*. This great centre of resistance lay thirty miles eastward of the camp, in the middle of a natural basin surrounded by precipitous hills.

Through these hills lay a pass, to hold which, and secure a retreat, Buller left thirty troopers, while, about half-past twelve p.m. he descended towards the *kraal*. As two other *kraals*, those of Umbelini and Ingatini, were in the vicinity, the greatest caution and secrecy in movement were necessary.

When the *kraal* came in sight, great herds of fine cattle were seen quietly grazing on the green hillsides. The *kraal* was very well built, and whether it held a strong force or not was quite unknown to Buller's men, and this doubt added largely to the excitement of the raid. No alarm or suspicion had been roused as yet, and the double fact of the smallness of the force, and of its being composed entirely of mounted men, contributed to the success of the attack.

Throwing out a few vedettes, Buller felt his way carefully forward, and was ere long observed by some Zulus who were idling about, but who, on seeing his marksmen, fled to the hills, where they were speedily joined by others in some force. After exchanging a few shots, the troopers made a headlong dash at the *kraal*, which was captured almost without resistance, six men only being slain, and its huts, two hundred and fifty in number, with immense stores of grain, were instantly given to the flames. Then the troopers at a gallop, often using their swords as goads, gathered the cattle, to the number of 400, in one great herd, and drove them off in triumph, in the face of 300 men, who offered no opposition, either to the flankers or rear-guard.

Fort Kambula was finished on the 2nd of February, and armed with two guns, and before the 10th two more successful raids were achieved, under Buller, one into the Eloya Mountains, and another towards the Inhlobane Mountain, which resulted in the capture of 500 head of cattle, without any serious resistance.

While a new and stronger fort was being constructed, and occupied at Kambula, on the 15th Brigadier Wood made an attack on the great military *kraal* of a warlike chief named Manyanyoba, who had been killing and plundering in all directions in the valley traversed by the Intombe River. Prior to moving against this chief, who had been joined by Umbelini, known as the Swazi pretender, another turbulent warrior, who, in 1878, had expelled the German military colonists from their farms near Luneberg, several careful reconnaissances had been made, and from the local knowledge of a Dutch trooper of Piet Uys', Colonel Buller was enabled to carry out the instructions of Colonel Wood with success.

On the night of the 14th, at ten p.m., the force detailed for this service got under arms; they were composed of thirteen sabres of Buller's Horse, and fifty *burghers* under Piet Uys, 417 of Wood's Irregulars, eight Kaffrarian Rifles, and 100 Luneberg Natives. In profound silence, without lights, bugles, or other accessories, they moved off to the bush, not even a scabbard being permitted to clink; and the single gun which accompanied them had its wheels bandaged with strips of raw hide, for the double purpose of muffling their sound, and protecting them from the sharp rocks and boulders amid which lay a portion of the route.

The bright moon rose, and by its silent light they crossed the river at a ford, and got quickly into the bush, without being heard or seen by the occupants of some adjacent villages. A two hours' brisk march brought them to an open plain, traversed by a watercourse, through which they rode, and just as the grey dawn stole quietly in, the gun was got into position, and Buller gave the troopers their final instructions. Before them rose a range of mountains that averaged 1,000 feet in height.

This range ran along the valley leading to the smaller *kraals* in the distance. Half the cavalry were now sent away by Colonel Buller to the left, with instructions to gain the bush, and wait dismounted, until the shells were heard. They were then to dash forward at a swinging canter, and cut off the cattle seen to be feeding on the slopes, which manoeuvre, if carried out, would drive them into the hands of Piet Uys and his men posted on the right. Just as the sun began to appear above the horizon, the gunners managed to hit off the range to a nicety, and the second shell crushed and burst right into the centre of the interior circle, where the cattle are placed at night, and which is usually surrounded by the beehive-shaped huts in which the Zulus live.

The sudden explosion of these dreaded and—to them—inconceivable missiles caused the wildest commotion instantly in the *kraal*; flames burst forth, and mighty columns of white smoke began to ascend from it; amid these, dark figures were seen rushing about, and yells of men mingled with the bellowing of terrified oxen.

As Buller's Horse dashed forward on the *kraal*, the male occupants fired a ragged volley, and fled up the steep rocks, where no cavalry could follow them, and from whence they opened a file firing. The fighting and collection of cattle lasted about half an hour; of the Zulus, 34 were shot, and our losses were two killed, three wounded, and one missing; but 400 head of cattle and two large flocks of sheep and goats, were brought off by Colonel Buller, whose men got safely into camp at Kambula, after having been in the saddle for about nine hours.

On the same day a force under Colonel Rowlands, CB., late of the 34th Foot, and one of the nine officers "specially employed," was also engaged. That officer had been ordered to join Brigadier Wood, with a mixed force, composed of 103 Transvaal Rangers, 15 Boers, 240 of Fairlie's Swazis, and 75 Vos' Natives. While marching on the road from Luneberg to Derby, where a wing of the 80th was entrenched with two guns, Rowlands found the Talia Mountain occupied by the enemy, who manned the rocks and caverns on its southern side.

He attacked with only partial success, killed seven Zulus, and captured 197 head of cattle. After another affair on the 20th at the Eloya Mountains, Colonel Rowlands and his men started for Pretoria, as the attitude of the Boers in the Transvaal had become menacing, and then all the troops in the Luneberg and Derby district were placed under Brigadier Wood's command.

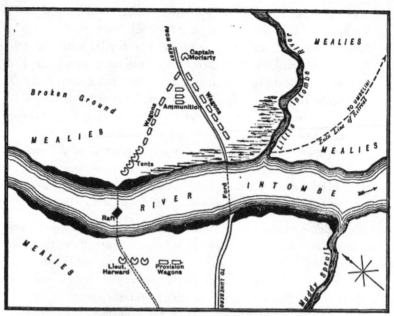

These and a few other petty movements, preluded what was known as the disaster on the Intombe River—an event somewhat similar to the calamity at Isandhlwana, though, fortunately, less in magnitude.

Luneberg was at this time occupied by five slender companies of the Both (Staffordshire Volunteers) under Major Charles Tucker, who had served in the Bhotan Expedition in 1865. He had also with him for a term Schembrucker's Kaffrarian Rifles, a corps raised from the survivors or descendants of the German Legion settled in British Kaffraria after the Crimean War, but they had now gone to join Wood's column at Kambula. Supplies for the garrison at Luneberg were being forwarded from Derby, and as twenty waggons laden with various stores were known to be on the road on the 7th of March, a company of the 80th under Captain David B. Moriarty, who had served with the 6th Foot in the Hazara campaign of 1868, was ordered to march from Luneberg, to meet and escort the convoy, which had arrived at the ford on the Intombe.

At first only a portion of the waggons of the convoy came, but with these the construction of a V-shaped *laager* was begun, resting on the river's bank. The situation was perilous, owing to the vicinity of a *kraal* belonging to Umbelini, the notorious Swazi freebooter, who had given much trouble of late.

The last of the convoy did not arrive till the 9th of March, when the waggon *laager* was completed, the flooded state of the Intombe rendering its passage impracticable. More rain fell; the river remained swollen, and on the 11th, when Major Tucker, full of anxiety, visited Captain Moriarty's company of seventy-one bayonets, he found it encamped on the bank, waiting for the water to subside.

Major Tucker, on inspecting the arrangements for defence, considered the waggons too far apart, and objected to the space left between the last waggon of the *laager* and the river bank, but did not order any change to be made. (Report, Intelligence Department.)

On that day it was reported by the native waggon drivers that Umbelini's people were gathering in arms. The camp has been described as being "pitched in a most dangerous position, with its face towards some high ground, covered here and there with dense bush, while its rear was resting upon the swollen river, across which Lieutenant Harward and thirty-four men were posted. No particular precautions appear to have been taken, excepting that a sentry was posted about fifteen paces from the front of the camp, on the Derby side," according to one account; or, according to another, with the exception of a guard stationed on each bank, each furnishing two sentries, but no pickets, the force being probably too slender to provide them.

On the morning of the 12th, at half-past four, while a thick haze rested on the swollen river, a shot was heard from the unfortunate sentry, while he shouted, mechanically, "Guard, turn out!" at a time when the officers and men on both sides of the river "were lying asleep and undressed." The shot and call made all stand to arms, for which there was barely time, as a force of 4,000 Zulus led, it is said, by Umbelini, was upon them!

Lieutenant Harward placed his thirty-four men under cover of a solitary waggon on his side, and made what dispositions he could to fire on the enemy's flank, while amid the dim light and gauzy mist, the whole valley could be seen swarming with dark-skinned savages, who at once surrounded the waggons, and *assegaied* the soldiers, in some instances ere they could leave their tents. The butchery—for it was no fight—was soon over, since all was confusion in a moment

Captain Moriarty was killed just as he left his tent, sword in hand, and his detachment on the left bank, being completely surprised, could offer no resistance to an attack so sudden and overwhelming.

The party on the other bank, taking advantage of the cover afforded by the waggons and also by some ant-hills, near the Intombe, opened a close fire on the Zulus, but failed to prevent 200 of them from crossing.

Lieutenant Harward, who commanded the party on the right bank, ordered his men to fall back on a farmhouse in their rear, and mounting his horse, galloped off to Luneberg for aid, leaving his handful of men to struggle as best they could without an officer to lead them.

Meanwhile, Colour-Sergeant Anthony Booth, of the 80th, did what Harward should have done. He rallied the few men who survived on the south bank of the river, and covered the retreat of fifty soldiers and others. The commanding officer of the 80th reported that, but for the coolness and bravery of this non-commissioned officer, not a man would have escaped with life; and so, Sergeant Booth was awarded the Victoria Cross.

The Zulus followed his party, consisting of only ten men, for three miles, but so bold was the front he showed, that he held them in check and retired without further loss. His resolute valour secured the escape of several fugitives from the left bank, who were without arms and some without clothes, and who were now in headlong flight for Luneberg.

Major Tucker, on receiving the report of Lieutenant Harward, started at once with a small mounted party for the Intombe, followed by 150 bayonets of the 80th, and on his arrival found that the Zulus had retired, carrying off with them the whole of the oxen, small-arm ammunition, rifles, blankets, and every scattered object of value, though, curiously enough, the waggons were only half pillaged.

Of the twenty-one men of the 80th, posted on the left bank of the Intombe, only twelve escaped, and some of those on the right bank also fell; making the total casualties 62 out of 106. Dr. Cobbin, two conductors, and fifteen drivers and leaders belonging to the Transport Department, also perished.

The dead were buried by Major Tucker, where they lay. They had all been stripped by the enemy.

Exaggerated details of this catastrophe renewed the terror which had been excited during the previous month in Natal, where a local print had the following passage:—

There are only 10,000 whites—men, women, and children—in Natal, and if 30,000 savages, skilled in military movements, and now effectively armed with the best that a British general's captured camp could yield, had come down flushed with victory, they could have devastated the land most thoroughly . . . Her Majesty's forces are now, so to speak, sucked out of every garrison in South Africa, and drawn towards the scene of immediate danger. The gaps they leave have to be filled by the volunteer forces, and in many instances the individuals of the latter have forsaken business, family, and home, to do garrison duty for several months, wherever it may be required. More than that, every male civilian between the ages of eighteen and fifty, is now enrolled as a member of a *burgher* force to defend, if need be, the towns and villages which may be denuded of volunteers by the latter being sent to the front.

There were called into existence during the Zulu War, no less than thirty-six different corps of volunteers, horse and foot, making an average force of 9,114 men. When the Natal Native Contingent was first raised, ten *per cent* of the rank and file were supplied with fire-arms. Afterwards they were armed entirely with fire-arms, Martini-Henrys, Sniders, and muzzle-loaders. On the 20th February in the following year. Lieutenant Henry Harward, of the 80th Foot, was tried by a general court-martial, at Fort Napier, Pietermaritzburg, by order of the commander-in-chief, for abandoning his post at the Intombe in the face of the enemy; but the court recorded a verdict of "not guilty." The proceedings of the court were submitted to the commander-in-chief, who recorded the following minute:—

Disapproved and not confirmed—Lieutenant Harward to be released and to return to his duty.

And the animadversions that followed were ordered to be read at the head of every regiment in Her Majesty's service.

It was about the time of this catastrophe that Uhamu, a half-brother of Cetewayo, whom the latter kept prisoner in one of his *kraals*, escaped, and was brought by Captain Norman Macleod to Derby, accompanied by 700 followers. He urged that the Zulu Army was demoralised, that Cetewayo was unable to collect a strong fighting force, and he seemed to cherish the idea that his own submission might change the situation, and that he would be made king in place of Cetewayo, just as Panda was installed in place of Dingaan. For the time, he was sent to Utrecht

About the latter end of March, Colonel Wood received a letter

ATTACK OF THE ZULUS ON THE ESCORT OF THE EIGHTIETH REGIMENT AT THE INTOMBE RIVER.

from Lord Chelmsford, acquainting him with the steps he was about to take for the relief of Pearson's column at Etschowe, and giving instructions for a diversion that must be made on the 28th of the month.

Wood's force had been strengthened by Schembrucker's corps, 106 strong; Raaf's Transvaal Rangers, 100 men; and Weatherley's Border Horse, 61 troopers, with a squadron of 100 mounted infantry, under Lieutenant-Colonel J. Cecil Russell, of the 12th Lancers.

On the 26th of March he summoned to his tent Colonel Buller and Piet Uys, and told them that he had received information, that a great herd of cattle—the chief wealth of the Zulus—had been seen on the Inhlobane Mountain, about twelve miles distant from the camp at Kambula, from which it was quite visible. The hill was well wooded, full of caves, and was in fact a natural fastness; and as several reconnaissances had been made of it, the brigadier and Buller were familiar with its features. Captain Tomasson says:

> This mountain was deemed impregnable by the Zulus, it was a huge square mass with precipitous sides, a flat top, some four or five miles long, and of a good breadth. There was only one way up, which was hard and difficult, and at the other end there was a way down, but it was well-nigh impracticable. Possibly there may have been unknown cattle-paths down its sides.

Colonel Wood was aware that bands of Zulus guarding herds of cattle had been for some time lurking amid its rocky recesses, and that in compliance with orders from Cetewayo, these bands had been reinforced by regiments sent from Ulundi, for the purpose of delivering an assault upon the camp at Kambula. Thus, to take the initiative and strike a decisive blow before more forces were concentrated, was now necessary, and would effect the diversion desired by Lord Chelmsford.

On the southern side of the Inhlobane Mountain there is an almost inaccessible ledge or terrace, on which the dome-roofed *kraals* of the natives were built, but the summit, which could only be reached with the greatest difficulty, was uninhabited, and used as a place of safety for the cattle of the people who dwelt below.

The attacking force was to be furnished by the Mounted Infantry and native levies, operating against the mountain simultaneously at both ends of it. That sent against the eastern flank was to be the chief attack, while the other was to create a diversion and act as a support, but was not to assault if a desperate resistance was encountered.

The total of the mounted force was 495 men, according to Major

COLONEL WEATHERLEY.

Ashe (but the details of it differ), each furnished with three days' rations and 100 rounds of ball cartridge. All were picked swordsmen and marksmen. The horses were carefully inspected, and any that seemed faulty, were retained and others substituted for them, and all these animals were so well trained and docile, that many would come from grass when summoned by their masters' whistle.

The eastern reconnaissance was to be under Lieutenant-Colonel Buller, and the western under Lieutenant-Colonel Russell, both of whom were to send out scouts to watch for a Zulu Army, said to be advancing on Kambula. On the 27th, Buller marched from camp with 400 horse and some natives, 675 in all, and after a thirty miles' circuitous route, bivouacked five miles south-east of the mountain; and about noon the same day, Russell, with 250 horse, a rocket battery, a battalion of Wood's Irregulars, and 150 of Uhamu's warriors, in all 640, after a fifteen miles' march, bivouacked four miles from the western flank of the mountain. In the evening the brigadier followed with his staff, including Captain the Hon. Ronald Campbell.

The night was damp and gloomy. The steep and precipitous Inhlobane could be seen in the gleams of the fitful moonshine, now in light, and *anon* in shadow, while the passing clouds seemed to foretell a day of storm.

Buller was for no more delay, and at half past three a.m., the word was passed quietly and quickly round for the men to stand to their horses, mount and march.

Under cover of the morning mist he reached the mountain, and ultimately, under the same friendly cover, the summit. Prior to this, the brigadier having been distinctly informed by Umtongo, the youngest of Cetewayo's innumerable brothers, that a Zulu Army was on the way from Ulundi, pushed on to make a junction with Colonel Buller and Weatherley and Piet Uys, lest they should be cut off.

The steep path by which Buller led his column was scarcely passable for mounted men, yet Captain Tomasson states that the Irregulars led up their horses by the bridle, and on arriving at the top:

> The men scattered and fired at their foes below them on the rocks. Captain the Baron von Sleitenkvon was here shot, as he was leaning over the edge of the hill.

He was a lieutenant of the Frontier Horse.

The firing on the summit of the hill could now be heard by the other column, which the brigadier ordered to push on, and as the ruddy sun was now up, a broken or bloody *assegai*, a battered shield, a dead troop-horse, and some Zulu corpses, could be seen here and there, indicating the line by which Buller had fought his way upward.

Most of the party with the brigadier had now dismounted, and, quitting their horses below a ledge of rock, ascended on foot. Wood himself leading his horse, with his staff and a small escort, was a little in front of Weatherley's men, when, at a short distance from the summit, a heavy and well-directed fire was poured upon them, flashing out from some dark crevices in the rocks above. Here Mr. Lloyd, Political Agent, fell mortally wounded while riding at a savage to cut him down, and the brigadier's horse was killed—disembowelled by a dreadful *assegai* wound

The shot which killed Lloyd tore one of Colonel Wood's sleeves to pieces.

As these and other casualties seemed to proceed from one cavern in particular, the brigadier ordered Colonel Weatherley to send a few bayonets to clear the place, at a time when he and his son, a gallant and chivalrous boy, aged only fifteen, were cheering on their men. As there was some delay in having this order obeyed, Captain the Hon. Ronald Campbell, of the Coldstream Guards, Chief Officer of the Staff, dashed forward, sword in hand, followed by Lieutenant Henry Lysons, Corporal Fowler, and three others of the Perthshire (later Cameronian) Regiment; but just as they reached the dark entrance, Campbell was shot through the head, after which every Zulu in the place was slain. He was the second son of John Campbell, Earl of Cawdor.

Colonel Weatherley and his men now moved on briskly to join Buller's force on the summit, while the brigadier and his escort descended to a ledge of rock where Mr. Lloyd lay. He was now dead, so his body and that of Captain Campbell were buried together near the foot of the mountain.

Colonel Buller, on gaining the high plateau—and to reach it more than one man had to clamber by clinging to vine creepers—saw how great was the area of the flat mountain top, where some 2,000 cattle were now collected, and that the Zulus who had been guarding them were dispersed. Accompanied by Piet Uys the colonel examined the plateau and the tracks by which a descent from it might be made, and of these there appeared to be three, *viz.*, that at the north-eastern end by which the ascent had been made, and two at the western end, both more difficult to traverse than the first, which, as it was secure from a flanking fire, Buller resolved to use for the retreat of at least a part of his force.

It was now the hour of nine a.m., and all seemed quiet on the summit, the Zulus having concealed themselves among the rocks and in caverns and crevices. Buller returned to the east end of the mountain, and sent Captain Barton, of the Coldstream Guards, his second in command, in search of Colonel Weatherley, with orders to return with him to Kambula by the route south of the mountain, which had been adopted on the preceding day.

Barton had scarcely departed on this errand when Buller saw a Zulu army, fully 30,000 strong, approaching the mountain from the south-east, looking, from the colour of their shields and the hue of their skins, like huge grey-speckled masses, moving amid the morning haze.

This army, the approach of which was known to Colonel Wood, who never could conceive it capable of compassing the distance it had marched in three days, was still about six miles distant; and it was calculated that the force on the mountain might thus have an hour's start

The retreat of that portion of the force now ordered back to the fortified camp at Kambula, was then so seriously threatened that two troopers were sent after Captain Barton with orders "to return by the right of the mountain," an expression by which Buller intended to convey the idea that he was to adopt the homeward route by the north, instead of the south, as at first proposed.

By this time the captured cattle had been collected by Raaf's Trans-vaal Rangers and Wood's Irregulars (two corps, about 138 and 460 strong, respectively), near the western extremity of the tabular summit of Inhlobane, and towards this point Buller and the men with him at once proceeded, in hopes that they would gain the support of Colonel Russell's force, which had been directed to that end of the mountain.

But mistakes had already occurred, and these led to another disaster. Had Wood's column, or portion of the attack, together with that of Weatherley, come on the scene of action in time to support the brilliant advance of Buller in the first place, all would have gone well:

But a delay caused by their missing the track, had enabled the Inhlobane followers of Umbelini and Manyanyoba to hold their own ground until the arrival of the Ulundi Army. Buller did all that a skilled general could do to bring off his men with small loss; but from the nature of the ground it was, in this instance, impossible for cavalry to work with any degree of celerity.

Russell's force was now in position on a small plateau, about 150 feet below that occupied by Buller. Viewed from thence, the path upward seemed totally impracticable for horsemen, consequently Russell made no attempt to ascend.

As it was impossible to see, from the place where he was posted, what was occurring above, Colonel Russell—about seven in the morning—sent Captain Browne with twenty mounted infantry, to communicate with Buller's party on the upper plateau. Without opposition he reached it, and after conferring with Major Tremlett, R.A., and Major W. Knox Leet of the 13th Regiment, a veteran of the wars in India, he returned to report "that all was quiet on the upper plateau, but that the path was almost impracticable even for men on foot."

By nine a.m., Colonel Russell saw the approaching Zulus, and to all who noticed the rapidity with which they advanced, it must have been apparent that there was a decided prospect of all on the mountain being cut off and pitilessly slaughtered. He ordered his men to abandon some cattle they had collected and to secure their own retreat to the open country below. He sent the native troops back towards Kambula, and drew up his mounted men at the base of the mountain to cover the retreat of Buller, instead of joining Colonel Wood, for here some instructions would seem to have been misconstrued, and the latter officer had taken post at the eastern end of Zungi Mountain, six miles from the spot towards which Russell had hastened with his mounted men.

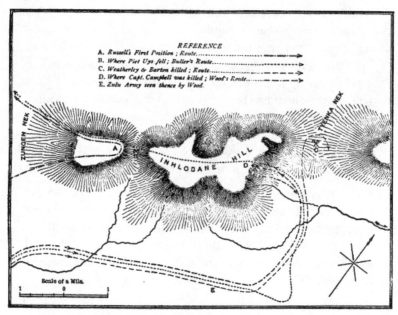

PLAN OF THE FIGHT ON THE INHLOBANE MOUNTAIN (MARCH 28, 1879).

Meanwhile the Zulus were coming on, advancing, in a line of five contiguous columns, with a cloud, of skirmishers thrown out in front and both flanks, forming as usual, two horns and a centre.

The approach of the army was now seen by the Zulu inhabitants of the mountain, who came out of their hiding-places in increasing numbers and began to harass the movements of Buller towards the western end of the plateau. The difficulties of the descent became more evident than ever; no support came from Russell's party, and Buller had no alternative but to continue the perilous line of retreat to which he had committed himself.

> The mountain side could be considered passable by horses only, by reason of the fact that the rocks of the encircling precipice here presented some appearance of regularity, and formed a series of ledges from eight to twelve feet wide, in which an insecure foot-hold could be obtained, the drop from one ledge to the next being about three or four feet.

How horses were got either up or down such ground, seems a riddle, yet such is the description of it as given in the Report of the Intelligence Department.

The native portion of Buller's force descended first, their rear be-

96

ing covered by the Frontier Light Horse, and now the dire havoc began. The Zulus of the mountain promptly occupied the rocks close to the line of the descent and poured a hot fire at point blank range into those who were helplessly endeavouring to get their struggling and scrambling horses over the almost impassable obstacles that barred their descent, and the casualties now became serious indeed.

In many instances the poor horses had to jump down three or four feet, then falling they broke their legs or necks, while the riders after discharging their carbines, became helpless, and were at the mercy of *assegais* thrust or launched.

Captain Tomasson says:

> Save for the heroic efforts of Colonel Buller, it would have been extermination. Six lives he is known to have saved that day personally, and how many more by his orders and example, it would be impossible to tell Major Knox Leet of the 13th Light Infantry, serving with some native allies, brought out Lieutenant Smith, of the Frontier Light Horse, on a pack-horse—his own being shot—and earned the V.C. Some of the Light Horse kept, in some measure, the advancing Zulus back and enabled the rear-guard to extricate themselves.

An officer and sixteen men were lost, and here fell the gallant old Dutch farmer, Piet Uys, the leader of the Boer contingent—"splendid, manly, honest, simple and taciturn Piet Uys, whose father, uncles and cousins, fought and fell in the old wars with Dingaan." He was last seen with his back to a rock, standing across the dead body of his favourite grey horse, with six Zulus lying dead at his feet, his empty revolver in his left hand, a bloody sabre in his right, and two *assegais* quivering in his body.

At last the lower plateau was reached down that rocky way, strewn with bodies and splashed with blood. The force was now disorganised; many were dismounted, their horses having escaped their hands and fallen over the rocks, and if the fears which all entertained, of an immediate attack of the great army from Ulundi had been realised, no man would have escaped to tell the tale. No attack was made as yet, and Buller, who had been forty-eight hours in the saddle, and was severely contused by a bullet, rallying his men drew them towards the Zungen Mountain, unmolested save by the fire from the Inhlobane Zulus.

It would appear that Captain Barton, on joining Colonel Weatherley, proceeded with him towards Kambula, till they found themselves near the Zulu Army, which by this time had approached the fatal In-hlobane so close as to leave no outlet between its right flank and the mountain. From this position, a most perilous and critical one, they thought to extricate themselves by wheeling about and endeavouring to cross the Ityenka Nek, and obtain a safe line of retreat on the north. The passage to this was already barred on one hand by Zulus who had come down from the mountain, and on the other by a portion of the advancing army.

Desperate was the fighting now, as they attempted to hew out a passage through the holders of the Ityenka Nek, and to the valour and coolness, the devotion and heroism of Buller, it was due that any ever reached the camp at Kambula. With his own hand he covered the rear of the retiring column, charging again and again into the dense masses of ferocious Zulus, who were all athirst for blood and carnage; and not until he saw the last of his men out of that terrible gorge in the rocks did he take time to draw breath or think of his own safety.

All the Border Horse except eight troopers were slain. Captain Barton and eighteen of the Frontier Horse perished, with Colonel Weatherley and his son, a boy in his fifteenth year, a sub-lieutenant .Great were the slaughter and confusion, so that in some instances adjutants and sergeants had much trouble in making out the lists.

Major Ashe says:

> Nothing could be more sad than Weatherley's death. At the fatal hour when all save honour seemed lost, he placed his beloved boy upon his best horse, and, kissing him on the forehead, commended him to another Father's care, and implored him to overtake the nearest column of the British horse, which seemed at that time to be cutting its way out. The boy clung to his father, and begged to be allowed to stay by his side, and share his life or death. The contrast was characteristic—the man, a bearded, bronzed, and hardy *sabreur*, with a father's tears upon his cheek, while the blue-eyed and fair-haired lad, with much of the beauty of a girl in his appearance, was calmly and with a smile of delight loading his father's favourite carbine. When the two noble hearts were last seen, the father, wounded to death with cruel *assegais*, was clasping his boy's hand with his left, while the right cut down the brawny savages who came to despoil him of his charge.

Colonel Frederick Augustus Weatherley had previously served Her

Majesty as a lieutenant in the 4th Light Dragoons (now Hussars), and as a captain in the Inniskilling Dragoons, under date 28th January, 1862.

So steady was the advance of the Zulu Army, and so dense their formation, that a broad tract of grass, over which they advanced, was completely destroyed by their bare feet. Brigadier Wood, after ordering Lieutenant-Colonel Russell to the Zungen Nek in the early part of the day, went himself about noon to this place—*viz.*, the low ground at the eastern base of the Zungi Mountain, and, finding that he was not joined by that officer and his force, he sent a fresh order, directing him:

> To move eastward from the point to which he had gone, and cover the retreat of the natives belonging to Buller's force, who were suffering heavy loss at this time.

Before this order could be delivered, Russell, in consequence of a mistake in the term "Zungen Nek," had already taken up a position at the end of the Zungi Mountain, and ere he could push on to the assistance of the native troops they had been cut off, almost to a man, and his force reached Kambula about nine p.m., unmolested by the Zulu Army, which was worn out by its long and rapid march. The Zulu loss was estimated at 3,000, and Cetewayo was said to have been a spectator of the conflict. (*Daily News,*)

Heavy indeed were the casualties of the day. There were killed about fifteen officers and seventy-nine non-commissioned officers and men; one officer and seven men wounded. But the number killed was uncertain, as several were reported missing, among others Captain Robert Johnstone Barton, of the Coldstream Guards, and formerly of the 9th Lancers, whose remains were not found and identified till the 28th of May, 1880, by a small party sent from the Ityotyosi River by Brigadier—afterwards Sir Evelyn—Wood, K.C.B., and then accompanying the Empress Eugenie.

It would appear that Captain Barton had descended safely to the open country north of the mountain, and was endeavouring to make his way back to Kambula, but, having taken a dismounted soldier up behind him, he was pursued, and thus easily overtaken near the Monzana River by some mounted Zulus, who were pursuing him and other fugitives from the Ityenka Nek. Finding escape together impossible, Captain Barton and his comrade separated, and the latter, being unarmed, was slain at once; and Barton, whose revolver was out of order and thus thrice missed fire, was shot from behind and *assegaied* by the same Zulu who, fourteen months after, guided the party to where his remains were found undisturbed amid the solitude of the African *veldt*. Redvers Buller obtained the V.C.:

For his gallant conduct in the retreat at Inhlobane, in having assisted, while hotly pursued by Zulus, in rescuing Captain D'Arcy, of the Frontier Light Horse, who was retiring on foot, and carrying him on his horse, until he overtook the rear-guard; also, for having, on the same date and under the same circumstances, conveyed Lieutenant C. Everitt, of the Frontier Light Horse, whose horse had been killed under him, to a place of safety. Later on. Colonel Buller, in the same manner, saved a trooper of the Frontier Light Horse, whose horse was completely exhausted, and who otherwise would have been killed by the Zulus, who were within 80 yards of him.

The V.C. was also given by Her Majesty to Lieutenant Henry Lysons:

2nd battalion, Cameronians (Scottish Rifles), and Private Fowler, of the same corps (then 90th), for having, in a most determined manner, advanced over a mass of fallen boulders, and between walls, that led to a cave in which the enemy were hidden. It being impossible for two men to walk abreast, the assailants were, consequently, obliged to keep in single file, and, as Captain Campbell was leading, he arrived first at the mouth of the cave from which the Zulus were firing, and there met his death. Lieutenant Lysons and Private Fowler immediately dashed into the cave, from which led several subterranean passages, and fir-

CAPTAIN THE HON. RONALD CAMPBELL.

ing into the chasm below succeeded in forcing the occupants to forsake their stronghold. Lieutenant Lysons remained at the cave's mouth for some minutes during the attack, during which Captain Campbell's body was carried down the slopes.

Doubts have sometimes been expressed as to whether the Zulus always mutilated the slain—at least, beyond ripping them open. Of this they make a particular point, according to a Natal correspondent of the *Daily News*, in consequence of a universally prevalent superstition, that if an enemy is killed in battle, and his body afterwards swells and bursts, so will that of his slayer burst open alive. So intense is this belief of theirs, that at the attack on Rorke's Drift, after the fate of the day had been decided, several Zulus were seen to pause under a heavy fire, and deliberately rip up the few who were killed on our side, outside the entrenchment. Cases have been known in which Zulus, who have been unable to perform this ghastly ceremony, have committed suicide, rather than await what they conceived to be their inevitable fate.

CHAPTER 7

Brigadier Wood Attacked at Kambula

Flushed with their next unexpected success in the affair at Inhlobane, the Zulus resolved to attack the British camp on Kambula Hill, but of this intention the brigadier had fortunately timely notice.

On the morning of the 29th March, a party of Raaf's Transvaal Rangers had left the camp to reconnoitre at daybreak. Tempted by the splendour of the African morning, when the parrots and monkeys were screaming and chattering, and when the vultures wheeling aloft in circles, indicated where a carrion horse or a dead man lay, they rode on for more than ten miles till they reached the Umvolosi, where they met a follower of Uhamu, with whom they returned to camp.

On the preceding day, it would appear that this man had found himself close to the advancing Zulu Army, and to have joined some acquaintances in its ranks, who were ignorant that he had attached himself to the British. From them he learned that the Kambula camp was to be attacked on the 29th, "about dinner time," and he was bringing this intelligence to Brigadier Wood, at the time he fell in with Raaf's Rangers.

He added, that he believed a very bad feeling existed in the ranks of the Zulu Army, where numbers of men were serving quite against their inclination, and were finding that instead of getting booty in the

COMMANDANT PIEI UYS, OF THE TRANSVAAL MOUNTED VOLUNTEERS.

form of cattle and sheep, arms and plunder, their *kraals* were being burned by the British, and their flocks and herds carried off.

This was not the only source of information Colonel Wood had, as spies were constantly passing, and moreover, he had received a detailed report of the enemy's force from a Zulu on the evening of the 27th.

On this eventful morning, two companies of the 13th Light Infantry were absent in the mountains cutting wood for fuel, and as the latter was absolutely necessary the brigadier did not recall them until that duty was carried out, which was done, fortunately, before the enemy appeared.

The brigadier had but few preparations to make, as in his camp every corps and company had their allotted place to repair to, the moment the bugle sounded. The position occupied by the fort was exceptionally strong, at the end of a long and isolated hill, and the fortifications, if they could be called so, were three in number. The first, which was manned by parties of the 13th and 90th Regiments of Light Infantry, was on the highest ground, and faced with stone; and this Wood commanded in person.

On the gentle slope below it, was a square cattle *laager* formed of waggons, averaging about 50 yards square, on the brow of some rocks, and held by one company of the 13th; and about 50 yards distant was another *laager* having seven sides, 200 yards in length, by 150 in breadth, manned by the main bodies of the 13th and 90th Regiments, and some Irregulars. This *laager* had within it all the horses, and the hospital.

Between the fort, as the stone-faced entrenchment was called, were placed the guns, four in number. Two more mountain guns, seven-pounders, were close to it.

The ground on the north of the position sloped gently down; but to the south some abrupt ledges afforded a considerable amount of cover close at hand, unseen by the defenders. Dinner was over by a quarter to one; the tents were then struck; the men repaired to their posts, and the boxes of reserve ammunition were opened and placed in convenient spots. This was done rapidly and without the least confusion, as all the preparations for defence had been practised previously.

From eleven p.m. the Zulus were reported to be in sight, and were perceived advancing in dense masses from the direction of the Zungi Mountain, and, as on the previous day, in five deep columns. At first the brigadier feared that, as the point to which they were directed did not seem very apparent, their object was to pass Kambula and advance on Utrecht, which, though provided with a strong fort into which the inhabitants might retreat, offered a somewhat tempting bait to invaders.

In their alarm after Isandhlwana the authorities of that town had besought the brigadier to quit Kambula, and garrison Utrecht, but he had declined to do so, believing that it was sufficiently protected and covered by the position he had taken up.

About noon, and for some time after it, the general line of the enemy's advance had been westward, but when they reached a point nearly due south of the camp they made a change of direction, and, while one portion of the army moved to its right and circled round the north side of Wood's position, the columns of the other continued to advance for some distance, and then wheeled up against its western side. The right horn, having a shorter distance to march, had by this time reached its point of attack, and halted, but out of gun-shot

Some mounted men, led by Russell and the indefatigable Buller, now rode out, for the double purpose of reconnoitring and luring on the enemy, as the brigadier wished to irritate them into an attack on one side before the other, and beat them in detail; and the action commenced by the mounted men riding up to within range of the right horn, dismounting, and opening fire. Though the discipline of the Zulus was good, it was not strong enough to restrain a column—said by one authority to be 2,000 strong, by another 7,000—when attacked by only a hundred men; thus the whole of the right horn sprang up, broke from line into column, and ran at a tremendous pace along a ledge situated at the beginning of some cultivated land, hoping to entice the cavalry to attack them on broken and difficult ground.

But Buller and Russell restrained their men from attempting anything of the kind, and fell back towards the *laager*, in which movement Lieutenant Edward S. Browne, of the 24th, won the V.C., by galloping back and twice assisting on his horse, under a heavy fire and when within a few yards of the enemy, one of the Mounted Infantry, who otherwise would have fallen into their hands.

Fed by supports and reserves, a cloud of agile skirmishers began to scale the north front of Wood's position at a quarter past two o'clock. The mounted men had now retired within the *laager*, and fire was opened by the artillery and infantry from their strong defensive position, and so tremendous was the first volley poured in by the Perthshire, says Captain Tomasson, that the Zulus "never again attacked the face of it" Here, as elsewhere, the sturdy Boers of poor Piet Uys, then lying dead on the distant mountain, handled with deadly precision their old national weapon, the long, single-barrelled *roer*, carrying an enormous bullet, suited for the destruction of big game, and whenever a dark head or a grey shield appeared above a rock or tuft of grass their fire was planted in with terrible effect.

The Zulu left now worked round to the west of the camp, while the centre advanced against its southern face, and, availing themselves of the cover afforded by its steepness, they crowded there in vast numbers, and assaulted the lesser *laager*, where the cattle were, with such fury that the company of the 13th posted there had to fall back into the other, after losing heavily. It was led by Captain William Cox, who commanded the skirmishers at Almora in the Indian campaign.

Encouraged by this success, a Zulu column 1,500 strong now formed up on the west of the captured cattle *kraal*, where they were sheltered from the fire of the main *laager*, on which they evidently contemplated a very serious attack; but before it could be delivered. Colonel Wood directed a counter movement to be made by two companies of the 90th, under Major Robert Henry Hackett. They advanced over the slope steadily, as if on parade, and, getting into the rear of the *laager*, took the Zulus completely by surprise by pouring upon them a steady and most destructive fire. Dark bodies with buffalo shields soon strewed all the ground, or rolled down the rocks with bloody and gaping wounds; but other athletic warriors, with yells of vengeance, sprang into the places of the fallen, and still the human stream came onward and upward, and these two companies soon became exposed to such a severe enfilade fire from a number of Zulus posted on a lofty spur to the westward, that they were withdrawn by sound of bugle, and took post again within the defences.

In falling back upon these. Major Hackett fell severely wounded, and was carried out of the fire. Lieutenant Bright of the 90th—a mere boy—fell mortally wounded, and died soon after. He has been described as:

A clever, cheery fellow, a capital artist, a good musician, and a most accomplished officer. It was in running forward to pick up Hackett that poor Bright received his death-wound.

Hackett had been shot in the head, yet the doctors expected to save him, but with, the loss of his eyesight.

Meanwhile, from the redoubt on the height, the two 7-pounders were smiting the naked masses heavily with grape and canister, till ere long the whole face of the rocks, up which they struggled, became slippery with blood. Lieutenant Nicholson, who fought his guns with

105

ardour, was mortally wounded in the temple, fell forward upon one of them, and died soon after.

The Zulus who occupied the cattle *laager* were unable to remove any of the beasts; but as the position on Kambula consisted now of only the main *laager* and the little redoubt, they were enabled to crowd below the rocks and steep ground, to within 200 yards of the former, and hence to assault it, which they did several times with undaunted bravery:

> But the two English and Scotch Light Infantry Regiments vied with each other in noble rivalry, and beat back the hordes of the Zulus upon the two most exposed flanks.

Meanwhile, four field-pieces that were without the *laager*, yet under the shelter of it, were worked with the most tremendous effect by Major Tremlett, R.A., who shifted them from time to time, as the movements of the enemy necessitated, and to the brilliant practice they made, much of the subsequent victory was due; while issuing out at the head of their mounted men, Buller and Russell executed some brilliant and destructive charges, which had a terrible effect upon savages totally unaccustomed to cavalry.

The action was a protracted one, but in time the Zulus began to see the impossibility of crossing the open space which separated them from the *laager*. At half-past five p.m. a shiver seemed to pervade the

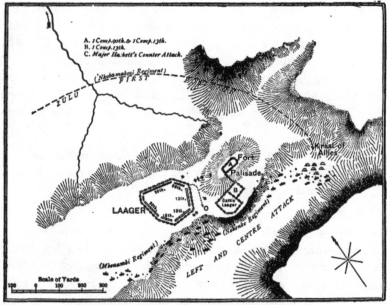

PLAN OF THE BATTLE OF KAMBULA (MARCH 29, 1879).

106

masses, and the vigour of their attack began to slacken. Lieutenants Smith and Lysons, seeing some Zulus advancing to *assegai* a wounded soldier of the 13th, who was lying under fire in the open, rushed out, and, led by Captain Woodgate, carried him into shelter, and in doing so, Woodgate had his helmet smashed by a bullet; yet so incessant was the clatter of the breech-loaders, that the Zulus were strewn like leaves in autumn beneath the biting fire.

Brigadier Wood now ordered a company of the 13th to retake the cattle *laager*, and one of the 90th to advance on the right to the edge of the precipitous rocks, from whence they poured a heavy fire into the Zulus who were now giving way. Captain Cox of the 13th, though suffering greatly from a wound and loss of blood, gallantly led his men on this arduous duty.

The mounted men, who, after having placed their horses within the *laager*, had been assisting in the defence of it with their carbines, now sprang into their saddles, betook them to their swords, and were led by Buller and Russell against the now retreating enemy, whom, for more than seven miles, they pursued like a flock of sheep until night fell, while the infantry and native levies scoured the immediate vicinity of the camp, and killed all whom they found in concealment.

The attack lasted from half-past one p.m. to half-past five, when the retreat commenced. It was greeted with a ringing cheer, and when the mounted pursuers filed out of camp at full speed, they were saluted from the forts with shouts of applause, which told them how much the infantry would have liked to join in the work of vengeance.

The army which fought this day at Kambula, was subsequently ascertained to have comprised—with Umbelini's men—25,000 in all, and had been assembled at Ulundi specially to deliver an attack on Brigadier Wood's camp. The right horn was composed of the N'kobamakosi regiment, which, in consequence of its losses at Isandhlwana, was eager for distinction and revenge, and suffered very severely by prematurely commencing the action in attacking Buller's Horse.

The loss inflicted on the Zulus this day is stated in the public prints as 3,000; but the War Office Report reduces this number to 2,000; 1,500 dead bodies lay in the vicinity of the camp at nightfall, but in the morning, many were found to have been carried off. By the 3rd April, 800 Zulus were buried, and 326 firearms were gleaned up; some of these were our own Tower weapons.

The British force engaged numbered in all only 1,998, and its casualties amounted to eighteen non-commissioned officers and men killed, eight officers and fifty-seven non-commissioned officers and men wounded. Many died of their wounds, among these were Lieutenants Nicholson, White, and Bright.

On the day after the engagement our dead were all buried on Kambula Hill, the burial service being read in the most impressive manner by Brigadier Wood in person.

Many wounded Zulus were brought into camp, where their wounds were dressed, and finding the soldiers kind to them, they became wonderfully communicative. Their army dispersed immediately after the action, which is generally believed to have saved the Transvaal from a Zulu invasion.

The gallant Major Hackett of the Perthshire lost the sight of both eyes from his wound, and in the July of the following year, was presented to Her Majesty, by his brother. Colonel J. B. Hackett, V.C, a veteran officer of long and distinguished service.

The wounded were sent to Utrecht, a distance of about thirty miles, under protection of an escort, and the author of *With the Irregulars in the Transvaal*, who was on this duty, describes their sufferings as great, owing to the rough roads that were like tracks, and the ill-hung waggons and ambulances. The first halt was made at the Blood River, so named from some old battle between the Zulus and the Boers, on which occasion it was dyed with the blood of the slain. It divides the Transvaal from Zululand, and was now in full flood

> The flood was so high that the waggons could not cross, and ambulances had to be sent for from Balte Spruit on the opposite side; they arrived at ten p.m., a light span bridge was thrown across the river by a company of the 13th Regiment, and the camp entrenched for the night. A most miserable night was then passed by the Irregulars, who had crossed to the opposite bank; the swamp was four inches deep in water, the mosquitoes aggressive in the extreme, and the only way to rest was to lean against a waggon wheel. Towards day the bridge, which had broken down by the force of the current during the night, was repaired. The sick and wounded had to be carried through the worst part of the swamp to the waggons, a quarter of a mile off. They could not be got nearer, the ground was so soft. The sufferings of the wounded must have been extreme, as they were carried in *dhoolies* over the rough ground and through deep pools. It was curious to observe the difference in men thus

equally suffering; some never uttered a sound, others groaned most horribly; some expressed fierce anxiety to be getting on; others were sunk in profound apathy, and seemed utterly indifferent to all around them. . . . . We often had to halt to administer brandy to some poor fellows who were sinking, and once or twice to find that some of the number had breathed their last in spite of all the care that under such circumstances could be given them.

A day or two afterwards, this escort rejoined Wood's column at Kambula, bringing fresh ammunition to replace that recently expended on the 28th and 29th of March; and once, when on escort duty, they discovered a trooper of Weatherley's Border Horse, named Grandier, who had been taken at Inhlobane, and sent back from Ulundi, to undergo torture at the hands of Umbelini's men. He had escaped, and when found, was naked, famished, and all but dead from exhaustion. Some days before this, Umbelini's career had been cut short by the pistol of Captain Prior, of the 80th Regiment, after a twelve miles' pursuit.

The effects of the officers who fell on the 28th and 29th of March, were sold in camp, and high indeed were the prices realised for provisions. Tins of preserved meat, sold at home for one shilling, went for six or eight; matches fetched ninepence per box; while cigars and tobacco brought fabulous prices.

Reinforcements were now coming out fast from England, and about this time the *Colonist* newspaper says:—

The Zulus are dispirited; Cetewayo means to await the attack in the heart of his own country, and is said to be preparing a last retreat for himself. It is in a ravine between high rocks, said to be accessible only in front, and through a morass impassable, or nearly impassable, in wet weather. If defeated, he says he will retire and make his last stand there, and kill himself, rather than fall into the hands of his enemies. It is added, that he says he will however first kill his *indunas*—not a very likely threat for him to have given utterance to, whatever he may intend.

As related, it had been determined by Lord Chelmsford that the position at Etschowe should be completely abandoned after the relief of the blockaded garrison, which reached the Tugela on the 7th April; and the 9th saw the general at Durban, where the bulk of the welcome reinforcements had already disembarked, and where he could see no less than sixteen magnificent steam transports, some of them the largest afloat, in the outer anchorage, twenty-three store and other vessels in the inner harbour, and thirty more in the roads, while steam cranes were at work on every wharf, landing all the munitions of war.

Among the arrivals were the 1st Dragoon Guards and the 17th Lancers; two batteries of Royal Artillery and an ammunition column; a company and a half of Engineers; the Royal Scots Fusiliers; the 58th, 60th, 91st Argyleshire Highlanders; the 94th, and drafts for all the other corps in Cape Colony, making a grand total of 418 officers, 9,996 men, 1,868 horses, and 238 waggons; and not the least remarkable figure, among the brilliant group of staff officers who were there to greet Lord Chelmsford, was that of the ill-starred Prince Louis Napoleon, who had reached Durban two days after the conflict at Kambula, and was appointed an extra A.D.C. on the headquarter staff.

The conveyance of all these troops to Natal had been marked by only two misfortunes worth mention—one, when the *City of Paris* ran ashore in Simon's Bay on the 23rd of March, and had to transfer her living freight to H.M.S. *Tamar;* and the other, the disaster that befell the *Clyde,* which was totally wrecked near Dyer's Island, seventy miles farther eastward.

She had left the docks at Capetown on the 2nd April, after bringing from home fifteen officers and 534 men, all volunteers to make up the shattered strength of the 24th Regiment, the whole under the command of Colonel Davis, of the Grenadier Guards. After being twelve hours enveloped in fog, the watch suddenly found her, within a few lengths of herself, close among rocks and breakers, and though the engines were instantly reversed, she went crash ashore at twenty minutes past six a.m., on a rock between the island and the mainland. Discipline was never relaxed, and the weather was calm and beautiful. By half-past eleven Colonel Davis had all the troops rowed ashore, and the vessel was abandoned. She sank in the night, with 15,000,000 rounds of rifle ammunition, four Gatling guns, and other stores.

The soldiers who first reached the shore selected a convenient place whereon to bivouac, and provisions from the beach were conveyed to them in the waggon of a neighbouring farmer, and there they remained till brought to Durban by the Tamar,

As all fear of an invasion of Natal was now at an end, and as it was resolved to carry an offensive war into the very heart of Zululand, Lord Chelmsford found the reorganisation of his forces and a change of plans alike necessary. After some alterations, the following arrange-

MAJOR-GENERAL E. NEWDIGATE, C.B.

ments were made on the 13th of April, and these must be borne in mind with reference to the operations about to be detailed. No. 1 column was now designated No. 1 Division South African Field Force, under the command of Major-General Hope Crealock, C.B. Brigadier Wood's force was to act independently, as "a flying column;" and the remainder of the troops in Utrecht were to constitute No. 2 Division, the command of which was given to Major-General Newdigate.

On landing, the infantry began the forward march at once, but the cavalry were retained for a week at Durban to get the horses into condition for service. The greater portion of the force took fresh ground at Kambula on the 14th of April. There the redoubt was still occupied, but a new entrenched camp was formed 700 yards westward of the old one. Sanitary reasons compelled this. The whole air was redolent with a horrid odour, for in the crevices and among the long, rank grass lay in corruption the bodies of Zulus who had crawled away to die, undiscovered and unseen.

On the 15th of April, and before new operations began, the following was the general position of our troops in South Africa. Lord Chelmsford, with the Lancers, Dragoon Guards, and Artillery, was still at Durban. The 2nd Brigade of the 1st Division (57th, 60th, and 91st), with a portion of the Naval Brigade, held Ghingilovo, while the 1st Brigade (Buffs, 88th, and 99th Regiments) held the left bank of the Lower Tugela. The 2nd Division (Scots Fusiliers, 58th, and 94th) were on the march for Doornberg, a wooded mountain between the Blood and Buffalo streams, and Wood's flying column, constituted as before

FRONTIER LIGHT HORSE, ON VEDETTE DUTY, DISCOVERING ZULUS NEAR WOOD'S CAMP, ON KAMBULA HILL.

described, held the entrenched position at Kambula, while Utrecht was garrisoned by the 80th Regiment

CHAPTER 8

Arrival of Sir Garnet Wolseley

The chief features of the new campaign against the Zulus were these.

The two divisions operating from separate bases, one at Utrecht and the other at Durban, while holding communication with Brigadier Wood's Flying Column and Major-General Marshall's cavalry brigade, were to have one common object in view—an advance upon Ulundi—the chief *kraal*, or capital of Cetewayo.

Major-General Crealock, commanding the 1st Division, left Durban, and on the 18th April his headquarters were established at Fort Pearson, near the mouth of the Tugela. He had served with the Perthshire Regiment at the siege of Sebastopol, at the storming of the Quarries, and in the attacks upon the Redan. He had been D.A. Quartermaster-General in China in 1857, in several Indian campaigns, and lastly at the capture of the forts of Tangkoo and Taku.

By Lord Chelmsford's orders, he was to march upon the Emangwene and Undi military *kraals*, on the north bank of the Umlatoosi River, attack and burn them; he was to form a strong and permanent fort at Inyezane—the scene of Pearson's fighting on the 22nd January—and store therein two months' provisions for his column, while an intermediate fort was to be established between that point and the Tugela. After the destruction of the *kraals*, the further movements of his command were to be at Crealock's discretion, Ulundi being the object of the northern force, in support of which, an entrenched post and supply depot should be established by General Crealock near St. Paul's Mission Station.

In obedience to these orders, two forts were formed, at the points indicated on the 24th and 29th of April, and named respectively Forts Crealock and Chelmsford. After much delay, caused by the extreme difficulty of carrying the requisite materials from Durban, a pontoon bridge was constructed across the Tugela by the 7th May, which was replaced in the subsequent month by a semi-permanent trestle and pontoon bridge, while the telegraph had been previously extended to Fort Chelmsford.

Up country the climate is usually bracing and healthy, but the low-lying coast region in which the 1st Division encamped, was very unhealthy and much enteric fever broke out .The 2nd Brigade, under

Colonel Clarke, though its camp at Fort Chelmsford and its position was better in a sanitary way than that of Ghingilovo, suffered so severely that 18 officers and 479 men of the line were sent back sick from Forts Chelmsford and Pearson before the 17th June, and 71 officers and men died. The troops suffered from the effluvia caused by the decomposition of dead oxen and horses, lying in *kloofs* and along the waysides, tainting and poisoning the air.

Great were the transport difficulties of the position, and by the middle of May forage was always apt to fail from the almost universal practice of grass-burning by the natives; and the oxen which were thus obliged to travel farther for their food, fell off in condition and became unfitted for hard work. Waggon owners grew very chary about encountering the risks which journeying in Zululand necessitated; and by May large numbers of animals perished, the daily average being ten, and as these were all hired, the indemnity paid by the British Government for each ox that died, or was lost, was £20.

Great difficulty, too, was experienced in obtaining natives to drive the transport teams; but eventually their numbers were made up, and the requisite two months' provisions having been amassed at Fort Chelmsford, the division was ready to march, but the month of June was advanced before this was achieved, and on the 13th the forward movement began.

On that day, with the intention of concentrating the division at Fort Chelmsford, a portion of the 1st Brigade, consisting of the 2nd battalion of the Buffs, Lonsdale's Horse, a corps raised by Commandant Lonsdale in Cape Colony, in February, 1879, and two guns, marched from the Tugela. The rest of that brigade followed on the 17th, on which day the actual advance of the division may be said to have commenced, and two days after the Major-General and his staff were at Fort Chelmsford with the Naval Brigade under Commodore Richards, R.N.

The march to that place was up a steep ascent, and then along grassy table-land to the westward, and then by a steep descent into the valley of the Amatikula, where masses of crystalline pebbles were seen glittering amid the silver sand, and the scene was made beautiful by yellow convolvuli, tiger lilies, and osier bushes.

On the 19th, in the afternoon, Major-General Crealock rode out to reconnoitre the Umlalaz River for six miles. A camping ground was chosen, and on the 20th a column, under Major Bruce of the 91st Highlanders, composed of that regiment, two Royal Artillery guns, a detachment of Engineers, and the 4th battalion of the Natal Native

Contingent, went forward in that direction. It was about this time, we are told, that:

An enlightened *Kaffir*, being spoken to by a gentleman with reference to the arrival of the 91st Highlanders, remarked in the coolest manner possible—'Oh, your English soldiers are nearly all killed, and you are obliged to get Scotchmen to assist you now.'

On the 21st the remainder of the division advanced, and on the following day the passage of the Umlalaz was effected without opposition, a pontoon bridge being thrown across, where it was thirty-five yards wide and ten feet deep. The valleys through which the troops marched were observed to be very fertile, with swelling undulations often cultivated, with alternations of pine timber, rich grass and prickly jungle.

The eminence on the right bank of the stream, where the 1st Division encamped, was named Napoleon Hill, in honour of Prince Louis Napoleon, whose fate has to be recorded when we refer to the other columns.

On the 23rd of June, General Crealock and Commodore Richards, with the mounted men, made a reconnaissance eastward of Napoleon Hill, and approaching the coast they ascertained that Port Durnford was about six miles north of the mouth of the Umlalaz, and was merely an open, lonely and sandy beach, on which the surf is ever thundering with unusual violence. There signals were afterwards exchanged with H.M.S. *Forester*, which the commodore ordered to sail for Durban, with orders for the transports to be at Port Durnford by the 29th June.

The only result of the reconnaissance of the 23rd was, that the troops accompanying Crealock, *viz.*, the 91st Highlanders and two guns, came upon some 250 Zulus driving a large herd of cattle, which, after a little skirmish, they captured (with the loss of only one man), besides a number of women and children, who implored protection and food, and to whom, as they seemed famishing, biscuits and mealies were served out at once.

On the 25th June, a small fort to hold one company was formed on the left bank of the Umlalaz. It occupied the crest of a hill, covering the pontoon bridge, and was named Fort Napoleon. The following day, the mounted men made an expedition towards the Ungoya Hills, supported by the 3rd battalion of the 60th, two guns and 200 natives under Brigadier Clarke, while the Naval Brigade, the Buffs, and 200 natives moved towards Port Durnford and encamped for the night

On the same day, some stalwart Zulus, fully equipped and armed for war—one of them a corpulent chief, named Umsintwanga, clad in an old horse blanket, with a tippet of leopard skin, and bearing an elephant's tusk—came from Cetewayo with proposals for peace, through an interpreter, and, as a symbol of friendship, laid the huge ivory offering at the feet of General Crealock, who informed him that all communications on that matter must be made to Lord Chelmsford; but eventually he sent the tusk to the Secretary of State for the Colonies.

The 27th saw the divisional headquarters at a place called Five Kraal Hill.

> The long ranges of mountains which completely separate the coastline from the interior, here stand out in magnificent relief, and though they are at a distance of sixty or seventy miles, they present a sharply defined outline in the morning air, their ravines, watercourses and terraced heights, appearing with almost supernatural distinctness.

As yet nothing was seen of the enemy in arms, but knowing the wily and crafty nature of the people, every movement and advance was made with the greatest care. On the 28th of June, the division reached camping ground on a plain about a mile from the coast, where the Umlalaz flows into the Indian Ocean. Southward lay the coast range of sandy hills through which the broad stream forces its solitary way, and on the other three sides were wide and desolate marshes.

The transports were now seen off shore, and the Naval Brigade ran out hawsers, by which surf boats could be drawn up and stores landed, while the general was giving to the flames a number of *kraals* on the banks of the Umlatoosi River.

Sixty tons of supplies and thirty mules were got on shore, and a work, called Fort Richards—after the commodore—was formed between the camp of the 1st Brigade and the sea. On the 2nd of June the weather was so wet and stormy, with such a dreadful sea on, that all communication with the vessels in the anchorage was suspended. Among these vessels was H.M.S. *Shah*, which having left Durban the day before with his Excellency Sir Garnet Wolseley and his staff, had arrived off Port Durnford that day.

Sir Garnet, who was not only to be governor, but commander-in-chief and high commissioner in Natal and the Transvaal, had reached Durban from London on the 28th June, and been sworn in at Pietermaritzburg; after which he had re-embarked at Durban, and sailed along the coast in the *Shah*, to join the 1st Division; but as the weather and the surf showed no sign whatever of abatement, he returned to Durban, and the transports all put to sea.

On the 4th of July, the Emangwene military *kraal* was burned by the mounted men and 200 of John Dunn's scouts, the whole being commanded by Major Barrow of the 19th Hussars. It stood nine miles from the Umlatoosi River, and seemed to have been long unoccupied, so not a shot was fired on the occasion, though about 200 Zulus were seen hovering on the green hill slopes at some distance, and a few were made prisoners.

Next day the destruction of the old Undi *kraal* was resolved on, by the same force under Barrow, while Brigadier Clarke followed him with a supporting force, consisting of one battalion, one Gatling, one 9-pounder, the Naval Brigade, and 500 natives, as resistance was expected, and Major-General Crealock, with his staff, was present.

Marching by the light of a brilliant moon, at half-past three a.m., from their bivouac at the lower drift of the Umlatoosi, the force came to a deserted Norwegian mission station, and the military *kraal* was reached at a quarter to ten a.m. It consisted of 640 huts, which were destroyed by fire, and a few Zulus who lurked near it were made prisoners.

On the 7th of July Major Barrow's force and the Native Contingent, returned to the camp near Port Durnford; and Sir Garnet Wolseley, having again left Durban, rode into it in the evening, and with his arrival ends for a time the somewhat uninteresting operations of the 1st Division of the South African Field Force.

CHAPTER 9

Buller's Scouts

We have now to detail some of the movements of the 2nd Division, preluding the tragedy in which Prince Louis Napoleon so speedily closed his mortal career.

The 16th April saw the infantry regiments of the 2nd Division marching towards the north of Natal, by Greytown, Estcourt, and Ladysmith; while, on the following day, the mounted men left Durban and proceeded, by ten-mile marches, with a halt every third or fourth day.

On the 17th Lord Chelmsford moved his headquarters from Durban to Pietermaritzburg, and was accompanied by the prince. Before leaving Britain, the latter had obtained permission to serve with our troops in Zululand as a spectator. He was the bearer of a letter from the commander-in-chief to Lord Chelmsford, requesting assistance to his views, and accordingly his lordship attached him to his personal staff.

Lord Chelmsford sought, in vain, to bring about such a change in the existing laws of Natal as would enable the military authorities to impress transport, as at that time none was forthcoming, and the Isandhlwana disaster had struck such terror into the class who became drivers and leaders of waggon teams, that desertions were numerous; and the majority of those who undertook such duty, stipulated that the engagement should end at the frontiers.

On the 22nd April, Lord Chelmsford set out for the scene of active operations, and on his departure Major-General the Hon. H. H. Clifford, V.C., C.B., took command at Pietermaritzburg.

General E. Newdigate, who had served in the Eastern campaign, and won the Cross of the Legion of Honour, while his division was on the march contrived to visit Brigadier Wood at Kambula to consult for future operations, and on the 2nd of May an entrenched camp was formed at Landmann's Drift, on the Buffalo River, in which the bulk of the division remained for some time, till the arrangements for its advance were completed. On the 3rd, Lord Chelmsford, accompanied by Prince Louis Napoleon and others visited Wood's camp at Kambula, and the former expressed himself greatly satisfied with all the arrangements for the defence of the place.

On Sunday, the 4th of May, after church parade. Lord Chelmsford suggested that a reconnaissance should be made towards the White Umvolosi Valley, to select ground for an entrenched camp within easy distance of Doornberg and Conference Hill. The former post was midway between the Blood and Buffalo Rivers, and the scenery thereabouts was somewhat similar to that of Natal—grassy plateaux, broken by stony and rugged hills, and tufted with trees of what our soldiers called "cabbage-tree wood," the leaves being like those of the cabbage, and the wood like that of the alder, moist and full of pith.

The day was bright and pleasant, and Buller paraded a party of his Horse, which, when first raised, had worn any kind of dress they chose, but now were almost uniformly clad in broad-leaved hats with coloured *puggarees*, baggy brown-cord breeches—all now copiously patched with untanned leather—patrol jackets of mimosa colour, also patched, laced gaiters coming high over the knee, and coloured flannel shirts open at the bronzed neck of the weather-beaten wearer. Their firearms were rifles of various patterns, slung across the back; their other weapon was a long sabre.

118

Their horses were more useful than showy, and often somewhat of the cob kind, but wiry and active as antelopes.

Buller rode off on his reconnaissance with his party, but was soon signalled back, by an announcement that his movements were watched by a body of Zulus on some adjacent hills. A three miles' ride, however, brought him into a rugged plain south-west of the Zungen Nek, where the winding track was bordered by mimosa thorns. There a couple of bullets whizzed past, but no enemy could be seen, till after a time, by Wood and some others, who had cantered to the front, some dark figures were detected creeping along in the bush, and so intently watching this distant group of staff officers, that they were unaware of their retreat being nearly cut off by some twenty of Buller's sabres; but the latter found themselves suddenly on the verge of some precipitous rocks, about 300 feet in height, down which they descended by a narrow track, their horses' hoofs throwing showers of loose stones and sand on every side, as they half slid, half scrambled to level ground.

Thinking it possible to capture some prisoners, from whom information might be obtained, the general's escort was detached for that purpose. Accordingly, they reached a *kraal*, and having collected some cattle, began to return through the dense thorns that covered the sides of a narrow valley, in which they found themselves. The precipice we have referred to barred their way, and, while seeking to find a ford in the Umvolosi River, they perceived one of Buller's troopers making signs of danger, for the bush in their rear teemed with the enemy. A few minutes later the escort came upon a horde of dark, copper skinned savages, loading the air with unearthly yells, leaping and brandishing their *assegais* and firearms. The ford was found in time, and the escort splashed through girth-deep, and two men, who had been left to drive the cattle, also escaped, their movements being covered by a few well-directed shots.

The Zulus, with yells of baffled rage, followed so close that more than once the rear sections had to face about and charge to silence their fire, till the open ground was reached. But the whole country seemed alarmed now. In quick succession signal-fires of dry grass blazed up, columns of smoke rose high in the clear air, and they were repeated from *kop* to *kop*, showing that the whole place was garrisoned, and that the movements of the scouts and escort were alike watched; and the cattle in wild herds could be seen, as they were driven out of the wooded *kloofs* and little valleys into inaccessible places.

After his escort rejoined him, the general resumed the reconnaissance, and about twelve miles from Kambula had, from an eminence, a complete view of the beautiful valley of the White Umvolosi, with the southern slopes of the fatal Inhlobane, and, near Conference Hill, the white tents of the 2nd Division gleaming in the blaze of the bright sunshine

On the summit of the Zungen Nek, they were met by Buller, whose men were still skirmishing with some Zulus, who were in force and in a position from which to annoy the invaders, who were now in a kind of natural amphitheatre, the outer edges of which were sometimes 1,000 feet in height, scored with ghastly fissures and perforated by dark caverns, from which white jets of smoke and bullets were perpetually issuing, while the dismounted men, availing themselves of every cover, worked their way upward on two sides, and shot back into the holes as opportunity offered.

> The Zulus finding the situation rather too hot, one by one began to escape, and the moment a dusky form was seen gliding through the thorns, half-a-dozen rifles rang out, sometimes succeeded by the crushing sound of the body of a huge savage rolling from a high rock to the stones below. It was wonderful to see into what small crevices these big Zulus had squeezed themselves. Sometimes three or four would get together in one spot, generally a small cave almost inaccessible from above or below, and could be approached only by working along the sides, under the fire of dozens of other caves and loopholes, every one of which seemed scooped out for the purpose of creating a crossfire. (*Story of the Zulu Campaign.*)

COLONEL DRURY LOWE, C.B.

120

As Lord Chelmsford had now achieved his object—an examina-
tion of the country—he gave the orders to fall back, remount, and
return to camp, a movement that was greeted by defiant and exult-
ant yells from the savages who were left in their holes unearthed. It
was now known that a line suitable for the advance of Wood's Flying
Column, led from Conference Hill to Ibabanango, but no other route
had been found as yet, by which the 2nd Division under Newdigate
could join in the advance. However, hopes were entertained that the
necessity for making a detour so long might be avoided by a more
direct way from the new camp at Landmann's Drift, after some cavalry
reconnaissances beyond the frontier were accomplished

Lord William Beresford of the 9th Lancers, who had got leave for
six months from India, after he had served at the capture of Ali Musjid,
in Afghanistan, and had come to Africa in the sheer love of fighting
and adventure, was appointed staff officer to Colonel Buller.

Several reconnaissances were made; one on the 16th of May, by a
squadron of the 17th Lancers, who rode to Vecht Kop, while Bettington's Horse searched round Conference Hill, without either meeting with the enemy. On the 21st May at four a.m., Colonel Drury
Lowe—whose name is now a household word—with a wing of the
King's Dragoon Guards, a wing of the lancers, and ten Natal Carbineers, dashed across the Buffalo, proceeded up the Bashee, and past
the ruins of Sirayo's *kraal*, as far as Isandhlwana, while General Marshall, with the remainder of the mounted troops, two guns and four
companies of the 24th, swept the heights on the eastern side of the
stream. And on the 23rd of May Colonel Harrison, A.Q.M.G., established the fact from his own observation that the Ibabanango Mountain could be reached from Landmann's Drift by a practicable track
leading by the Itelezi Hill, so this line was chosen for the advance of
the 2nd Division, which was now to enter Zululand at Koppie Allein,
where Bengough's Natives, the 2nd battalion of the 1st Natal Regiment, was sent on the queen's birthday.

Much useful information regarding the geographical features of
the country in which the new campaign would lie, had been furnished by the reports and sketches, made by Colonel Buller, Lord
William Beresford, and Prince Louis Napoleon, whose pen and pencil
sketches were alike clear and vivid, and who had won all hearts in the
camp. One day when out on a reconnaissance with Captain Bettington, they were fired on from a *kraal*. At once drawing his sword, the
prince dashed forward, crying, "Come along—come along, Betting-

PRINCE LOUIS NAPOLEON AND PARTY BEFORE THE ZULU SURPRISE.

ton!" and it was all that brave officer could do to moderate his ardour.

On another occasion, when on a three days' patrol with Buller, some Zulus were seen on the top of a hill. The advance was ordered to feel their strength. The prince was spurring forward and trying to head the charge, when he was recalled and kept in check by Buller. It was now known that no large bodies of Zulus were within twenty miles of the Blood River, or indeed anywhere between the Buffalo and the White Umvolosi.

On the 27th May, the advance of the 2nd Division was resumed, and by the 30th it was concentrated on the Blood River, by which time the Flying Column from Kambula was at Munhla Hill, eighteen miles distant. Wood having received orders to move parallel with, and slightly in advance of, Newdigate, in a south-easterly direction towards the Itelezi Hill. The force of the latter was about 10,000 strong, with 480 baggage waggons, with provisions for thirty-one days.

Continuing the advance, on the 31st May, General Newdigate, with the 1st Brigade of his division, and Harness's battery, crossed the river and encamped on its left bank. The country in front had been by this time fully examined, and it was decided that the division should march north of the Itelezi Hill, and between the Tombokala and Ityotyosi streams. The selection of the route, and the choice of the camping ground upon it, fell of course to the department of the quartermaster-general, and Prince Louis Napoleon, who had tired of the partially inactive life of an extra A.D.C, was now fully attached to this important branch of the staff.

No large body of the enemy was yet seen, and the Zulus appeared to have gained military wisdom from experience. They seemed no longer to hurl their strength against the bayonet and the deadly breech-loader, or face the "fiery *assegais*," as they designated the rockets. Their new rule was to avoid fortified camps and armed detachments, and to content themselves by overrunning defenceless territory and carrying off cattle.

Each division had to march accompanied by its supplies. These and reserve ammunition a writer says:

> For 5,000 soldiers for five months will extend a distance of two and a half miles, the rest of the train will be nearly as long, and remember that adequate protection will have to be afforded against a Zulu rush from adjacent caves. You will then understand something of the difficulties and risks in our path in transport alone.

About this time John Dunn met two ambassadors at Fort Chelmsford, who confirmed the previous message brought by Umgwene from the Zulu chiefs, with the sanction of Cetewayo. This message they repeated, adding, "Take the soldiers from Zululand, and then we will conform to terms."

General Crealock replied that the negotiations must be conducted with Major-General Newdigate's column. The ambassadors then presented to John Dunn the following message from Cetewayo:—

Dunn,—I was wrong not to take your advice, and accept the hard terms of the British. You knew all from the beginning. Then why not show them their injustice to me?

Dunn answered:

It is too late now—I am powerless.

Two clever scouts about the same date, May 31, interviewed several Zulu chiefs, and held indirect communication with the scouts of the king. They reported that the chiefs generally wished for peace, but were too afraid of the king, who was resolved on battle unless favourable terms were granted to him.

On Sunday, the 1st of June, the 2nd Division moved from the Blood River to the Itelezi Hill, a long and lumpy mass, the brown slopes of which are serrated with ravines and *kloofs*. It stands some little distance within the Zulu frontier, is precipitous in some places and had many *kraals* upon its lower slopes, and was the lurking-place of many Zulus, who acted as spies along the border and otherwise made themselves objectionable.

The original intention of the general had been to harass out these skulkers and scour the hill. With this object, a detachment of the Dragoon Guards from Dundee had been detailed to cross the Buffalo at Robson's Drift, to push round the south-western extremity of the hill, and then to cut off all fugitives; while the 17th Lancers from Landmann's Drift, were to encircle the hill on the west. On the north were to be posted Bettington's Horse, while Bengough's battalion of natives was to penetrate into the heart of the mountain, and thoroughly search its defiles and crannies, but circumstances prevented this programme from being carried out

On the morning of the 1st of June, Prince Louis Napoleon started in advance of the column, to select camping ground for the division to occupy at the close of the next day's march, and with instructions to examine the nature of the country through which that movement must lie. It had been arranged that the temporary camp should be on the banks of the Ityotyosi River, and, as the district up to that point had been fully reconnoitred some days before, and no Zulus had been seen, the only escort detailed on this occasion to guard the prince, consisted of six troopers of Bettington's Horse (No. 3 Troop Natal Horse), and six of Shepstone's Basutos—Native Horse.

The prince was accompanied by Lieutenant J. B. Carey, of the 98th, or Prince of Wales's Regiment, D. A.Q.M.G., who applied for permission to join the party in order to verify some observations he had previously made, and at a quarter past nine in the morning they started from the camp at Koppie Allein, where a friendly Zulu volunteered to act as guide, but only Bettington's six European troopers reported themselves to Lieutenant Carey, Shepstone's six Basutos having failed to appear. With this slender escort, the prince pushed on over an open and grassy country, and reached the Itelezi Hill a little after ten o'clock, and when General Wood's column was in motion from Munhla Hill towards the Ityotyosi River. On that same day, Wood—whose orders were to keep one day's march ahead of the 2nd Division—was reconnoitring in advance of his column. On his left were Buller's Horse scattered over the undulations on either flank of him; in his front lay grassy slopes, scored and torn by watercourses. Rain had fallen over-night to swell the latter, but the morning was clear and bright, and the sky cloudless.

On emerging from a thick and thorny underwood, interspersed with tall wavy bamboos and drooping date-palms, General Wood came to the placid waters of a deep river, on which, however, a ford was discovered at a place shaded by fan-palms and acacias, and soon he perceived some of the vedettes on higher ground signalling the approach of mounted men, whom they afterwards reported to be evidently fugitives. Then came Colonel Buller, with twelve of his troopers, as curious as the brigadier and his men were, to discover who these riders could be. They all spurred on together, and on rounding the base of a cliff came upon Lieutenant Carey, and four troopers of Bettington's Horse, riding at a furious pace

In a few minutes more the secret was revealed, and Lieutenant Carey, whose horse was almost dead beat and covered with foam, related to General Wood the circumstances under which Prince Louis Napoleon had been killed.

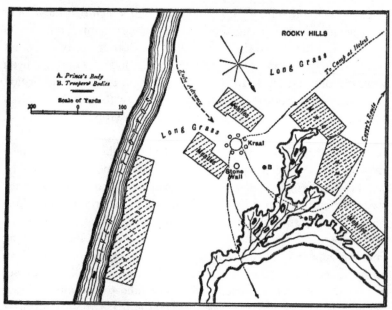

PLAN OF THE GROUND WHERE PRINCE LOUIS NAPOLEON WAS KILLED (JUNE 1, 1879).

CHAPTER 10

Death of the Prince Louis Napoleon

The horse ridden by the prince when he left the camp at Koppie Allein, and which was, perhaps, eventually the cause of his death, was a large grey, awkward, clumsy, and an inveterate buck-jumper. At the place on which the 2nd Division was to march, near the Itelezi Hill, the prince and Lieutenant Carey were met by Lieutenant-Colonel Harrison, A.Q.M.G., and after some little time spent in discussing the water supply necessary and available for the intended camp, the two became separated from the colonel, and the prince moved forward with his eight companions to complete the reconnaissance for which he had come.

The *Cape Argus* of that date says:

> After crossing the *spruit*, which in rainy weather helps to fill the Ityotyosi River, they arrived at a flat-topped hill, nameless in our maps, but which is a conspicuous feature in the landscape of this portion of the Zulu frontier, and here the prince, directing his men to slacken girths for a while, took a sketch of the country.
>
> After spending nearly an hour on the flat-topped mountain, which

126

was steeped in all the light and splendour of a real South African noon-tide, the party rode along the ridge between the Tombokala and Ityoty-osi Rivers, and about two o'clock p.m. descended from the high ground towards a *kraal*, 200 yards distant from the latter stream. The *kraal* was of the usual native kind, consisting of a circular stone enclosure, about twenty-five yards in diameter, with five huts built on the outside.

These were empty, but as some dogs were prowling about, and the remains of food were found, it was evident they had become unten-anted only recently.

Between the empty *kraal* and the river, stretched a luxuriant growth of coarse Tambookie grass, about six feet high, with mealies and Indian corn interspersed. This closely surrounded the huts on every side except the north and north-east, where lay the ashes and broken earthenware strewn about, as of a common cooking-ground It was open for about 200 yards, and at that distance from the *kraal* was a *donga*, or dry water-course, about eight feet deep, through which, in rainy seasons, the storm waters of the mountains found their way into the bed of the Ityotyosi.

On reaching the *kraal* at three p.m., the prince ordered the party to off-saddle and knee-halter for grazing. This was done and the men made some coffee and rested. The *Cape Argus* says:

> As the dogs were seen lingering near the huts, the presumption of course was, that the animals, attached to their masters' homes, had remained there after the Zulus had deserted the *kraal*; but seen in the light of the dreadful event that immediately followed, it is more than probable that the dogs belonged to the Zulus, who were actually then stalking the prince and his companions, who were completely off their guard and chatting together.

All the party having turned their horses into the grass and grain crops, the hour wore on, and it is horrible to think of what was pass-ing so near them!

All this time, concealed by the deep *donga* and the tall grass, and along the path afterwards taken by the fugitives, some forty or fifty Zu-lus—the exact number was never known—were creeping slowly and stealthily towards their unsuspecting victims. Stealing noiselessly out of the *donga*, they made their way, completely concealed by the Tam-bookie grass and other rank vegetation to the water's edge, and there, it is supposed, lay lurking until the bustle of preparation for a start, should afford them an opportunity of rushing upon the prince's party.

At about ten minutes to four o'clock the native guide reported that he had seen a Zulu come over an adjacent hill, and this was interpreted to the prince by Corporal Grubb, who knew the language well

"You can give your horses ten minutes more," said the prince looking at his watch. But the *Kaffir's* intelligence had roused suspicion, and the order was given to "saddle-up at once!" Every man went in search of his horse; and the escort, whose Martini-Henry carbines had not yet been loaded, were soon standing by their horses in different places near the *kraal*, waiting for the order to mount—waiting for death!

"Prepare to mount!" cried the prince. The order had scarcely left his lips, when with a startling crash, there burst through the cover a volley from at least forty rifles, and the long reedy grass swayed as if beneath a stormy wind, when the hidden Zulus, with fiendish shouts, rushed towards the prince and his companions.

"*Usula!*" was their cry; "death to the English cowards!" The latter epithet had often been hurled at our men elsewhere by the Zulus, particularly at Inhlobane and Etschowe.

The horses all swerved at the suddenness of the tumult and some broke away. Private Rogers, of Bettington's Horse, was shot before he could mount, and those who did mount, could hardly control their horses, which, terrified by the shots, shouts and yells of the Zulus, bore them wildly across the open ground, and towards the deep and perilous *donga*.

The prince was unable to mount his horse, which was sixteen hands high, difficult to mount at all times, and still more so in its then state of terror; and one by one the party galloped past, while the prince, who was extremely active, endeavoured to mount by vaulting.

"*Dépêchez-vous, s'il vous plaît. Monsieur!*" cried Private Letocq, of Bettington's Horse, a Frenchman, as he dashed past lying across his saddle; but the unfortunate prince made no answer, already striving his best, and in a minute he was face to face with the savages!

Yelling and firing after the fugitives, the Zulus burst from their covert. The prince's horse followed the rest, and he was last seen by Letocq, holding his stirrup leather with the left hand, trying to keep up with the animal and mount. He must have made one desperate and despairing attempt to leap into the saddle by clutching a holster; but the strap gave way, he fell to the ground, and the horse as it shot away after the rest, trod on him; for a moment, he covered his face with his hands on finding himself abandoned.

Turning in his saddle for a second, Letocq looked back again, and saw the prince running on foot, pursued by the swift Zulus only a few feet behind him; they had all *assegais* in their hands. Then Letocq looked the way he had to ride, and no one—save the foe—saw the awful end. The *Argus* says:

> The rest galloped on towards General Wood's camp, and after going three miles met the general himself and Colonel Buller. They made their report, and those officers looking through their glasses, saw the Zulus leading away the horses they had taken, the trophies of their successful attack. Troopers Rogers, Abel, and the *Kaffir* guide were killed, Abel being shot in the back by a Martini-Henry bullet as he was galloping from the *kraal*.

The remainder of the party, consisting of Lieutenant Carey and four troopers, achieved the passage of the *donga* unhurt, at different points, and reached Brigadier Wood, as stated, after crossing the Tombokala, and proceeded at seven p.m. to the camp of the 2nd Division, now pitched at the Itelezi Hill.

Lieutenant Carey, on whom much obloquy—rightly or wrongly—rested, was not an Irishman, as many supposed from his name, but a native of the south of England.

When the party returned to headquarters it was dark, and nothing could be done then towards ascertaining the fate of the prince.

An officer who was in the camp wrote:

The news of his death fell like a thunderbolt on all! At first

PRINCE LOUIS NAPOLEON.

it was regarded as one of those reports that so often went the rounds. Bit by bit, however, it assumed a form. . . . Even then people were incredulous, only half-believing the dreadful tale.

There was little sleep in the camp that night, and long after the bugles had sounded "lights out," the soldiers lingered in groups and talked with bated breath of this new disaster.

When morning dawned, strong parties were sent alike from Wood's camp and that of the 2nd Division, to visit the scene of the catastrophe. A grim silence prevailed in the ranks of the searching parties; the pennons of the lancers fluttered gaily in the wind, but the hoofs of their horses made no sound on the soft and elastic turf. Low whispers and murmurs were heard occasionally as the troopers neared the fatal spot, and lance and sword seemed to be held with a stronger grasp than usual, and then a malediction escaped more than one bearded soldier when some vultures and hawks were seen to rise like a covey, and wing their way upward from the long Tambookie grass and other rank luxuriance near the deserted *kraal*.

About 100 Zulus who were found lurking in some bushes and caves, were speedily and roughly dislodged by some of the 17th Lancers, dismounted and led by Adjutant Frith, and advancing in extended order, the troops approached the *donga*, which General Marshall and three other officers crossed on foot. Among those taking part in the search, and somewhat in advance of the rest, was Lieutenant Dundonald Cochrane of the 32nd Regiment, then in command of some Basutos; he was seen to pause suddenly, and with reverence to take off his cap. Then all knew what he saw, and on a small bank of sand, within the *donga*, with some wild flowers under his head as a pillow, naked, all save one foot, and the reliquary and locket containing his father's miniature on his neck and a gold armlet on his wrist, lay the handsome young prince—dead, and pierced by sixteen *assegai* wounds.

Near him lay the body of his little white terrier, which, at least, was faithful to the last, and remained till an *assegai* laid him dead by his master's side.

The correspondent of the Paris *Figaro*, with the unrestrainable passion of a Frenchman, flung himself down by the prince, weeping and wringing his hands.

The prince's face was composed and almost smiling, the eyes were open, though one was injured by the cruel wound which gashed the lid and eyebrow, and must have caused instant death. Save the wounds

KRAAL WHERE PRINCE LOUIS NAPOLEON AND HIS PARTY OFF-SADDLED AND WERE FIRED AT.

in the chest and front, the body was not mutilated, and no desecration of it had occurred, and even the usual *coup de grace*—the Zulu gash in the stomach—was, says Captain Tomasson, inflicted lightly, as if something in the look of the dead had impressed the ferocious savages that they had struck down no common foe, for the body of Trooper Abel was found riddled with *assegai* wounds and the final gash given with more than ordinary vigour. In the *donga*, at a little distance, was the body of Rogers, not lying, but propped against a bank, and though pierced with wounds and gashed, the eyes were open and glaring into space with a ghastly and horrid expression.

The prince's right hand grasped a tuft of human hair, conclusive evidence that he had not perished without a close and deadly struggle; all the ground around where he lay was trampled and torn, and tracks of blood showed the way his slayers had fled. Whether he had used his revolver was then unknown, but he had certainly not used the sword he loved so well—the sword of his father, the emperor. His spurs lay near him, together with his watch and rings, which, like the relics at his neck, were supposed to be potent charms, and which the savages dared not take away.

Some interesting particulars of his death were afterwards gathered by General Wood from eighteen Zulus, who were concerned in the tragedy. They were these:—

The attacking party numbered forty, of whom twelve followed the prince, and were concerned immediately in his death. The Zulus having surrounded the party, fired and rushed on them as they were in the act of mounting. The prince not having succeeded in doing so, ran alongside of his horse till it broke away from him, on the further side of the *donga*, about 220 yards from the *kraal* where the party had off-saddled. The prince followed his horse into the *donga*, until closely pressed by his pursuers, when he turned upon them, in the words of the Zulus themselves, "like a lion at bay." Struck by an *assegai* inside the left shoulder, he rushed at his nearest opponent, who fled out of the *donga* and got behind another Zulu, who, coming up, fired at the prince when only ten yards from him.

The prince returned the fire with his pistol, and faced his now rapidly-increasing foes, until, menaced from his right rear and struck by another *assegai*, he regained the level spot on which he had first stood in the *donga*, and where he was completely surrounded. He then seized an *assegai* which had been thrown at him, for in struggling with his terrified horse his sword had fallen from its scabbard. He thus defended himself against seven or eight Zulus, who stated that they did not dare to close on him till he sank exhausted by loss of blood in a sitting position.

Thus, though an accomplished swordsman, he had been by accident deprived of his sword, but sold his life dearly, fighting to the last.

Our soldiers raised the body, and laid it on a bier formed by lances of the 17th covered by cut rushes, mealies, and a cavalry cloak, and in relays the loving and respectful hands of his comrades bore it along by difficult and rough ground towards the camp at the Itelezi Hill.

When the camp was reached, the body was received by General Newdigate, with the entire 2nd Division under arms. When the sad *cortège* came within the lines, a gun-carriage was brought; the body was laid thereon wrapped in linen and covered by the Union Jack, and then a funeral service was performed by the Rev. Charles Ballard, the Roman Catholic Chaplain to the Forces, Lord Chelmsford, who was deeply affected, being chief mourner.

The same evening it was enclosed in a rough deal coffin, and sent by mule-cart to Pietermaritzburg. On arriving near Ladysmith, there occurred one of the most touching, because simple, scenes in the whole of the long, sad progress that ended at Chiselhurst. The body remained for the night upon the *veldt* at the entrance of the village, with a guard of honour round it. From the schoolhouse there came, and lined each side of the way, a long procession of black children with their harmonium, and as the body was taken away they sang a hymn.

> There was much of pathos in the sound of the sweet sad strain uprising in the chill morning air; this entirely spontaneous mark of sympathy for the 'young chief' was but one proof of the feeling that all in the colony, whatever their age, colour, position, or sex, had in the sadden close of that bright young life.

The body was escorted by a party of the 58th Regiment to Pietermaritzburg; and ultimately, after mass at the Catholic Church in Durban—it was embarked on the 11th June, on board H.M.S. *Boadicea*, and afterwards on board the *Orontes* for conveyance to England.

The prince's *major-domo* was for some reason left behind. As might be expected, he was inconsolable for the death of his young master.

It seems but fitting to close this—the most remarkable episode of the Zulu War—by a brief reference to the court-martial on Lieutenant Carey, with whose name all Europe was familiar then. It was preceded by a Court of Inquiry, held on the 10th June, in the camp of the 2nd

Division upon the Upoko River, and the following is the finding:—

> The court is of opinion that Lieutenant Carey did not understand the position in which he stood to the prince, and, in consequence, failed to estimate the responsibility which fell to his lot Quartermaster-General Harrison states in evidence, that Lieutenant Carey was in charge of the escort, while Lieutenant Carey alluding to it says:—'I do not consider that I had any authority over it.' After the precise and careful instructions of Lord Chelmsford, stating, as he did, the position the prince held, and that he was invariably to be accompanied by an escort in charge of an officer, the court considers that such difference of opinion should not have existed between officers of the same department
>
> Secondly, the court is of opinion that Lieutenant Carey is much to blame in having proceeded on duty with part of the escort detailed by the quartermaster-general. The court cannot admit the plea of irresponsibility on Lieutenant Carey's part, inasmuch as he took steps to obtain the escort and failed; moreover, the fact that the quartermaster-general was present at the Itelezi Ridge, gave Lieutenant Carey the opportunity of consulting him on the matter, of which he failed to avail himself.
>
> Thirdly, the court is of opinion that the selection of the *kraal* where the halt was made, surrounded as it was by cover for the enemy, showed a lamentable want of military prudence.
>
> Fourthly, the court deeply regrets that no effort was made to rally the escort and show a front to the enemy, whereby the possibility of aiding those who had failed to make good their retreat might have been ascertained

A general court-martial, of which Colonel Glyn was president, was held on Lieutenant Carey on the 12th June, in the Upoko Camp, on the charge of having behaved in an unsoldierlike manner before the enemy; but the sentence was kept secret, awaiting its confirmation by H.R.H. the Commander-in-Chief in Britain; and meanwhile Carey was sent home under arrest. But, in consequence of some technical irregularity, the proceedings of the court were declared null and void, and he was ordered to return to his duty.

Although the prince held a somewhat undefined position in the South African Field Force, he had formed friends innumerable, and the general feeling was one of intense regret that his high-spirited impulses were not more controlled by those into whose hands his life had been entrusted

A writer at the time said:

The excitement is too great, to reason calmly upon this subject; but the reflection is forced upon us, that here has been solved one of the most difficult problems of French history.

CHAPTER 11

Resumed Advance of the Second Division

On the 3rd of June, the 2nd Division again moved forward, and encamped near the junction of the Tombokala and Ityotyosi Rivers, within half a mile of the spot where Prince Louis Napoleon had been killed Brigadier Wood's column, which had marched on the preceding day, was now on the left front of the division, and advanced on the further side of the Ityotyosi

By this time the horses of our cavalry were rapidly deteriorating under reduced rations of eight pounds of bad oats and no hay, and some officers were beginning to fear that horses unfitted for cavalry work would prove an encumbrance rather than an advantage.

For a wonder, the hospital organisation of the force seemed adequate. By May, two field hospitals had been formed at Landmann's Drift; No. 1 with seventy-five beds under Surgeon-Major Elgee, and six surgeons on service with it, with medicines, ambulances and transport then all ready to move. No. 2 field hospital, under Surgeon-Major Heather, with fifty beds and five surgeons, was in the same state of preparedness. The base hospital for the 2nd Division was constituted at Ladysmith, having 150 beds with four surgeons.

On the 4th of June, the division crossed the Ityotyosi River, and encamped on the ground just vacated by the Flying Column, which had moved onward to the further bank of the Nondwene River. On the evening of this day, news was received that a considerable force of the enemy was a few miles in front of Wood's camp.

Indeed, a cavalry patrol under Colonel Buller, had a narrow escape from being entrapped by 2,500 Zulus, who were discovered in time, and the attempt failed; but on receipt of this intelligence all the cavalry were ordered out, and an earth-work was formed round the tents, as the enemy's force was thought to be but the vanguard of a larger body.

General Marshall with the cavalry—Lancers and Dragoon Guards—of the division, started at half-past four a.m., on the 5th, and proceeding by the camp of Wood's column, reconnoitred the track in advance, as far as the Upoko River (sometimes called the Tenemi) when he effected a junction with Buller and his Irregular Horse, and on reaching the ground where the ambuscade had been planned on the previous day, a dark mass of Zulus were seen in the plain below it, and near them were some *kraals* which Buller had fired, all blazing at once—yet the scene was a beautiful one.

The morning sun had just risen over the opposite mountain, and turned to golden sheen the river that rolled at its base. Between these, on a green plain, were the blazing huts. The hill was seamed with stony ravines, and clothed with mimosa bushes. Away on the left, toward Inhlazatye, or the greenstone mountain, gleaming redly in the sunshine, and beyond it, was known to lie the great *kraal* of Cetewayo, the object of the combined operations.

The order was given to advance.

"Frontier Light Horse, the centre—Buller's Horse, the left—Whalley's the right," cried Colonel Buller. In the meantime, the Zulus had massed, moved off by companies, and taken up a position in the *dongas* at the base of the Erzungayan Hill, where thick bush and high reedy grass gave them cover. When the river was crossed, Buller's force advanced at a gallop, to within 300 yards of the enemy, and dismounted. The horses were then led rearward, out of the hottest fire, by those men told off for the purpose.

Cover was taken in long grass and behind ant-heaps, from whence a steady fire was opened; but there the hill side was studded with aloes, which amid the eddying smoke of the musketry, frequently looked like dark Zulu figures, and there many a shot was thrown away. On an ant-heap stood Buller, watching through his field-glass the effect of the firing, which went on for some time, till the enemy made a flank movement on the right, and poured in a volley at eighty yards from the edge of a mealie field into which they had crept Buller saw this, and knew that a large Zulu force was in reserve.

The order was consequently issued to "retire," the movement was well performed, the river was recrossed and the Irregulars were formed on its other side. One who was present wrote:

Apart from the chances of getting hit, the scene was pretty in the extreme, to see the whole face of the hill dotted with little puffs of white smoke. We had eight or ten men hit—none mortally, and fifteen horses, killed or wounded. The Imperial cavalry had meanwhile come on the scene, and by General Marshall's order advanced to the attack.

Led by Colonel Drury Lowe, the troops of the 17th Lancers, with all their pennons fluttering, advanced in gallant and imposing order.

Drury Lowe, whose name will occur frequently in these pages, entered the army as a cornet in the 17th Lancers in 1854, after taking degrees at Oxford. He joined his regiment in the Crimea in the following year, and was present at the Battle of Tchernaya and the siege and fall of Sebastopol. He was next in the Indian War, and served in the pursuit of the rebel forces under Tantia Topee, and in the action at Zurapore. After having been in command for twelve years he was placed on half-pay, but was reinstated in his old regiment in February, 1879 (the then colonel having met with a serious accident, just before embarking for the scene of war in South Africa), and he it was who led in the charge and pursuit of the Zulus at Ulundi.

The correspondent of the *Daily News*, whose details of these operations are very ample says :

Marshall could hardly hope to succeed in such a country, with his serried squadrons, where Buller had confessed himself foiled, with his light skirmishing sharpshooters mounted on nimble rats. He was conscious of the lack of opening for him, and thus told Drury Lowe to take his lancers down to water in the stream, while he sent a troop of dragoons to the right to guard against the contingency of Zulus creeping down the river bed. One squadron of lancers had been left, halted in reserve on the slope behind us. Lowe took his three squadrons down into the river bed, and crossing, deployed on the plain beyond. He was full of soldierly eagerness to give his young troopers their 'baptism of fire,' and he had the genuine cavalryman's conviction that there are few things within the scope of fighting that resolute cavalry cannot accomplish. Marshall sent Lord Downe (of the 2nd Life Guards, his *aide-de-camp*) galloping after him to enjoin caution. Nelson had a blind eye; Lowe has a deaf ear to any injunction he does not relish.

The Irregular Cavalry who now looked on, expressed regret to see these splendid lancers sent on this service, believing it to be a mere waste of life, as the enemy were too strongly posted to have any serious damage done to them, and it seemed hopeless to expect cavalry to ferret them out of their holes and cover.

Lowe trotted them up into a line with the now smoking *kraals*, and saw between him and the thorn-clad hill slopes the tall and waving stalks of the mealie fields. Through these he resolved to sweep with his men, and let those who might lurk therein feel the points of British lances. One squadron he despatched to the left beyond the burning *kraals*, with the rest he rode straight at the mealie fields. "Gallop!" rang out the trumpets, and the fine English horses stretched themselves over the smooth springy sward that led to the mealies.

With lances unslung the troopers dashed on, the Zulu bullets from the hill—all aimed too high—whistling over their heads. The reedy stalks of the dead mealies rustled as they were crushed beneath the hoofs, but no Zulus were hidden there; and leading his men close to the edge of the thorns, Lowe ordered some to dismount and open fire with their carbines against those who lurked therein and behind the adjacent rocks, and there twenty-five Zulu corpses were found in August by Colonel Russell's column when cutting firewood.

Mounted and passive, the remainder of the squadron formed a very conspicuous mark, and had the Zulus fired better than they did, they must have emptied many a saddle.

The cavalry were now ordered to fall back, but not before the Lancers lost one of their best officers, Lieutenant and Adjutant E. F. C Frith, a capital soldier and general favourite. Three mounted men were close together—Frith, Colonel Lowe, and another—and their horses being all of a light colour offered an excellent mark for the enemy's bullets. One shot from a Martini-Henry struck Frith, who threw up his arms and fell forward on his saddlebow. Those nearest lifted him, but he was dead when they touched him—shot through the heart. His body was placed across his saddle, and his horse was led slowly to the rear.

The firing party and advanced squadron now began to fall back; but for retiring cavalry the nature of the ground was extremely awkward. From their inaccessible fastness, beyond the undergrowth of prickly thorns, the Zulus continued to fire, while other savages, running swiftly along the bed of the river, opened on one flank, while a third party hovered on the other, and the whole position of our little cavalry force would become perilous should the fire be concentrated on the only point where the stream could be crossed—its sweep or convexity.

The time had come for Marshall's cool courage and prompt grasp of the situation. One stretch of the river he had covered

LORD CHELMSFORD (A PORTRAIT SKETCH BY AN OFFICER
MADE SHORTLY BEFORE THE BATTLE OF ULUNDI).

with dragoons. The charge of the other he had entrusted to
Shepstone's Basutos. He withdrew the regular cavalry slowly
across by alternate squadrons, continually keeping a front to
the Zulus, and striving, but in vain, to lure them from their
fastnesses and give him a chance at them in the open. Having
recrossed the river, we halted on the slope, and then for some
time, the Zulus came out and made us long for artillery. They
formed companies out in the open, and swarmed all about their
blazing *kraals*. They hooted so loudly that we could hear them,
and they gave us a lesson in tactics! Keeping our attention fixed
by their evolutions in the open, they sent men creeping down
along the river-bed from both flanks, till they opened fire on us
down at the bulge of the convexity.

Over the broken ground it was impossible to charge, and reinforcements were seen swarming round both shoulders of the Erzungayan Hill; Marshall had no infantry, British or native, and no alternative was left him. Again, the trumpets sounded the "retire," and the
two parties of cavalry rode back to camp and their respective columns;
after which the 2nd Division occupied new ground, by marching to

PEACE MESSENGERS FROM CETEWAYO

the Isandhlwana Hill.

Three Zulu envoys of rank had presented themselves at Wood's camp on the evening of the 4th, and as Lord Chelmsford happened to be there, he had an interview with them. The party in all consisted of nine—three seniors, three juniors, and three lads, who were mat bearers. The six men carried shields and *assegais*, and the principal one had a dingy, faded shawl, tied round his brown and muscular throat. He and his suite were very sullen and sulky, because, through some mistake, no food was offered to them.

On the evening of the 5th, after the fighting. Lord Chelmsford resumed the interview.

Various communications had passed previously between the British authorities and Zulus purporting to bear peaceful proposals from Cetewayo, but up to this time they had generally been deemed spies or impostors, and the original ultimatum was the only definite statement of the British demands which had been announced. Though not of the highest rank, these envoys seemed to have really come from the Zulu king, and they were desired to return and inform him, that before any terms of peace could be considered, the following conditions must be complied with:—

1. The restoration of the captured oxen at the king's *kraal*, together with the two 7-pounders taken at Isandhlwana.

2. A promise to be given by Cetewayo, that all arms taken during the war should be collected and surrendered.

3. That one Zulu regiment, to be named by Lord Chelmsford, should come in under a flag of truce and lay down its arms at the distance of one thousand yards from the British camp.

A written statement of these conditions was given to the envoys, who were then dismissed to Ulundi. Prior to their departure, Lord Chelmsford gave no promise of the arrestment of operations. These envoys seemed greatly impressed by the appearance of our forces, particularly the Dragoon Guards and lancers; and the younger men pointed to the infantry, saying, "There is the wall we could never break through." They knew nothing about the colours of the and 24th, left or lost at Isandhlwana; nor could they be made to understand what "colours" meant, and on being shown a British flag, they said with great simplicity, that "Cetewayo would never wear anything like that"

Many attacks on our troops appeared about this time in prints at home; they were accused of inhumanity in burning down *kraals*, by writers who knew not what *kraals* were. There were three kinds of *kraals* in Zululand—the royal, the military, and the domestic, a hamlet of beehive-like *wigwams*. The first-named were filled with cattle and stores of mealies to reward the warriors; and the second were fortified depots, rallying points, and each was a sort of barrack, or garrison.

In the South African Field Force at this time, the use of the razor was almost entirely abolished, and so beards became very fashionable. General Newdigate trimmed his grizzled beard square in the fashion of Henry VIII., while Brigadier Wood wore his cut in a peak; those under their command are said to have trimmed their beards after the same style. Concerning the bearing of the troops, a writer says:—

> Field service, with, please Providence, some genuine fighting experience thrown in, evokes the finest qualities of the soldier. It forges the true link of mutual good feeling between officers and men; it stimulates *esprit de corps*; it brings good men to the front, and incites men less good to emulate the fine examples they see before them; it blots out the baser phases of garrison life at home; it teaches self-reliance, manliness, and a rude homely patriotism, quite different from the gassy swagger of the music hall.

This observer also remarked that in the camp there was less foul speech than in barracks; that the men were kindlier one to another, and generally graver and more earnest than when in garrison.

On the 6th of June the 2nd Division remained halted on the bank of the Nondwene River, and a long train of waggons containing a fortnight's provisions were unloaded, that they might be sent to the rear for more supplies; two forts of solid stone were commenced, and the post was named Fort Newdigate.

To be ready for any surprise at night, the camp was surrounded by parties of infantry with supports in rear, and a chain formed by the native levies between. At nine p.m. on the 6th of June one of the latter thought he saw a Zulu creeping in the gloom towards them, and fired three shots, the recognised signal that the camp was attacked, and the soldiers of the 58th, or Rutlandshire Regiment, ran in on their supports, the officer in command of which fired two volleys, blindly and at random, and retired into one of the unfinished works, which, in consequence, was named by the soldiers "Fort Funk."

The alarm spread, the tents were struck, and the troops manned the waggon *laager*, and, fearing his pickets might be shot down. General Newdigate ordered the bugles to sound the "close," and two rounds to be fired by the heavy artillery, while the troops opened fire from every face of the *laager* upon—nothing!

Orders were promptly issued for this blind and blundering fire to cease, as the outposts had not been withdrawn; but not until two sergeants and seven men had received several gunshot wounds—one mortal—from their own comrades. Several oxen were shot, their drivers frightened almost to death, and the heaped-up tents riddled with shot. Order was restored when the moon shone out bright, and showed there was no enemy near, so the tents were pitched again.

Two companies of the Scots Fusiliers, with two Gatlings, and a company of the Native Contingent, were left to garrison Fort Newdigate, with a squadron of Dragoon Guards to keep open communications, and the 2nd Division moved forward to the Upoko River, the scene of the skirmish on the 5th of June.

The duty of escorting the empty waggons referred to, was entrusted to Brigadier Wood's Flying Column, which was joined by half the cavalry of the 2nd Division, and during its absence on escort duty Buller's mounted men took its place.

On the next advance Colonel W. P. Collingwood, of the Scots Fusiliers, a Crimean officer, who displayed great courage and presence of mind when the *Spartan* troopship was wrecked on the African coast in 1856, was left in command of Fort Newdigate, and Fort Marshall, five miles distant, was garrisoned by the remaining companies of his regiment

The delays which had occurred in the progress of the war, and the manifest want of harmony between the military and civil authorities in Natal led, as related, to a change in the supreme command, and it was in the camp at Upoko that Lord Chelmsford received, on the 16th of June, the somewhat mortifying telegram, announcing his super, session by Lieutenant-General Sir Garnet Wolseley.

With the force now welded together, consisting of 4,062 Europeans, 1,103 natives, and 14 pieces of cannon (including two Gatlings) at that time. Lord Chelmsford deemed himself certain of striking a final blow at Ulundi. Considering all the difficulties that General Crealock with the 1st Division had encountered, the commander-in-chief had thought it would be only fair to give him and his force the honour of drawing the first blood in the final attack, but the coast sickness had proved so fatal to Crealock's commissariat train that he was unable to avail himself of Lord Chelmsford's chivalrous kindness.

The operations of the 2nd Division and of the Flying Column were now combined

All longed to wipe out the stain of Prince Louis Napoleon's death. On the 19th of June the forward march was resumed, and the ascent of a steep spur of the great Ibabanango Mountain having been accomplished, Wood encamped on the left bank of the river there, with the division a little way in his rear. On the 20th, when marching between two branches of the Umlatoosi River, a skirmish took place between some Zulus and Buller's Horse, a corps raised by Major F. C Buller, of the Ceylon Rifles, an officer who had served through various African wars and in Borneo. The Irregulars forming the advance guard had left the camp before dawn, to examine the ground over which the column was to pass. Forming two detachments, they examined the hills on the right and left of the route. Buller's Horse were on the former flank and unearthed some Zulus, who fired a volley and then fled over the crest of a hill, ere the troopers could climb its steep side.

On the summit was a long plateau covered with rich short grass, and bordered by, a deep gorge some miles below. Through this some Zulus were seen driving cattle towards a river. This Major Buller suspected to be a mere lure, and issued orders that no capture was to be attempted, and this, as the sequel showed, was fortunate. Riding to the spur of the ridge that overhung the gorge, his troopers opened fire with their carbines, and no sooner had they done so, than a volley from rifles was given from a knoll, 200 yards off on the right. An officer was despatched with twenty-five troopers to dislodge these Zulus, and took ground on another spur, outflanking them, and both parties of Irregulars now opened on the stragglers 600 yards below. The latter took shelter in a *donga*, which was fired into whenever a dark head appeared. About 300 Zulus were seen stealing out of the lower end of the gorge and down the river bed, to make a two miles' detour, and cut off Buller's Horse, while those in the *donga* fled out of it and attempted a charge, but were repulsed with the loss of thirty killed.

The detouring body had in the meantime crept round the base of the hill, so Buller ordered his party to fall back, which they did with some captured cows and sheep. Such skirmishes were of daily occurrence. One who was engaged, says:

In the face of much superior numbers, our small force of fifty men, had inflicted a loss of about forty on them. Their total numbers were about 700. The party which had early in the day gone to the left, had exchanged shots with an enemy posted in an inaccessible *kloof.*

On the 21st of June, the Flying Column made a short march of about three miles, and crossed the left bank of the eastern Umlatoosi, while the division came up from the Ibabanango Spruit, and encamped on the right bank.

As it was evident that these continued advances menaced Ulundi every day, more Zulus were now seen, and small skirmishes took place, while the enemy made many determined attempts to burn up the tall grass along the line of march, and all vigilance was requisite to prevent them from doing so, for being dry as tinder, it caught fire at once, imperilling the ammunition boxes, and what the men carried in their pouches. Every day a broad strip was cut around the camp lest tents and all might be burned; but sometimes the enemy would fire a large strip within rifle range and then take to flight, and on some occasions the troops lay among black ashes.

CHAPTER 12

The Expedition Beyond the Umvolosi

Though the Home Government, influenced by a section of the English press, sent out Sir Garnet Wolseley to supersede Lord Chelmsford as Commander-in-Chief, the latter was fortunately able, as we shall soon relate, to complete his plans for the final blow before that supersession took effect.

On the 22nd of June, Wood moved forward a few miles, while the division remained in camp, and Newdigate, whose teams of oxen required rest, gave the troops a holiday. Wood as he advanced carefully noted every stream, rock, and feature of the route, which lay through jungle, long grass, and among sandstone boulders, while the trumpet of the elephant could be heard at times in the thickets. Two companies of the Perthshire, with two of the 58th, one of Engineers, two 7-pounders of Colonel Harness's battery, R.A., and Bengough's natives were now detached to construct and garrison a work to be called Fort Evelyn, on the left bank of the Umlatoosi; and so quickly did they toil, that by the next evening it was quite defensible, with an outwork constructed on an bland in the stream, situated amid rapids and picturesque cascades, overhung by thornwood and wild lemon trees. It was reached by garlands of sweet-scented creepers like baboon-ropes—a work of great peril, the slightest mistake involving death.

On the 24th, the Flying Column marched to the summit of the Jackal Ridge, while the 2nd Division encamped at the base of it.

While patrolling in front of the column that day, Buller and his Horse came on some eighty or so Zulus busy burning the grass, to destroy the forage for horses and oxen: of these he made short work, and might have slain them all if he had chosen; but it was afterwards decided that an attack in force should be made upon five *kraals*, which he reported having seen in the district of Usipezi, guarded by a rather formidable Zulu *impi*.

The natural features of the country as seen from the ridge were beautiful The valleys on the left were full of green bush, wherein the cotton tree and castor-oil plant grew wild; in the foreground in some places the hills were of red rock, and crested with luxuriant timber, while at their bases grew the aloe with its spear-like leaves and tall scarlet spikes, and the pale green foliage of the *spekboom*, which is said to be the favourite food of the elephant

From the heights could be seen in the distance what was supposed to be Ulundi—that mysterious royal *kraal* of which traders had circulated such fabulous accounts. Vague stories of the wealth of Cetewayo went about, says an officer of the Irregulars, with splendid visions of loot in the shape of ostrich feathers, diamonds, and gold dust. He adds:

> Incredible stories of the amount of treasure taken at Isandhlwana were circulated. We believe the real amount was £300. It is needless to say these golden visions were (eventually) broken, not a man of the Regulars being a sovereign the better for any loot taken. Some of the Irregulars got small sums from deserted *kraals*. The amount taken altogether was small. The men took pains to conceal anything they did take, as they were afraid of being made to disgorge.

On the 25th, prior to the intended attack on the *kraals*. Wood's column advanced again, and early in the day an unknown stream with steep banks and a soft muddy bed had to be crossed, a difficulty achieved by laying down grass mattings found in deserted *kraals*; but as there was only one crossing-place the delay was great, and the time occupied seven hours, the division following.

The advance now brought the troops in sight of the *kraals* seen by Buller, and while the column halted, at daybreak on the 26th a force to attack them paraded for Lord Chelmsford's inspection. It consisted of two squadrons of the 17th Lancers, Buller's mounted men, two

9-pounder Royal Artillery guns, and two companies of Bengough's natives.

The *kraals* stood in the 'Mpembene Valley, five miles north of the camp, and hot work was expected there. The guns, and Drury Lowe's gallant lancers in their blue and white-faced uniform, with red and white pennons fluttering, took a circuitous path, and speedily crowned some heights above the *kraals*, which were shelled and all burned in succession without much opposition, for, though a skirmish ensued, not a British soldier was touched.

These *kraals* or barracks consisted in some instances of 2,500 huts each, and in them were found baths, buckets, canteens, a hymn book, and little prints of Roman Catholic saints, all brought from Isandhlwana. By the gunners on the hills, while the smoke of the blazing *kraals* ascended into the clear sky in five great columns, a compact body of Zulus, estimated by Tomasson at 2,000 strong, was seen advancing, but the guns opened fire, two shells exploded in their front, and they retired, pursued on the spur by the Frontier Light Horse and mounted Basutos, who killed only a few, however, perhaps because the atmosphere then was hot, stifling and fragrant, like that of a conservatory at home.

Both columns marched to the Enlonganeni Hill, and encamped there on the 27th, and Buller, who, with his unwearied Horse, was out reconnoitring between that point and the White Umvolosi, which there rolls in all its breadth through a valley covered with brushwood, met three envoys from Cetewayo, who bore two elephant's tusks, and were accompanied by a herd of 150 commissariat oxen captured at Isandhlwana. On being conveyed to the camp, they handed to Lord Chelmsford a letter written on behalf of the Zulu king by a Dutch trader named Vijn, who, having been among the Zulus when the war broke out, had remained with them since.

This letter was in reply to Lord Chelmsford's communication of the 5th of June, from his camp at Nondwene, and was to the effect that:

> The cattle sent were all that could be collected, the rest having died of lung disease; that the arms demanded could not be surrendered, as they were not in the king's possession; that the two 7-pounder guns were on their way, and that the British troops must now retire.

The Zulu messengers left the camp, bearing with them the elephant's tusks, and a written reply from the general, who informed

Cetewayo that:

> As the conditions had not been complied with, the British Army would still advance; but, that as some cattle had been delivered, this advance would be delayed until the evening of the 29th, to allow time for the fulfilment of the remainder of the conditions.

Lord Chelmsford also expressed his:

> Willingness to make peace, and modified the preliminary conditions by stating, that the surrender of such arms captured at Isandhlwana as were in possession of the Zulus now with the king would be accepted, and that a body of his retainers to the number of a regiment (1,000) might make their submission by laying down their arms, instead of this being done by a regiment named.

The troops had two entire days' rest during the halt by the Enlonganeni Hill. In the afternoon of the 28th, Lord Chelmsford received a telegram from Sir Garnet Wolseley, informing him of what he knew already, that Sir Garnet had assumed the command in South Africa, and requesting a plan of the campaign, with the positions of the troops, to be forwarded to him.

Sir Garnet had at that time assembled the Durban Kaffir chiefs, seventy of whom responded, some of them travelling a hundred miles to the meeting, when it was explained to them that a great white chief had come across the sea to talk with them and deliver the words of the Great White Queen. After thanking them, he said:—

> The Great Queen orders me to finish the war forthwith, and I shall do so, if loyal subjects will help me as I wish. I am informed by the generals in front that they have plenty of men, but that the cattle are dying. The British can easily beat the Zulus and all the tribes helping them. Even should the war continue for years, the Great Queen will go on sending out armies, as the British always do what they say they will do. I shall not leave Africa until the war is finished. This is a war against a king who has broken his promises, and not against the people, whom the queen does not wish to deprive of their cattle, their land, or their property. The queen desires the war to be finished quickly, and I can do so in six or eight weeks, if the chiefs provide carriers.

Hearty expressions of approval followed this address, and many chiefs stepped forward with offers of assistance, among them Sikalo, a young *induna*, whose father with forty of his tribe fell at Isandhlwana.

Sir Garnet wished 4,000 carriers to carry supplies in the Ashantee fashion, and on the 30th of June, he telegraphed to the Secretary of State for War, that he was organising them.

Ulundi was now not more than sixteen miles distant from Lord Chelmsford's camp at the Enlonganeni Hill, and it was decided that the troops moving from thence against it, should be in light marching order, without kits or tents, and with rations for ten days only. The latter supplies were to be borne in light ox-waggons, which, with the mule-carts for the regimental reserve ammunition, were the only transport vehicles, about 200 in all, that were to accompany the force.

On the 29th, while these waggons were sent back to Fort Marshall for more supplies, the rest of the ox-waggons were formed into a *laager* on the hill with entrenchments and strong abattis of trees, felled and pegged down for the protection of all stores, which were entrusted to the care of two companies of the 24th (full of disappointment at being left behind); and one non-commissioned officer and two privates from each company of both columns, which on the following day moved down from the hill into the valley of the White Umvolosi, and bivouacked by a small stream on the level ground between the hill and the river, which ran in the distance like a great silver flood through the green valley, its banks thickly studded with spiky aloes, mimosa and other tropical trees, including those strange stiff and gaunt-looking *euphorbias*, whose leafless outlines suggest the idea of Indian idols, and are so peculiar to South Africa.

Here, about midway, two other messengers from Cetewayo were received by Lord Chelmsford, before whom they laid the sword of Prince Louis Napoleon, which had been recovered from the small tribe by whom he was slain. It was easily recognisable by the cypher N, worked into the hilt, and was regarded with mournful interest and curiosity by all who saw it. Rumour said it had belonged to the Great Napoleon, but it certainly had been worn by Napoleon III.

They brought another letter written by the Dutch trader Vijn on behalf of Cetewayo. It promised that the two field-pieces and some more cattle would come in on the following day. It was addressed "From Cetewayo to Lord Chelmsford," and Vijn at the peril of his life, had written on the outside, "*If you come, come strong—there are 20,000 of them,*" a noble message, deserving of remembrance. There were many Zulus about Cetewayo who could read English, and had one of them seen this warning, torture and death would have been the doom of Vijn.

In Lord Chelmsford's reply, the terms of peace were further modified to the surrender of the guns and 1,000 rifles, in lieu of the submission of 1,000 men, and as water was scarce in his present camp, the general announced his intention of moving close to the Umvolosi, but promised to go no farther than the bank of that river before noon on the 3rd of July, to give ample time for the fulfilment of the conditions stipulated, adding that if the Zulus made no opposition to this trifling advance, he would burn no more *kraals*.

Next day, 1st July, saw the march of the columns continued, through a difficult country, covered with long reedy grass that swayed to and fro in the wind, and great sharp cactus and mimosa bush, and without opposition the White Umvolosi was reached.

At thirty minutes past one p.m., while Wood's column, which was leading, was getting into position on the bank of the stream, a large force of the enemy was seen advancing on the opposite bank, and as an immediate attack was apprehended, the 2nd Division instantly formed a *laager* on its leading waggon. The Zulus, however, did not cross, and no attack was made.

Next day saw its waggons parked with those of Wood's column, so as to form a double *laager*, and the whole of the 2nd was occupied in cutting down and clearing away the bush on all sides, and building a stone fort on a rising eminence close by.

At two a.m. on the morning of that day, the Irregulars of Wood's column had been ordered to get under arms for watching and reconnoitring work, and that hour saw them leave the camp amid moonless, starless, and pitchy darkness. They knew not upon whom they might fall, as for the four preceding days reviews of the Zulu troops had been in progress, and *impies* of 4,000 strong would march nearly to the banks of the river in a menacing manner, and then return, but every movement was closely watched.

Amid the gloom of the morning, the Irregulars rode for some miles in the strictest silence, till they reached a ridge that sloped down to where the dark current of the broad Umvolosi rolled noiselessly past, and there they dismounted to rest their horses. Then, at some miles' distance, rising and falling through the quiet air, was heard the war-song of the Zulu Army—at times a mighty volume of sound from many thousands of voices united; at other times dying away, weird and solemn.

They were supposed to be guarding the ford below, and every moment the Irregulars expected to be engaged, but their orders from Chelmsford were not to fire till fired on. As day came in, they mounted, and rode a little way to another ridge, from whence they could see the valley of the Umvolosi filled with the dark masses of the enemy, but chiefly posted at two fords below. Trotting back, they saw the long trains of baggage waggons descending the slopes in rear, and the sun flashing on the rifle-barrels of the columns as they got under arms for any emergency, while the weird music of the war-song still floated upward from the valley of the river. Thus far one account. Another states that during the 2nd no Zulu force was seen (this probably means by the headquarter force); and that Cetewayo's intentions still remained unknown.

A herd of those white cattle which are the peculiar property of the king was observed in the course of the day coming from the direction of Ulundi, and seemed to have been sent thence as a peace-offering; but before they could reach the fords on the river they were driven back by the Zulu troops, who were indignant at the prospect of these animals being surrendered. So passed the 2nd of July, and the dawn of the important 3rd—the last day of grace—stole in. The defensive preparations at the fort and *laager* continued all day, undisturbed by the enemy.

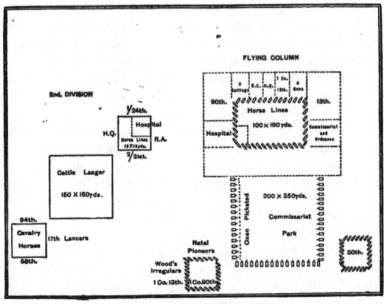

PLAN OF LAAGERS ON THE MARCH TO ULUNDI.

151

Noon came; the hour named for the receipt of a reply passed; none had arrived, and this silence was deemed as a rejection of the final proposals sent to Cetewayo. It was, however, known long after, that the messengers who had visited Lord Chelmsford on the 30th had been falsely informed on their return to Ulundi, that Vijn, "Cetewayo's Dutchman," as he was named, was gone thence, and no other translator being then available, the letter they bore was never delivered to the king, but remained in possession of one of them unopened till the 18th of the following October, though, as its purport had been explained to them, it might have been conveyed to Cetewayo orally, and thus averted much loss of life.

Two hours before noon on the 3rd a sputtering fire was opened by the Zulus from the rocks on the left bank of the river, at our men watering their horses in its bed, which was the sole source of water supply for the force; and as this straggling fire was maintained along the front for about two miles, after noon was passed, all negotiations were naturally deemed at an end A soldier of the 90th was wounded, more than one horse was hit; the Zulus became more insolent, and all the watering and bathing operations went on under fire, yet the orders for the day enforced comparative inaction.

Through glasses women could be seen hurriedly burying the valuables belonging to the different *kraals*, seven of which were in sight all at once.

At one p.m. a reconnaissance in force was undertaken by Colonel Buller with the mounted men of the Flying Column, while guns were brought up to cover his retreat, in case he should be hard pressed Accompanied by Lord William Beresford, Buller led his Irregulars down the river, crossed it in a rapid gallop to the left, turning the flank of a large bluff, the front of which was lined by the enemy's sharpshooters until they were dislodged by a couple of shells, that went whistling among them. Meanwhile every waggon in the *laager*, and every coign of vantage, was crowded by officers and men, to watch the movements of the Irregular Horse, whose object was twofold—to turn the enemy on the bluff, from whence their fire had been so annoying all morning, and to proceed as far as possible with safety on the way to Ulundi, observing the ground on every hand

Sending a portion of his force by the ford of a waggon-track, Buller with the main body crossed lower down, and moved round the southern end of the bluff. After galloping up the opposite bank, where the aloe, the mimosa, and other tropical shrubs grew thick, and from amid which the *steinbok* and *duiker* fled with affright, the Horse pushed on in a helter-skelter after the Zulus, who fled in hundreds towards the great *kraal* of Unodwengo. At the head of his best mounted men, the heroic Buller went galloping on towards Ulundi; but between it and him lay deep hollows, with one intersecting them at right angles.

Suddenly from each of these hollows, through the chief of which flowed a stream named the 'Imbilane, there sprang up a body of 5,000 Zulus in front and flanks, pushing boldly forward with the double object of encircling the force and cutting off its retreat

Buller's command consisted of the Frontier light Horse, the Mounted Infantry, the Basutos under Captain Cochrane, the Natal Light Horse under Captain Watt Whalley, a regular soldier of fortune, who had served in the Mutiny, China, and Abyssinia, in the Papal Zouaves, and in the Carlist War as colonel. The other corps were Rangers, mixed Hottentots, and broken men from the Diamond Fields.

"Halt, and fire, without dismounting," were now the orders of Buller; but, as several volleys responded, they had to wheel about and fall back with the Zulus after them. Commandant Raaf, who had seen many a fierce border raid and fray, had halted near the Unodwengo *kraal*, with his Rangers as supports, and their close fire kept the Zulus in check, but a steady retreat was all that could be achieved, and not without loss. In galloping back, with the fleet-footed Zulus in hot chase, some of our Irregulars went splashing girth-deep at the point where they had first crossed the Umvolosi, others went sweeping down by the bluff that overhung the river, pressed hard on both flanks by the horns of the advancing Zulu column, which threatened to cut them off entirely, and might have done so but for the fire of Major Tremlett's 9-pounders, and, as it was, on the left of the retreating force, the fighting was all but hand-to-hand, while many of Buller's horses were seen carrying double, thus saving those whose cattle had been shot under them.

To one of these the adjutant of the Light Horse gave his charger, and the fellow—a German—actually rode off on it, leaving his preserver helpless in the open. The Zulus were advancing rapidly. Lord William Beresford saw, after cutting his way through fifty Zulus, a trooper of the Light Horse dismounted and reeling, giddy with pain, and, wheeling his horse round, resolved to save life or lose his own. He ordered him to mount behind him, but, as the man did not know English, he delayed to obey it, and was with difficulty saved from a cruel death.

All this took place while the Zulus were racing over the 150 yards that separated them from the pair, therefore it occupied but little time—enough, however, to earn two or more V.C.'s. Commandant Cecil D'Arcy, who had earned his V.C over and again on the Inhlobane day, and who, though then recommended for the decoration, did not get it, as he was an Irregular, now earned it again. He likewise rode back to save a dismounted and stunned man. He jumped off his horse, and attempted to lift the man bodily into the saddle; this he could not do, and, while trying, strained his back, so severely indeed as to have to miss the battle of the next day—probably the first fight for three years he had missed in South Africa. The Zulus closed on him rapidly, and he was only able, crippled as he was, to avoid them and get away, without accomplishing his object. (*With the Irregulars.*)

The unfortunate trooper was overtaken and *assegai*ed, with four others, and thirteen horses were killed. The Zulu loss was at least a hundred.

Colonel Buller had penetrated altogether about six miles beyond the river, and the expedition might have had a better effect had some infantry and guns during the interim taken possession of the bluff referred to, and more effectually covered his retreat, which now the Zulus considered a victory, and their songs of triumph were heard loading the air in the early part of the night, as they marched and counter-marched from *kraal* to *kraal*. Buller had objected to firing the *kraals*, though close to them, lest the Zulus might charge under cover of the smoke.

During the whole night of the third July, the howls and singing of the Zulus could be heard, and a night attack on the British *laager* was anticipated but none was made.

They drank enormous quantities of *utywala*, or *Kaffir* beer, that night, a sour beverage like thin gruel; yet they contrived to get intoxicated on it, and it was seen flowing out of the mouths of the wounded and dying next day.

Lord Chelmsford was so pleased with the result of Buller's reconnaissance, that he resolved to lose no time in advancing at once on Ulundi. Accordingly a little before daybreak on the morning of the 4th July, Wood with his Flying Column crossed the White Umvolosi, leaving the 1st battalion of the 24th and other Europeans, to the number of 529, with ninety-three natives, under Colonel Bellairs, in *laager* with all the heavy baggage and supplies, and he occupied the bluff commanding the upper or waggon ford.

The river was crossed by the combined force, having a total strength of 4,166 Europeans, and 958 native troops, with two Gatlings and twelve pieces of cannon.

Under Buller, the Irregulars, who had been in the saddle long before dawn, pushed on ahead of the combined column. Each of the former had provisions for a day and a half, with 100 rounds of ball cartridge. They cantered through the river, scaring in flights the vultures, then gorging themselves on the slain of the previous day, that were lying there ghastly and torn, among the tamarind and acacia trees, the convolvuli, wild guava and sweet-scented bush, which fringed the bank of the rippling river, and amid which the great bees began to hum as the morning sun arose.

The order of march was as follows:—80th Regiment, with four Royal Artillery 7-pounders, two 9-pounders, and two Gatlings; 90th and 13th Regiments; 94th and 58th Regiments, with two 7 and four 9-pounders; the Royal Scots Fusiliers in rear, covered by three squadrons of the 17th Lancers. The infantry were drenched to their waist-belts in fording the river.

About half-past seven Buller's Irregulars, after pushing on unopposed, through rough and jungly ground, eastward of the Umvolosi, reached the open country. Nothing of the enemy was seen by them as yet, excepting dead bodies here and there, marking the line of yesterday's conflict. On passing the Unodwengo *kraal*, however, masses of them were seen on the adjacent hills moving rapidly, yet keeping out of sight as much as possible, as they evidently did not think the time had come to attack the invaders on the plain.

Detachments were now hurrying from the *kraals*, and through field-glasses it could be noticed how companies swelled into regiments, and regiments into *impies*. They were also seen massing in the bush, along the banks of the little river Unodwengine, and at Ulundi; and soon the riders came to the body of a poor prisoner whose shrieks had been heard over night. It was tied to a stake and mutilated beyond all description; but the sight called forth deep threats and imprecations from all who saw it

The Irregulars looked back from their saddles as the sun rose above the hills, and could see the imposing sight of the column coming on, the fluttering pennons of the lancers in their blue uniforms lapelled with white; the bright steel barrels and bayonets of the scarlet-clad infantry; while, in the hollows where the Zulus were gathering, all was gloom as yet, for they lay under the shadow of the great mountains.

The trumpets sounded—the forward movement began again, and ground was passed wherein the women of the *kraals* had buried their valuables, and then the horses began to stumble, as pits, to entrap them, had been dug and covered over with coarse creeping grass.

And now we have to relate the story of the advance of the force in hollow square, perhaps the first instance of such a movement in war.

CHAPTER 13

The Battle of Ulundi

The order was given for the troops to form a large hollow oblong square, with Engineers' tool-cart, ammunition and bearers in the centre, under Major Chard and Captain Ainsley. The Flying Column under Wood held the post of honour in front, and the general formation on this eventful day was as shown on the accompanying diagram.

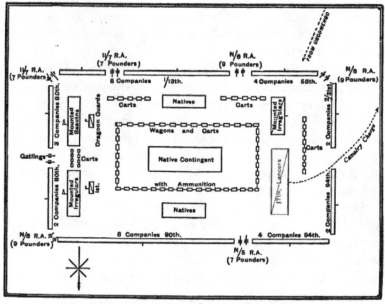

DISPOSITIONS IN THE "SQUARE" AT ULUNDI (JULY 4, 1879).

The infantry on the sides of this hollow square marched in sections of fours, those in the front and rear faces being deployed, and thus formed, the advance began about eight in the morning, covered by cavalry scouring the front and both flanks under Buller, while two squadrons of the 17th Lancers, under Colonel Drury Lowe, with Captain Shepstone's Basutos, formed the rear-guard.

In the centre, with all his staff, rode Lord Chelmsford in rear of the front face, and ever and *anon* as circumstances required, his clear voice rang out the order, "The square will wheel to the left" or "right," as the case might be. This advance in hollow square was a most imposing sight. At first the formation was somewhat loose, but only so that a few minutes would close all up and make a human wall. The colours—the first time for many days—were all flying, and the bands were playing, a very unusual circumstance, as the bagpipe is generally the only instrument heard before or in action. The stirring music, says Tomasson, vibrated through every heart and made all impatient for battle. The guns were marched parallel with the infantry.

The general march of this huge rectangle was north-eastward, between the Ndabakaombe and Unodwengo *kraals*. It soon reached propitious ground.

"Are we to fight here?" asked Colonel Buller.

"No," replied Lord Chelmsford, "a little farther on."

Past the two *kraals*, about 2,000 yards north of which lay the great circular grave of Panda, the father of Cetewayo, the march was continued till a favourable position was reached; then Lord Chelmsford wheeled the rectangle half-right and halted it, with its front towards Ulundi, which lay due east and about half a mile distant, with a ruined mission church and a group of gum trees half way between.

About two miles off were steep hills, the sides of which were strewn with grey boulders. To the right of the square rose lower hills covered with thorn trees, running towards the mouth of the White Umvolosi. In the rear and on the left spread a broken country, scarred by stony *dongas* and sloping valleys, studded with mimosa bush and strange, stiff, gaunt *euphorbias*. The position was in a kind of amphitheatre, where stood three great military *kraals*, the chief one being that of Ulundi.

Close by there, yawned a gloomy hollow, used by the Zulus as a place of execution since the days of King Chaka, and all around were the fields and demesne of Cetewayo.

Buller and his ubiquitous riders dashed about here and there to tempt on the Zulu columns, which were seen advancing from various quarters. This was about half-past eight in the morning. At the extreme end of the amphitheatre the sun shone strongly upon a long line of great white oval shields, marching in a species of double column, with skirmishers thrown out in front and on the flanks, in imitation of European tactics, as they emerged from the base of the hill, and occasionally the barrel of a rifle or the blade of a knife emitted an ominous gleam.

At the same time the mounted Irregulars under Buller were far out, hovering on three sides of the square, which was all closed up now, shoulder to shoulder, with every gun and rifle loaded, while the ammunition boxes were opened and the doctors got out their instruments; but from some error, the right, where it was thought the Lancers would have acted, was at first unprovided for. A remedy was soon found, as the mounted Basutos and Native Contingent under Dundonald Cochrane rapidly deployed in excellent style, and skirmishing towards the Ndabakaombe *kraal*, held the enemy pluckily in check. The first *kraal* was fired, some of the Basutos having applied flint and steel with great deliberation to the work, and the lapping flames and rolling smoke ascended skyward together.

The next was the *kraal* of King Panda, wherein he had dwelt of old, named Unodwengo, which was also fired, but the smoke, as it rolled along the ground, proved such a screen to the advancing Zulus that Lord Chelmsford ordered its immediate extinction.

Still anxious to lure them on, Buller sent forward twenty horsemen under Captain Parminter, with orders to "ride close and draw them, but not dismount, and to watch the *donga* on his right." Parminter obeyed, and on seeing so small a force advancing, the Zulu front in that quarter opened to make a trap, while sending a body down into the *donga* to cut them off. Enraged at being bearded by only twenty men, who rode right up to them and poured in a carbine fire, they began to advance firing at random.

A German trooper, in defiance of Buller's orders, dismounted to handle his carbine, and his horse, terrified by the yells of the Zulus, swerved wildly round and prevented him mounting. His peril was seen by Captain Parminter, who assisted him into his saddle, and, over ground pitted with artificial holes and covered with grass, the twenty troopers rode furiously back towards the square, which stood still and motionless in the morning sunshine, but which was soon to be girt by a spitting fire of flashes and glittering steel. Already the booming of the artillery was heard, and the fierce squishing sound of the rockets as they were launched into Ulundi—the royal *kraal*—and set more than one hut on fire.

Great was the Zulu terror of these fiery missiles, which, as they make a hideous rush and screaming sound through the air, produce always a great effect upon animals and uncivilised men; and savages sneaking in high grass or light bush will fly in terror from what seem to them, as they call them, living devils.

A little after nine saw the whole of the mounted men inside the square, standing by their horses' bridles and looking quietly about them, and the whole front being clear now, and almost free from bush, the artillery opened fire in a manner that proved most destructive in the ranks of the enemy.

Their circle gradually contracted as they came within musketry

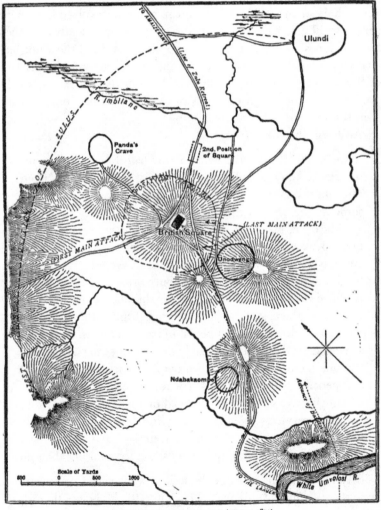

PLAN OF THE BATTLE OF ULUNDI (JULY 4, 1879).

159

range, and the action soon became general, with cannon, Gatlings and Martini-Henrys. Our ranks were four deep, the two front kneeling as if to receive cavalry. The casualties among the British troops, formed as they were in so dense an order, and exposed to a converging attack from so many thousands, would have been very serious, had the fire of the attacking foe been at all accurate, but as the sequel proved, the loss was comparatively small.

The enemy had extended their formation, so as to embrace the four sides of the square, advancing in skirmishing order, steadily and for a time silently, as yet not clashing their shields, but well-disciplined and orderly in aspect. The whole square was now involved in eddying smoke, amid which the dismounted cavalry looking silently on—their faces at times half seen, half hidden—while overhead the Zulu bullets whistled and screamed, but with different notes, the sharper ring of the Martini-Henry being discernible from the duller ping of the Snider, while the rough-cast balls of the Enfields and long elephant guns sounded more heavily than either.

An Irregular wrote:

If we are hit today, let it be by a rifle ball if possible. The unmistakable thud of bullets, as they strike horse or man, is not often heard. Horses spring up into the air as they are struck, sometimes crying in their agony. A stretcher party, the pillow already dyed, passes us. All things seem in pretty good form now, so we can take a walk round the square. . . . The doctors are busy at work with the red cross of St George flying overhead, and Army Hospital men are busy bringing them patients. Archibald Forbes, who had laid a level hundred there would be no fight, is there, looking not one whit dismayed by its loss; he stands with note book and pencil in hand, taking in everything at a glance, and knowing probably more about the business than any one there. Melton Prior is moving about also, sketch-book and pencil busily occupied. There too was the clergyman, Mr. Coar, who was standing at the head of a grave, quietly reading the burial service, while the bullets whistled overhead. A touching picture enough, as the bodies were laid in a hastily made grave—it was certainly a unique position for an army chaplain.

Meanwhile, rushing on like the rolling waves of the sea in a storm, came the swarming Zulus, with their white shields before them, leaping over the soft springy turf, with wild gestures and demon-like yells, fierce, stern, fearless, with set teeth and gleaming eyes, only to be hurled back from the faces of the square, all shattered, bloody and broken by the tempests of lead and iron from the shrapnel shells that were poured into them;—yet on they would come again. "Steady, my lads," Evelyn Wood was heard to cry more than once; "fire low and not so fast."

Under cover of the Unodwengo Kraal, northward of which grew clumps of *euphorbia* trees, one great *impi*, led by a daring chief on a white horse, who—imitatively perhaps—formed it in hollow square, with unearthly war-cries and piercing yells, dashed itself like a living sea upon the right rear angle of the square, where two 9-pounder guns were placed, flanked by two companies of the Scots Fusiliers under Major Hazelrigge, a Crimean officer, and four of the 58th Foot, and two of the 94th.

This was a skilful movement, as every engineer knows that the salient angle of a square, like that of a bastion, is its weakest point. But the shells of the two 9-pounders were sent into the mass with the deadliest effect, while the eight infantry companies pouring an oblique, yet concentrated fire, at the very moment when a hand-to-hand conflict, bayonet against *assegai*, seemed imminent, shattered their order, broke and rolled up the square, hurling back the living over the dying and dead, and after a pause the warriors of the white horseman fled in tumult and dismay.

Amid all this hurly-burly, in the centre of the square might be seen Chelmsford in his saddle amid his staff; Buller with a cigarette between his lips and the field-glass at his eyes; one or two of the mounted officers were hit, and as the enemy's bullets went high, it was a marvel they were not all shot down. Gunner Morshead, though severely wounded in the leg, crawled to the Gatling Battery, and assisted the sergeant to fill the carriage drums.

In the direction of Ulundi, large masses of the enemy could be seen, by those who were mounted, lying among the long grass, but affording no mark save the smoke of their firing, which there as everywhere flew high, probably from their ignorance of how to sight the rifle. Colonel Drury Lowe was knocked off his horse by a spent bullet, but sprang into his saddle again.

While the right rear angle of the square was repelling its assailants, the front attack was again developed, as a dip in the ground there enabled the Zulus to re-form out of fire, so that the gallant 80th under Major Tucker had to reserve theirs till the black shaven heads were seen to rise in line above the grassy mound, and then they poured in a volley so deadly and direct, that the attack slackened; the Zulu line wavered and ceased firing.

The Report of the Intelligence Department says:

The Zulus firing wildly, pressed forward in their usual loose order, and sought to close with the British troops; but the steady and well-sustained fire of the infantry, supported by the Gatlings and artillery, rendered this impossible, and at no point did they succeed in approaching nearer than thirty yards.

A want of concert in their action was perceptible, and though reserves were on the ground—those, however, lying among the grass in the direction of Ulundi not being brought up—the check which the advanced portions received was soon taken advantage of. In half an hour after our infantry fire opened, they were seen falling back in close masses that rapidly became disorganised under the storm of bullets and shells rained upon them, and then the wavering mob broke into headlong flight

This was at twenty-five minutes past nine a.m., and then Chelmsford resolved to let slip the lancers after them.

"Go at them, Lowe," he cried, waving his helmet to the men, who gripped their weapons with willing hands and fearless hearts; "but don't pursue too far."

Leading them out from an opening in the rear face of the rectangle, Drury Lowe advanced in column of troops from the right, while the guns were tearing up the flying masses with their shell fire.

"From troops, form squadron—trot!" cried Lowe; "form line— gallop—*Charge!*"

A roaring cheer burst from the infantry square, as the gallant Lancers swept at racing speed, with all their weapons lowered in the rest, the pennons streaming ahead of their horses' manes.

On they went like a whirlwind, driving the fugitives headlong into a *donga; anon* rooting them out of it, they forced them to fly for safety to the mountains, that rose northward of the battlefield; but when flanking the *donga*, half a Zulu regiment, that had been hidden among the long grass to cover the retreat, rose as one man and poured in a rifle volley. Many saddles were emptied, a splendid young officer. Captain the Hon. Edmond Verney Wyatt-Edgell, fell in the act of leading on his men, who, maddened when they saw him fall, dashed in their spurs all the deeper to take a sure and bloody vengeance.

His friend and collaborator in the *Story of the Zulu Campaign* wrote:

A moment more, and the bristling line of steel meets the black and shining wall of human flesh, rent, pierced, and gashed, by a weapon as death-dealing and unsparing as their own *assegai*. Still, though crushed and stabbed by the lances, and though their fierce army was scattered like sea-foam, the Zulus fought in stubborn knots, nor cried for quarter, stabbing at the horses' bellies as they went down, and trying to drag the men off them in the *mêlée*. The lance was now relegated in most instances to its sling, and the heavy sabres of the troopers became red with gore.

Deeply was Edgell's fall avenged by the 17th Lancers. He had been a cornet of 1866, and was the eldest son of Henrietta Baroness Brave (whose family was raised to the peerage by Henry VIII.) and grandson of Mr. Otway, of Otway Castle, Tipperary, and he had just qualified himself for admission into the Staff College.

In this pursuit the efficacy of the lance as a cavalry weapon was abundantly proved.

To follow up the lancers, a troop of the King's Dragoon Guards under Captain Brewster, with the mounted men of the Flying Column under Buller, issued together from the front of the square, and pursued, with Lord William Beresford many yards in advance of the whole, cutting down scores till they won the crests of the hills; but even there the Zulus were not safe, as the shrapnel shells, fired with time-fuses, were continually exploding amongst them.

Those bands which fled towards the hills were small and scattered;

CAPTAIN THE HON. E. V. WYATT-EDGELL.

but ere they could gain their eyries, the Irregulars came up with many of them, and then rifles were resorted to once more, as the former, diverging from the line of pursuit taken by Lowe and his lancers, swung on the spur round some hills on the right When overtaken, the Zulus fired and then used the *assegai*; the Irregulars used their carbines in pistol fashion. Many Zulus hid among the long grass, or feigned death, trusting to escape afterwards.

A lively musketry fire was opened by them from the summit of a hill too steep for horses, where a number of fugitive parties converged; and all who died, died hard, no cry for mercy or quarter ever escaping their lips. Amid the fury of the chase, one huge Zulu was seen with a muzzle-loading elephant gun, which had hung fire, and at the nipple of which he was prodding away with perfect coolness till a revolver shot settled him for ever.

The effects of the shell-fire and rockets were seen to be terrible, by the mutilation of the dead; while, on the other hand, those slain by the rifle were little disfigured, a very small orifice where the bullet went in, and a larger at its exit, alone being discernible.

After our wounded had been attended to, the troops of the two columns, still retaining their rectangular formation, moved about a mile nearer Ulundi, and halted on the banks of the Imbilane stream, where they rested and dined on the contents of their haversacks; and at two p.m. the troops marched, but slowly, as the wounded had to be carried on stretchers, back to their *laager* on the right bank of the Umvolosi, which was reached at four in the afternoon.

The British loss on this day amounted to two officers killed, including Captain Wyatt-Edgell, and the Hon. W. Drummond, reported missing, but whose body was afterwards found, and ten non-commissioned officers and men; the wounded were nineteen officers, including Lieutenant Pardoe of the 13th, mortally, and sixty-nine non-commissioned officers and men.

The attacking force consisted of twelve regiments, set down at 20,000 men, of whom not less than 1,500 fell. No Zulu wounded were found on the field of Ulundi. Our Native Contingent with their *assegais* and knives despatched all they could find. It was said, that had permission been given to the Zulus to remove their wounded, and our forces been withdrawn to enable them to do so, they would certainly have availed themselves of the privilege, and the moral effect of such clemency might have been great. The absence of hospitals was given as an excuse; but until the *kraals* were destroyed, the plea was scarcely valid; besides, the surgical staff was very numerous.

Native eye-witnesses of the conflict asserted that the Zulus fought without much heart, and only to save their national honour, made a show of resistance. They described with admiration and terror the terrible execution done by the Gatling guns, and the charges of the lancers; and when detailing Buller's reconnaissance on the previous day, they told how a party of his cavalry fell into an ambush, but burst through the Zulu force, losing fifteen men, but killing thrice that number.

Cetewayo was said to have been present on horseback; other accounts state that it was one of his brothers, and that he quitted Ulundi on the day before the battle; but, by the result of this action, the power of his people was completely broken, and a conviction brought home to his best-trained warriors, that their superiority in numbers was of no avail against the weapons and the discipline of the British troops, even when in the open and undefended by military works. The Zulu Army began to melt away, and the people returned to their own *kraals*.

Before the rearward movement began, Buller and his Irregulars were pushing on towards the great royal *kraal*.

"Now, then," cried he, "who is to be first in Ulundi?" thus waiving his own right to be so.

Every spur was applied then, and a dash was made for the *kraal*, round which was a stiff thorn hedge, its boundary measuring 700 yards by 550. Rushing his pony at it. Lord William Beresford flew over it like a bird, and landed himself among the dome-roofed huts. The residence of Cetewayo was found to be a square house built of mud, surrounded by tall wooden fences, evidently constructed to guard against surprise. The floor was of clay, and strewn with empty champagne and square Geneva bottles. Two elephant's tusks were found, and—most singular to say—a large box full of London newspapers, among which were the *Illustrated London News, Graphic, Times*, and others full of references to Cetewayo and his Zulus.

A troop was now despatched by Colonel Buller to burn a *kraal* farther on, and to Captains Tomasson, Prior of the 80th, and Parminter was assigned the duty of destroying the royal *kraal*. By these three officers the 10,000 huts which made up Ulundi were burned. Being dry, they were easily consumed. The first-named officer says:

> The burners rode from hut to hut with flaming torches of grass,
> and, after hard work, got everything in flames. The huts were

165

small and bad, save those around the king's house for his chief wives; the others were decidedly the worst huts we had seen in Zululand. At the bottom corner was a splendid pile of skins ready to make into shields.

Several Zulu women, who had been watching the fight from the hills, had been killed that day accidentally by our shells. Before the troops left the bank of the Umvolosi, the burial of Captain Wyatt-Edgell's body took place by the riverside, a sight that was very impressive, as he was lowered into his lonely grave by his sorrowing comrades in the dead of the night

Many were the surmises now in the two columns as to what the next move would be; but these were soon set at rest by an order, on the 5th of July, to effect a junction with the 1st Division under General Crealock. Both columns began their backward march to the camping ground below the Enlonganeni Heights, where Wood's troops bivouacked, while the 2nd Division ascended and encamped in the fortified *laager* above. There the tents awaiting them were pitched; the troops who had been drenched with rain were enabled to get dry and to refit; yet the men behaved admirably, and jocularity and good humour reigned supreme.

On Sunday morning, the 6th July, two of the 13th Light Infantry, who had died of their wounds, were buried. On the preceding evening Lord Chelmsford had received another communication from Sir Garnet Wolseley, brought by native runners, and sent up by General Crealock from Port Durnford, notifying the new movements he meant to inaugurate.

Lord Chelmsford's orders were that he was to return with the 2nd Division and all the wounded to Fort Newdigate, and march the Flying Column to join Sir Garnet Wolseley, by the way of Kwamagwasa and St Paul's.

The night of the 6th of July proved a stormy one, with torrents of rain and a bitterly cold wind, and these lasted with more or less violence during the two subsequent days, rendering all movement for the time impossible, and adding to the sufferings of the wounded. The horses and oxen had great mortality among them in consequence.

News of the victory of the 4th July reached Sir Garnet at Fort Pearson on the following day, and his congratulations, telegraphed from that place, were received by Lord Chelmsford on the 8th of the month. The news was conveyed to Fort Pearson by a telegram from Mr.

Archibald Forbes, the war correspondent of the *Daily News.* The latter came into Pietermaritzburg, looking gaunt, grizzly, and worn; and his clothes were almost in tatters by riding through thorns, and plastered with mud. He had ridden about 300 miles in fifty hours, with one thigh swollen by a spent bullet—the first hundred miles through the enemy's country, over rugged and mountainous ways, without proper roads and entirely alone, and at the no small risk of being cut off by the straggling bands, then scattered over all Zululand. He rode all through the night, which was dark, with a thick fog, and twice lost his way. Mr. Forbes's exploit was a notable deed

CHAPTER 14

A "Durbar" By the Umlatoosi

On the evening of the 8th of July, copies of the General Orders issued by Sir Garnet Wolseley on the 28th of June reached the camp at Enlonganeni, and Lord Chelmsford decided at once to resign his command and return to Britain without delay.

He ordered a parade of all arms that he might take farewell of the troops who had served him so faithfully. General Newdigate massed them in a hollow square of three sides—Lord Chelmsford with his staff forming the fourth. He kindly praised all for their good service in the field and good conduct in camp and bivouac, and added these words:—

> For the courage, coolness, and devotion you have all displayed wherever I have been with you my best and warmest thanks are due. For the unselfish devotion, untiring energy, and good humour with which you have encountered hardship, fatigue, and privation I find it hard to express my gratitude sufficiently. In all senses you have done your duty as British soldiers!

Cheers were on the lips and in the hearts of all, but discipline re-strained them.

On the 10th of July the retrograde movement began, and it was found that the sick and wounded, of whom there were about 100, bore the journey well; twenty five were in stretchers and cots, borne by natives, four men to a stretcher and six to a cot, and a company was told off daily to pitch the hospital tents. This most unexpected movement of course led Cetewayo and his chiefs to suppose that our losses at Ulundi, together with lack of military skill, and not the new plans of another commander-in-chief, led us to forego the advantages

167

CHARGE OF THE SEVENTEENTH LANCERS AT ULUNDI.

we had gained.

Four days' marching saw the 2nd Division and Flying Column passing Fort Marshall, on the Upoko River, and then the sick and wounded, escorted by two companies of the Scots Fusiliers and Bengough's Natives, were sent on to the convalescent hospital at Ladysmith.

The breaking up of the 2nd Division took place on the bank of the Upoko on the 26th of July, by the departure of one troop of the 17th Lancers, a company of Engineers, and four of the 94th, for Fort Newdigate, with orders to proceed to the valley of the White Umvolosi, and there construct a work to be called Fort Cambridge.

Major-General Newdigate now took leave of the troops. The 17th Lancers, then under orders for India, handed over their horses to the King's Dragoon Guards, and the rest of them moved to Dundee and elsewhere, prior to their employment in the Transvaal, where the cloud of war was gathering. Others formed garrisons for the various new forts; for when Sir Garnet Wolseley took over the command from Lord Chelmsford, he found a complete chain of these, such as had never before been seen in South Africa, along the whole Zulu frontier, from the Blood and Buffalo Rivers to the mouth of the Umvolosi and Port Durnford on the Indian Ocean, encompassing on three sides the kingdom of Cetewayo.

On the 5th of July, and before the victory at Ulundi could be known to the troops of Crealock's division, 700 Zulus, with all their women, children, and cattle, came into his camp near Port Durnford, to make submission and seek protection; They had all heard of the battle, yet, strange to say, not a whisper of it escaped them. To impress them, General Crealock ordered a muster of his entire division, letting every available man parade, yet his strength was but weak after all, even with the bluejackets of the *Active* and *Shah*.

When line was formed an *aide-de-camp* was sent to the Zulus, who were halted on the crest of a hill, to advance and disarm, on which 300 muscular-looking warriors approached in good order, proffered a salute, and laid down their *assegais*, with seventy muskets, nearly all of obsolete patterns.

Before leaving Durban, Sir Garnet had telegraphed to General Crealock to report direct to him and not to Lord Chelmsford.

All drafts marching to the front were ordered to halt, and volunteers were permitted to disband.

The published despatches of General Crealock proved amply his inability to form any junction with the 2nd Division before the battle of Ulundi, and it was the result of no want of exertion on his part, but solely owing to the manner in which the movements of his troops were crippled and hampered in a savage country, especially by sickness among his teams of oxen; but that his time had not been wasted was evinced by the extent of roads he had made, and by the many raids achieved, thus making harassing diversions, which rendered Cetewayo less able to repel or inflict any defeat upon the 2nd Division.

Sir Garnet Wolseley had brought out with him several of his old staff, and some joined him subsequently. Colonel Pomeroy Colley took up the duties of chief of the staff, and Captain Ederick and Lord Gifford, V.C., who had distinguished himself so much in Ashantee, joined from his own regiment, the 57th. Sir Garnet made many important changes. Among other orders issued was one which gave great dissatisfaction—to suspend military operations upon the still refractory Sekukuni, against whom several successful patrols had been sent; and Colonel Owen Lanyon having, after serious difficulties and unavoidable delays, completed all his arrangements for an attack, was ordered to fall back, and thus all that was now undone had to be done over again, in the close of the following year.

When Sir Garnet Wolseley, on the night of Sunday, 6th of July, rode into General Crealock's camp, amid a storm of rain and wind, accompanied by Major Brackenbury, Captains Creagh and Fitzmaurice (together with Dr. W. H. Russell, the veteran war correspondent), he did not attract much attention, though Crealock and his staff rode out a few hundred yards to meet him; but the cleanshaven chins, white helmets, and new uniforms of him and his party contrasted strongly with the war and weather worn aspect of the officers and men of the 1st Division. The severe storm which had swept the eastern coast of Zululand, as well as the heights of Enlonganeni, for fully sixty hours, abated somewhat on the morning of the 9th of July, and the tremendous surf on the white beach at Port Durnford having moderated, the landing of supplies for the troops was resumed.

When Sir Garnet came, the war was thought to be over so far as fighting went; but Cetewayo had to be captured, and Sekukuni crushed, and the north-west of Zululand was still in arms, though by the number of its dead and those that were fast submitting, the nation was deemed to be crippled beyond the power of doing us mischief now.

The news of the victory at Ulundi which reached Sir Garnet on his way to Port Durnford, led to an alteration in the proposed operations of the 1st Division, which it was decided should be exclusively

LANCERS RETURNING FROM A FORAY.

supplied from that place, as 120 tons of supplies could be landed there daily despite the surf, in fine weather, and it was calculated, that if landing could be carried on one day in the week, the division could not lack supplies, and its line of communications by Forts Chelmsford and Napoleon were to be abandoned; while Wood's Flying Column, which was ordered to remain at Enlonganeni was to draw its supplies by the old line through Fort Newdigate and Landmann's Drift.

All connection between the 1st Division and the garrisons in Forts Crealock and Chelmsford was now severed, and on the 10th July, Sir Garnet Wolseley transferred the troops there to the command of Major-General the Hon. H. H. Clifford, whose authority extended over all the lines of communication instead of being reduced to those within the borders of Natal.

On the 14th of July, a column consisting of the 5th Regiment, a troop and company of Royal Engineers, Dunnes Scouts, four companies of the Natal Native Contingent, Jantzi's and Mafunzi's Natives, and two guns, all under Lieutenant-Colonel Baker Russell, but only 1,600 men in all, marched from Port Durnford to the lower ford on the Umlatoosi River with ten days' provisions, and Sir Garnet Wolseley with his staff came to the camp there on the same evening.

Escorted by the mounted men under Major Barrow, Sir Garnet rode on the 15th to St Paul's Mission Station, when he found that Lord Chelmsford had just arrived with Wood's column, which he inspected on the following day (when the V.C was bestowed upon Major Chard, one of the heroes of Rorke's Drift), and then returned to the camp at the Umlatoosi, accompanied by Lord Chelmsford and his personal staff, and on the 17th, the latter—whose resignation had been accepted—started on his return to Natal. He accompanied Sir Garnet Wolseley for a short distance until their ways separated, the latter returning to the Umlatoosi, and Lord Chelmsford making his way back to the frontier by Etschowe.

He reached Durban on the 20th of July, and Pietermaritzburg next day; a ball at the former town, and a banquet at the latter were given him with all the brilliance, and certainly all the warmth and sincerity these new communities could afford; and on the 5th of August he sailed from Cape Town for England, where he and many of his brave comrades were welcomed with all the honours they deserved.

Meanwhile the Flying Column which had marched to a deserted mission station at Kwamagwasa, and commenced the construction of a fort, left there a company of Wood's Irregulars, 160 mounted men of

Buller's force, and two companies of the 94th with two 9-pounders, and then marched on the 13th towards St Paul's.

Prior to this, while the column had been posted on the Magnumbonum Heights, after enduring there storms of wind and icy rain, under which bullocks and horses perished in dozens, on the 7th July Colonel Buller made one of his raids. Starting with two troops at three am., he rode for a whole day amid the drenching and blinding rain of a thunder-storm and captured a fine herd of cattle. While at the mission station of Kwamagwasa they found the dead bodies of Lieutenant Scott Douglas, a signalling officer, and Corporal Cottier, of the 17th Lancers, who had escorted him. They had been missing for some days, having ridden from the Magnumbonum Heights to the next fort, and returning in the fog had lost their way, and fallen among some of the people of Dabulamanzi, by whom they had been surprised and slain while resting under a tree.

Corporal Cottier had evidently died hard, as evidences of a terrible struggle were seen all round where his body lay. Neither had been mutilated. They were buried where they were found. The mission station here had formerly been the residence of Bishop Robertson, and is described as being a beautiful spot, closely planted with fine lemon trees and gardens, then desolate, where the Cape gooseberries were growing wild.

The district between the Umlatoosi and St Paul's was found to be in a very quiet state, the people having returned to their usual avocations, after bringing in many Enfield muskets, but no Martinis. It was not certain, however, that resistance on the part of the northern chiefs and of Cetewayo was at an end, and on the 18th Sir Garnet Wolseley resolved to re-occupy Ulundi (although Lord Chelmsford had been ordered to fall back from that point), and from there to dictate the terms of settlement for Zululand.

To all the most powerful chiefs who could be communicated with, notices had been sent desiring them to meet the new commander-in-chief in the camp on the Umlatoosi on the 19th of July, and on that day a large number presented themselves, and surrendered arms and cattle belonging to Cetewayo; but all these chiefs belonged to the east coast tribes, and no sign of submission had been made as yet by those of the inland and northern clans.

On this day the camp by the Umlatoosi presented rather a picturesque spectacle.

With the Queen's Colours a guard of honour was drawn up out-

side the tent of Sir Garnet Wolseley, while for the reception of the
Zulu warriors a large space had been enclosed by mimosa branches,
and from an early hour of the morning the Zulus had come trooping
in dark bands down from the hills in every direction. As the deputation from each tribe, preceded by its chief and chief men, came into
camp, it was formed up in a mass, of some 18 feet deep; 250 chiefs
with their immediate followers were present, each man attired in his
best bravery, cow-tails, copper armlets and anklets, with plumes of
feathers, and all armed with carved *knobkeries*, which they laid before
them when they squatted on the mats and skins provided for them.

Among these were Cetewayo's two brothers, Dabulamanzi and
Magwendi, both contrasts to Uhamu. The two former were muscular
savages of considerable stature; the latter was a corpulent and un-
wieldy man. They wore fillets of ostrich feathers, heavy arm-rings of
burnished copper, and necklaces of monkeys' teeth and small shells.

Mr. Fynny, the Border Agent, acted as interpreter, and to Sir Garnet's speech—which we give somewhat abbreviated—they all listened
with rapt attention. It ran thus:—

Tell them, I am glad to see them; because their coming here
shows that they wish for peace, as the Great Queen does in
whose name I speak. We have been at war with Cetewayo—
not with his people. While he ruled, life and property were not
safe anywhere in Zululand. His marriage laws prevented people
from settling and becoming wealthy and prosperous; men were
slain and their cattle taken without trial. I wish to end a system
that left no peace along our borders, nor among the Zulus at
home. We have now beaten the king, and burned his *kraal*; he
is a fugitive in the bush, and shall never again rule in the land. I
rode over to St Paul's the other day, and there found the people
quietly living in their *kraals*.

All may do the same; but all must give up their arms and the
king's cattle, and the country shall be ruled according to the old
laws of Zululand I shall appoint the chiefs who are to rule, and
divide the kingdom into districts. Zululand shall be for the Zulus. All will be allowed to marry, to work, and become rich. The
Queen wishes the Zulus to be happy. Those who have arms
must give them up—they have no escape. The Swazies on the
north and the Tongas are only kept by my orders from invading
Zululand Uhamu and his soldiers are moving upon the west,

and I myself am going with my troops to Ulundi, when I shall announce to the Zulu people the arrangements I shall make for the future government of the country.

On this (according to the correspondent of the *Daily News*) two or three chiefs spoke, expressing their satisfaction at the words of the general Magwendi, however, had some high words with the chiefs who were present, and as they tried to shout him down, something of a scene ensued

At this "*durbar*," if we may term it so, the face of Redvers Buller, the gallant leader of the Irregular Horse, was missed, as was also that of Evelyn Wood, both of whom were returning home on medical certificates. On the preceding day there was a parade of the famous Flying Column at St Paul's, and both these favourite and brilliant officers came forth to say farewell. They were loudly cheered, and Buller's voice fairly broke when he addressed his hardy Irregulars, and long after he withdrew, says Captain Tomasson, did their eyes:

> Follow his figure as it went up the hill from us. After his departure the interest in everything was over, as he was the life and soul of the column. Many an Irregular read with honest pride the enthusiastic welcome that England gave to Sir Evelyn Wood and Colonel Buller, our leader and beloved chief. Not a few but owed their lives to the latter, and right glad we were to see that he got the CM.G. and was made A.D.C to the Queen, honours well deserved by him.

The command of the Flying Column then devolved upon Colonel Harrison of the Royal Engineers.

On the 19th the Frontier Light Horse started for Landmann's Drift, and Baker's Horse for Fort Tenedos, as both corps were to be disbanded Sir Garnet Wolseley supposed that for the measures he was about to inaugurate a large force would not be required, and thus he proceeded to reduce that already in the field. A marine battalion, consisting of 1,146 men of all ranks, which had arrived in Simon's Bay, he ordered home to Britain, while the Naval Brigade was embarked at Port Durnford It was 400 strong, and was conveyed away in the City of Venice transport

The Flying Column, after remaining for a time at St Paul's, making roads and reconnoitring, was denuded on the 21st July of Raaf's Rangers, the 1st Squadron of Mounted Infantry, and two companies of the Perthshire; the 13th Light Infantry were under orders for England, and began the march for Natal, so that by the end of the month Evelyn Wood's Flying Column had ceased to exist.

So had Crealock's division.

During its encampment at Port Durnford it had undergone much of inactivity and sickening delay, consequent on the weary and ir-regular advance to the Umtalazi, the misunderstanding of the naval and military authorities concerning the position and capabilities of Port Durnford, the waste in the commissariat, and the ignorance of transport arrangements. As Crealock, aware of the coming changes, had resolved to resign his command, he ordered a general parade on the 21st of July, and made a brief address to the troops.

There paraded the 3rd Buffs, 60th Rifles, 91st Highlanders, the Naval Brigade of the *Boadicea*, three troops of local horse, and a 7-pounder battery. They were drawn up on the bank of the thickly-wooded river, close down to the waters of which grew the tall reeds and over-arching date-palms, under which the crocodiles often bask in the mud and ooze—a scene overlooked on the east by the Libomba range, more than 2,000 feet in height

After the usual wheel into line and march past of the division, in worn, faded, patched, and tattered uniforms, the soldiers were addressed by General Crealock, who informed them that Sir Garnet Wolseley was about to disperse them; but he thanked them all for their good conduct and their constant work borne without a murmur, and ended by wishing every officer and soldier in the ranks prosperity, success, and a hearty farewell. Two days afterwards the division was broken up.

But Cetewayo was still King of the Zulus, and up to this date was reported to have a large force of fighting men with him. The details of his regiments present at Ulundi proved this, and many even then prognosticated, what was afterwards proved, the unwisdom of putting up puppet kings in his stead.

CHAPTER 15

Reorganisation of the Troops in South Africa

The future operations as planned by Sir Garnet Wolseley for the final conquest of Zululand were to be as follows:—A brigade was to hold St Paul's, and a military post for 400 men was to be established at Port Durnford, and another on the heights of Enlonganeni; on the Umlatoosi a regiment was to be entrenched, while a battalion of the Native Contingent was to hold the line of the Tugela. To co-operate with Uhamu in the west. Colonel Baker Russell was to advance immediately from St Paul's, while Colonel the Hon. George Villiers, of the Grenadier Guards, was also to join Uhamu (or Oham, as he is often called) and organise some corps of *burghers*, Natal men, and Zulus, to hem in Cetewayo in that quarter, while Macleod, late of the 74th Highlanders, was to organise and lead 5,000 Amaswazi warriors, and march them straight into Zululand if necessary.

Colonel Clarke was to march his column direct upon Ulundi, or rather the ashes of it; and meanwhile there was convened at St Paul's the great council of Zulu chiefs on the 19th of July, to arrange definitely for the temporary government of the country.

The troops were now formed in two great columns under Lieutenant-Colonel Charles Mansfield Clarke, of the 57th Regiment, and Lieutenant-Colonel Baker Russell, C.B., of the 13th Hussars, both officers of experience and distinction.

Colonel Clarke had served with the 57th in Warre's column on the Taptee River, in co-operation with the central India Field Force in 1858; in the New Zealand War three years afterwards, and was present at the action of Katikara, and the capture of many Maori positions, and was frequently mentioned with honour in the despatches of the general commanding; while the services of Colonel Baker Russell were still more varied.

He was at Meerut with the Carabineers when the Sepoy mutiny broke out, and at Kurnaul where Colonel Gerrard was killed; he was present with Seaton's column at the Battle of Gungaree, where, after his three senior officers were slain, he commanded the squadron of his regiment and a detachment of the 9th Lancers; again, he commanded the cavalry in the action of Putteali, where over 700 were killed. Sir Thomas Seaton wrote in his despatch:

> To Lieutenant Russell, who commanded the cavalry, as well as his brave companions in arms, my thanks are specially due for their gallantry in action and vigour in pursuit.

He led the cavalry at Mynpooree, when 250 rebels were cut down, and was with his regiment when Bareilly was taken and General Penny fell; he was at the relief of Bareilly and Shahjehanpore, the capture of Remai, and the destruction of Fort Mahundee. He was in all the operations in Oude, and served with the Agra Field Force under Brigadier Showers, in Central India, during the pursuit of Tantia Topee.

The component parts of these two commands were as follows:—

Royal Artillery and Gatling Battery—
Major J. F. Owen, R.A.

Royal Engineers, 20 men, Captain Blood, R.E.

Imp. Infty. { 57th Regt., Major Knox Tredennick.
6oth Rifles, Major Tuffnell.
8oth Regt., Major Charles Tucker.

2nd Squad. Mounted } Major Barrow.
Infty., 5 companies

Colonial Troops.

European.

1st Troop Natal Horse . . Captain de Burgh.
Lonsdale's Horse, 2 troops . Captain Lumley.

Native.

Jantzi's Horse . . . . . Captain C. D. Hay.
Mafunzi's Horse . . . . Captain Nourse.
Natal N. Contingent, 4 batt. Captain Barton.

LIEUTENANT-COLONEL B. RUSSELL'S COLUMN.

Imperial Troops.

Cavalry—1 Squad. 1st K.D.G.

Royal Artillery, No. 5 Battery Lieut.-Col. Harness,
R.A.

Royal Engineers, 2nd Company.

94th Regiment . . . . . Lt.-Col. Sydenham
Malthus.

1st Squad. Mounted Infantry Captain Browne, 24th
Foot.

Colonial Corps.

Lonsdale's Horse, 1 troop
Frontier Light Horse . . . Captain D'Arcy.
Transvaal Rangers. . . . Commandant Raaf.
Natal Mounted Police. . . Captain Mansell.

Native.

2nd Batt. N.N. Contingent } Major Harcourt M. Ben-
Mounted Natives . . } gough, 77th Regt.

Colonel Clarke's orders were to march northwards from Port Durnford and re-occupy Ulundi, as already stated.

As the submission or capture of Cetewayo was, of course, deemed essential to the permanent settlement of his country, in unison with the advance of the two columns, Uhamu with his followers was to advance from Luneberg and resume the occupation of his original district between the Black Umvolosi and the Pongola Rivers, while the Swazies, who were to assemble on the bank of the latter, under Captain Macleod, were to make a demonstration in the north, completing the circle destined to hem in Cetewayo, and prevent his escape—if he should attempt it—into the country of the Amatonga.

These Swazies, who were now to co-operate with our troops, are a people of whom very little is known. Their country lies north of

Zululand. Sir Arthur Cunynghame says:

> They are probably as brave as the Zulus, but have not the same
> military discipline. They are hereditary enemies of the Zulus,
> and if backed by Europeans, would probably fight against them.
> They assisted the Boers in their attack on Sekukuni's country
> in the North Transvaal, and fought while the Dutch ran away.

They are a mixed race—being a cross between the Zulus and the
aborigines of Swaziland. Those who dwelt along the frontiers of Wak-
kerstroom, a mountainous and woody district, north of the Transvaal,
and rich in coal, owed, until the war broke out, allegiance to Cetewayo; but quarrels arose and the races became bitter enemies, hence
their readiness to respond to the invitation of Sir Garnet Wolseley.
Their weapons are much the same as those of the Zulus, though their
shields are smaller, woven of stout reeds and covered with undressed
buffalo hide. Their lances are heavy, and they carry a *knobkerie* and
knife. Strings of teeth are their favourite decoration, and they are able
to brew a decoction that very closely resembles beer. They are rather a
race of hunters and agriculturists than warriors specially, as the Zulus
have been since the days of Dingaan and Panda.

Lieutenant-Colonel Clarke's Column began its march at ten in the
morning of the 24th July, and moved from Port Durnford to the left
bank of the Umlatoosi, where the 57th Regiment, which had held
the drift of this river since the 14th, joined him, together with the
mounted men under Major Barrow.

On the 25th, he left the Umlatoosi and continued his march. The
column was now accompanied by a field hospital and supply train of
106 waggons, which were to be filled with stores on reaching St Paul's,
where the commissariat depot was to be refilled by the carrier corps
from Port Durnford, and by the mule train from Fort Chelmsford.

On the 26th, Clarke's Column reached the middle drift of the
Umlatoosi and encamped on its right bank. Reports were now current that Cetewayo with his troops was in the Umvolosi swamps, and
that he had sent messengers to John Dunn, asking whether, if he surrendered, his life would be safe, and the answer sent was "yes."

On the 27th the march was resumed, to the carrier station on the
Umlatoosana, and on the following day, after moving ten miles farther,
the column passed the ruins of the Ondine *kraal*, which had been
burned on the 6th of July by the mounted men under Major Barrow.
On the 29th, the column once more crossed the winding Umlatoosi,

at the ford known as the Upper Drift, and encamped on the bank of the Idongo, which flows at the base of the Inkwenke Mountain.

Next day a convoy of fifty-six waggons with supplies overtook the column, and Colonel Clarke sent it forward immediately up the steep and richly-wooded hill, which was crowned by the ruined buildings of St Paul's mission station; but so great were the difficulties of the ascent there, that it was two p.m. before the convoy was clear of the road, and half-past eleven p.m. before the last waggon with its team of wearied oxen reached St Paul's.

There the colonel was joined by five companies of the 80th, the Natal Pioneers, and two Gatling guns, all of which were sent forward to Kwamagwasa, with seventy waggons. The main body followed next day, and the entire force, including drivers, leaders, and others, now mustered only 2,159 whites and 1,257 blacks, along with 198 waggons, fifty-four Scotch carts, and six ambulances, which were encamped a mile beyond the Fort of Kwamagwasa, formerly named Fort Robertson.

Here a battery of two 9-pounders joined Colonel Clarke, whose force, after suffering severely from rainstorms, encamped on the Heights of Enlonganeni on the 6th of August. Next day, halting on the same ground which had been occupied by Lord Chelmsford on his march to Ulundi, a site was chosen for a work to be called Fort Victoria, and during the afternoon Sir Garnet Wolseley rode into the

SWAZI SCOUT.

camp, escorted by a squadron of the King's Dragoon Guards.

Sir Garnet after leaving Durban had proceeded to Pietermaritzburg, which he reached on the 26th of July, and where he remained
four days. There he had tidings of serious disturbances in Pondoland,
where Diko, a subordinate chief, with about 500 men, had advanced
to attack the Xesibes, a tribe in alliance with England and under her
protection, and burned all their *kraals* up to the Residency, where
Captain Blythe lived. They also massed in the direction of Kokstadt,
which was garrisoned by volunteers, repulsing a party of twenty-five
of the Cape Mounted Rifles, under Mr. Hawthorne and friendly natives, with the loss of two killed and six wounded—the campaign in
Zululand having thus filled the minds of the usually slothful Pondos
with ambitious dreams.

Lieutenant-Colonel Bayley, with a detachment of the Cape
Mounted Rifles, was sent against them from Butterworth, and soon
put an end to the turmoil there. Malgora, the leader of the rebels, was
shot, and 150 of his men were taken prisoners, but Klas Lucas, the
only remaining insurgent chief, escaped. To add to growing troubles,
the Boers in the recently-annexed Transvaal were agitating for independence, and threatening to appeal to arms. To secure matters in that
quarter, the head-quarters of the King's Dragoon Guards were sent to
Pretoria, under Colonel Henry Alexander, who had served with that
regiment in the China War, and had been in the Battle of the Tchernaya five years before.

On the 28th of July Sir Garnet Wolseley telegraphed to the Secretary of State for War that he would leave Pietermaritzburg on the 30th
to join Clarke's column, and advance on Ulundi, adding:

> Cetewayo has lately sent messengers of inferior rank to some of
> our outposts, saying that he wishes to surrender, but fears being
> killed; answers have been sent advising surrender, and promising
> not only life safe, but good treatment; but I have reason to believe
> these messengers are only spies sent to ascertain our movements.

Pietermaritzburg, a town which will be frequently referred to in
subsequent chapters, is the chief one in Natal, and its name is stated to
be compounded from the names of the old Boer leaders, Pieter Retief
and Gert Maritz, and at the period at which we have now arrived its
population numbered about 6,500. It is so subject to thunderstorms
that every house has a lightning-conductor. In Dr. Mann's edition of
Brook's work on the colony, it is described as standing upon a plain

which runs from east to west, with lofty mountains sheltering it on the north. At the west end a ridge rises some feet above the town:

And is crowned by the military station of Fort Napier, a kind of barrack defended by an earth rampart. This work overlooks and entirely commands the town, but is itself dominated by higher ground to the north-west. The city retains exactly the same form of arrangement that it had when first laid out by its Dutch founders. It consists of eight parallel thoroughfares, about 180 yards asunder and a mile and a half long, and these are crossed at convenient intervals by transverse streets of similar character, something more than a mile in length.

These streets were often crowded by idle Zulus, armed with *assegais* and *knobkeries*, though such were forbidden by law.

Of the organised forces of the town, the most popular was the corps of Carbineers, formed in 1864. The Pietermaritzburg Rifles and City Guard comprised a total of 250 men, but the inhabitants could furnish 1,000 in arms. Fort Napier was armed by about twelve pieces of cannon, of various dates, shapes and calibre.

On the 30th, Sir Garnet Wolseley quitted Pietermaritzburg with his staff, rode to Greytown, and from thence with his escort proceeded to a temporary camp at Umsinger, and reached Rorke's Drift on the morning of the 3rd August, and there he bestowed the Victoria Cross upon Private Hook, of the 24th, at a parade of the troops, remarking truly in a brief speech, that it seldom fell to the lot of a general to confer the highest reward the sovereign could bestow on a soldier, on the very scene of his achievements.

He critically examined the position, and received some despatches which determined the movements of the subsequent week. It was reported that Cetewayo was lurking in a *kraal* in the Ngome Forest, and Colonel Villiers had but an indifferent report to give of the king's brother Uhamu and of his levies, while Captain Macleod asked for European troops to keep his Swazies under control, suggesting that he should content himself with watching to prevent Cetewayo's escape, and not tempt the former by a sight of the Zulu *kraals* and cattle. He wrote:

For, to allow them to cross the border, would be risking murder, rapine and all sorts of atrocities, which, if once begun, it would be impossible to stop.

Continuing his route by Forts Marshall and Evelyn, with escorts furnished by their garrisons, he reached Enlonganeni, and came up with Colonel Clarke's column at Fort Victoria. Critics now began to aver that he was not acting as if peace at any price were his object; he had made great efforts to reduce the field force and the expenditure, yet nevertheless considerable friction ensued.

Severe storms of wind and rain began on the 7th of August, and continued for two days. The weather became piercing, causing a serious loss of oxen; 452 belonging to the column perished in sixty hours, and in addition to these 195 were left sick at Fort Victoria with fifty-four store waggons. It was one of these storms which our troops so frequently experienced in South Africa during the months of June, July, and August. Mrs. Wood says:

> The air at one moment is perfectly calm, and the next wild with terrific storms. The sky so sweetly serene at noon, will before half an hour passes be darkened by clouds which shroud the land as a pall. For months the long draughts parch the earth, the rivers may be forded on foot, the flocks and herds pant for refreshing waters and green herbage. Suddenly a cloud no bigger than a man's hand appears at the horizon, and lo! the elements rage and swell, thunder booms upon the air, darkness covers the land, the arrows of the Almighty dart from the angry heavens, striking death and terror wheresoever they fall.

Many chiefs promised to be present at Ulundi on the 10th of August, and a satisfactory meeting was held with a powerful one named Mbelebele, at the foot of that beautiful mountain range, the Libomba. He brought above 200 guns, and many others promised to surrender arms, cattle and ammunition, if peacefully amnestied. He also brought tidings that another powerful chief named Mangondo, whose principal *kraal* was near the Inklankla River, would make submission, could he be assured of escaping the vengeance of Cetewayo.

Sometime after, two chiefs named Mangumana and Sintwayo, explained to Mr. John Shepstone that the reason they did not come in sooner, was their inability to collect their people. The Battle of Ulundi, they said, had utterly crushed the Zulu nation; and in answer to the question, "Why did you not bring in your arms?" they replied, "Most of them are lost or concealed, and we had not time to collect them."

They were told that they and three other chiefs would be detained as hostages till the two pieces of cannon were sent in. This displeased them, but they became more assured when Mr. Shepstone told them they might occupy the few huts in the *kraal* at Ulundi that had escaped the conflagration; and the presence of John Dunn inspired them with greater confidence. They seemed to long for peace, and were sick of war, "which," they said, "had been waged against them for offences of which they were innocent"

They gave up 600 head of cattle.

On the 10th of August, Sir Garnet Wolseley arrived at Ulundi, and found the valley completely deserted, but soon after messages came in from various chiefs expressing their desire to make submission. The few huts that had escaped the torches of the Irregulars were thoroughly examined, and several relics of Isandhlwana were discovered. There were also found portraits of the Queen and Prince of Wales, presented to Cetewayo on his coronation, if his ceremony of installation can be termed so.

Leaving Sir Garnet at Ulundi, where on the very day of his arrival, he obtained information which eventually led to the capture of Cetewayo, we shall briefly refer to the movements of the two columns of Colonels Clarke and Baker Russell.

On the 10th August, the former encamped on the right bank of the White Umvolosi, and on the following day joined the headquarters' camp at Ulundi. While on the march in that direction, his Mounted Infantry pushed on towards the Black Umvolosi, and reached a *kraal* of Cetewayo's named Mayizekane, which was supposed to be a formidable place for the protection of one of his great arsenals, but was found to be only an ordinary military *kraal*, circular in form, and about 100 yards in diameter. It had already been destroyed by the retreating Zulus.

Some rockets and 7-pounder shells were found in it, and in a ravine about a mile distant Major Hugh M'Calmont, of the 7th Hussars, found the two 7-pounders captured at Isandhlwana. The Zulus had made these guns—of which they scarcely knew the use—serviceable by screwing ordinary rifle nipples into their vents, but otherwise they were quite uninjured. They were re-mounted on their carriages, which were standing close by, and brought into the camp at Ulundi by the Mounted Infantry.

The military *kraal* at Mayizekane was again visited on the 12th by a patrol, which was accompanied by Sir Garnet Wolseley. More rockets and captured stores were found, and a large quantity of powder which had been secreted in some adjacent caves was blown up.

In all this we have anticipated the movements of Colonel Baker Russell, who had marched from St Paul's on the 26th of July with his column, which reached Kwamagwasa seven days after, and two companies of the Perthshire which had been stationed in that post were replaced by two of the 94th.

On the 30th he halted on the Jackal Ridge, and was joined by the artillery with two 7-pounder guns from Fort Evelyn, and two more joined him on the 2nd of August. On the 9th, after being joined by Lieutenant-Colonel Harness, with the rest of the artillery, he moved eastward, adding to the meshes of the net which was closing around the fugitive Cetewayo, and crossed the White Umvolosi, while his cavalry pushed rapidly on and reconnoitred the country as far as Bethel, a deserted and ruined German mission station.

Next day he reached another abandoned station at Elongana, on the site of which a redoubt, named Fort George, was commenced. Leaving there his infantry, artillery, and waggons. Colonel Russell at dawn on the 13th of August at the head of only 340 mounted men (80 of whom were natives) started eastward, and rode beyond the Black Umvolosi. The country was steep, wild, rugged, and occupied in great numbers by Zulus. These seemed prepared to dispute the further advance of the slender patrol, but ultimately it reached unmolested the mission station at a place named Rheinstorf.

The immediate object of this swift expedition of Baker Russell was to reach Umkondo, where Cetewayo was reported to be lurking; but at Rheinstorf it was ascertained that fully thirty-five miles of most difficult country would have to be traversed ere Umkondo could be reached; and as during the night the only native guide had lost courage and deserted, and many of the horses were already exhausted by the march from Fort George, the colonel decided to proceed no farther, but to return by a different route, and thus see more of country.

On the 14th, the column moved westward, and crossing the head waters of the 'Mhlusi River, bivouacked ten miles eastward of the Black Umvolosi, still in pursuit of Cetewayo, who was then in the recesses of the Ngome Forest At daylight next morning the march was resumed back to Fort George.

While this detachment was away, many Zulus had arrived there, surrendering to the garrison their arms and the cattle of the king, and during the week that followed, reconnaissances made through the adjacent country secured the submission of those chiefs who were not disposed to tender it voluntarily. "All this was accomplished without a shot being fired," according to the quartermaster-general's report, yet the newspapers under date the 19th have it thus:—

With the exception of a raid into the Luneberg district, in which Zulus were killed, and of small parties firing on Baker Russell's cavalry, no sign of a hostile spirit has been evinced during the recent expeditions, but the attitude of the people is not always amicable. The country is generally described as desolate. Few cattle were seen, and the people often fled from the *kraals* on Baker Russell's march, which was effected in the face of immense difficulties, the weather at times being very bad.

Colonel Baker Russell now began to move towards the northern district of Zululand.

Leaving a garrison of two companies of the 94th Regiment and some native troops in Fort George, on the 25th of August he began his march towards Fort Cambridge, about twenty miles distant, and halted on the White Umvolosi. Ascending the valley through which this stream flows, he reached the Inseke Mountain on the 26th, and sent 200 mounted men on a scouting expedition as far forward as the Zungen Nek. Thither his column moved on the 28th, and afterwards all the neighbourhood of the great Inhlobane Mountain was patrolled by the Mounted Infantry without any hostile natives being seen.

In fact, the land seemed to have become empty and desolate.

Near the mountain a redoubt was constructed, and named Fort Piet Uys, in honour of the gallant Dutch leader; and a mounted party when patrolling in the vicinity of the Dumbi Mountain, discovered and buried the remains of some poor fellows who had fallen after the attack at Inhlobane on the 28th March, and been lying there exposed to the weather and the vultures for six months. These men had belonged to Weatherley's Border Horse and Barton's Corps.

Leaving one company of the 94th as a garrison for Fort Piet Uys, Colonel Baker Russell marched his column on the 1st of September to the Pivan River, and crossing it next day, entered the Transvaal and marched in the direction of Luneberg.

By this time, he had learned that Colonel Villiers, who was then with the people of Uhamu, had effected a junction with Captain Macleod's Swazies beyond the Pongola River; and more than all, that Cetewayo had been captured on the 30th of August

Why the latter had resisted all the terms offered to him, had been long beyond conjecture, unless he, with the natural instincts of a savage mind, distrusted them. It was said that Dabulamanzi had warned him, that if he surrendered, he would be sent beyond the seas, and that chief was escorted to the rear in consequence.

Dabulamanzi, however, was a thorough traitor, whose hope was, that if Cetewayo committed suicide in his despair, or died in the forest, of starvation, he would be Sir Garnet's or the government's nominee to the kingdom of Zululand.

CHAPTER 16
Pursuit and Capture of Cetewayo.

The result of the various movements of the two columns under Colonels Clarke and Baker Russell was, that many Zulu chiefs tendered their submission to Sir Garnet Wolseley at Ulundi. And ere long there seemed good reason for hope that Cetewayo might act in a similar manner.

Colonel Villiers of the Grenadier Guards, with a force composed of sixty-five Europeans and 3,050 natives, pretty well organised, held the district belonging to Uhamu, and by the 13th of August had effected the junction referred to, with the 5,000 Swazies of Macleod, thus completing the chain on that side of Zululand.

Meanwhile, Lord Gifford, of Ashantee fame, with a band of Jantzi's men, was closely following up the king, and 200 of the 57th Regiment patrolled the hills beyond Amanse Kranze, supported by 500 natives under Captain Barton. A chain of pickets held the Enlonganeni district, from the Middle Drift on the Umvolosi to St Paul's, and there seemed no avenue for Cetewayo to escape by. A correspondent at the time wrote:

> One very remarkable refutation of the theory that Cetewayo was universally, or much hated by his people, is the tenacity with which they shield him. It is a native of Holland, named Viljoen, a cripple, who has been in his service as a powder maker, who has now gone out from our headquarters as guide to Barrow's cavalry, to the place where the king and his wives with a few men are said to be hiding, and Barrow has been ordered not to come back without his prisoner. Some of the ladies of his house are said to have gone off with their protectors to various *kraals*, but none of his own people have tried to betray him.

This Cornelius Viljoen (or Vijn, of whom mention has been already made) is by others said to have acted as a kind of secretary to Cetewayo, to whom he transferred his services, after having been in the employment of Sekukuni, when that powerful chief was at war with the Boers, and no doubt he had been waiting for some time past an opportunity to abandon the falling fortunes of the Zulu king. He had from time to time given his conquerors much useful information, and he it was who jotted the warning on the piece of paper that was sent in with the sword of Prince Louis Napoleon, regarding the strength of the army that was assembled at Ulundi.

By the result of that field, as of others elsewhere, it had become evident that the strategy and tactics of the Zulus had proved their own destruction. The writer before quoted says:

> They never seemed to know where their strength lay, or to understand their weakness. In the work supplied by authority as guidance to our officers, it was stated that the Zulus were given to night attacks. It is a remarkable fact that they never made one at all the force which came down on the position at Rorke's Drift, began the assault at four p.m. or thereabouts, and although they continued their efforts to break down the heroic defence of the front long after midnight, their energy was expended by that time, and serious assaults were relinquished after five or six hours' irregular demonstrations and fearful onslaughts. Night attacks, especially after Isandhlwana, would, if we are to judge from what occurred there, when there was no attack at all, have probably produced great demoralisation. The advantage to be gained by them would have been obvious to an intelligent foe . .
> A mass of black men would offer a very poor mark for the rifle under cloud of night. The Zulus, acquainted with the country, and possessed of an overwhelming superiority of force, could easily move round and encircle a camp in the dark.

A rush on the *laager* would have given them all the benefit to be gained by numbers, surprise, and physical strength, when opposing the shield and *assegai* to the fixed bayonet. They had not availed themselves of the advantages they really possessed, and now were ready to admit that "their heart was gone," and that all hope of successful resistance, even if they wished for it, was past.

It would appear that on the afternoon of Sunday the 10th of August, as Sir Garnet Wolseley, with another officer, was walking near the camp, or headquarters, which had been established on the site of the king's *kraal* at Ulundi, he observed a lame man, worn with toil apparently, making his way towards that place. Through the glass it could be seen that he often looked behind him, as if dreading pursuit This footsore traveller proved to be no other than Mr. Vijn, or Cornelius Viljoen, the Natal trader, popularly known as "Cetewayo's Dutchman," and who had latterly been a kind of prisoner in his *kraal*. Major Ashe says:

> His aspect and general appearance were, to put it mildly, more those of a badly-dressed scarecrow than those of a human being, and his haggard and hungry contour, his wearied look, lean and meagre, with eyes deeply sunk in their orbits, and his parchment-like cheeks, hollow and cavernous, all spoke with an eloquent voice of the ordeal he must have undergone while the enforced guest of King Cetewayo.

Food and wine were given him to restore his wasted strength, and he announced himself as the bearer of a verbal message from the fugitive king to the effect that, his army being dispersed, he was collecting cattle and was about to surrender them.

A personal surrender on the part of Cetewayo was not referred to in any way in this message, and thus, at the request of Sir Garnet Wolseley, Vijn ventured to return to him, with the object of inducing him to submit peacefully, his safety and good treatment being solemnly guaranteed.

At noon on the 13th of August, Cornelius Vijn once more appeared at Ulundi, and reported that his mission had failed, as Cetewayo had left the *kraal* where he had last been seen, and retired into the Ngome Forest, a wild and savage district between the Isquebesana and Ibululwane Rivers, tributaries of the Black Umvolosi, and overlooked by the Ngome range of mountains. Thus, a party of mounted men was promptly detailed, under the guidance of Vijn, to proceed to the *kraal* where Cetewayo had been the day before, and, if possible, to effect his capture.

This party was under the command of Major Percy H. S. Barrow, of the 19th Hussars, and consisted of a troop of the 1st Dragoon Guards, 60 Mounted Infantry, and some natives, making a total of only 300 men, with orders to traverse that district where the chiefs were still holding out, and among whom the king was supposed to have taken refuge. This party had taken with it but three days' preserved rations, as the forest was only about thirty miles distant from Ulundi as the crow flies, and all were in light marching order. With the party under Barrow went Major Richard Marter, K.D.G., Lord Gifford, Captains Hay and Hardy, and Mr. Herbert.

189

As the ways to be traversed were rough, steep, and devious, all detailed for the expedition were carefully inspected as to harness and accoutrements by Sir Garnet and Colonel Pomeroy Colley, and they started from the camp at three in the afternoon of the 13th of August

Traversing the dense bush, through which the Umbellan, a tiny river, flows, in many places almost hidden by the jungle, they reached the Black Umvolosi about midnight, and halted for some time and marked a large tamarind tree as a guiding post when returning, as they hoped to do, by the same route, and then the march northwards was resumed.

The chief difficulty the force experienced was that of keeping together while proceeding along a narrow path, through dark and thorny bush, infested by baboons, rock rabbits, and huge toads, causing great delay during the dark hours, and no small anxiety also, as John Dunn had warned them that the district they had to traverse had become infested by lions, and on that very morning an ox had been carried off by one outside a Zulu *kraal* close by.

Two varieties of the lion are stated to infest South Africa, the yellow and the brown, but these colours are said by Colonel Harris to depend upon the animal's age, and belong to one distinct species. Be that as it may, John Dunn's warning was not forgotten by Barrow's party after the Black Umvolosi was left in the rear.

Morning saw the party riding amid rich forest and other scenery, where the graceful date-palms drooped their long leaves, and the purple peaks of the Libomba Mountains stood up against the deep dark blue of a cloudless sky. In their scarlet tunics, white helmets, and glittering accoutrements,' the King's Dragoon Guards looked very picturesque as they rode in file amid the strange tropical trees and giant undergrowth of trailers and brilliant flowers, but there were no eyes to see the effect other than their own. Antelopes glided past, and occasionally scared troops of the eland, with greyish bodies, brown heads, and long twisted horns, each large as a bullock, went crashing through the woody *vistas*.

It was not until one p.m. on the 14th that the party rode up, and surrounded, with arms loaded, the *kraal* where Vijn had seen Cetewayo on the 12th. By this time nearly all the party had their clothes torn, and their hands and faces cut and bleeding by the thorny and spiky shrubs through which they had to force their way. The *kraal* was found deserted, but the fact was ascertained that Cetewayo had left it only on the previous afternoon, and consequently could not be very far off, though he had been warned to fly by unseen scouts and signal fires.

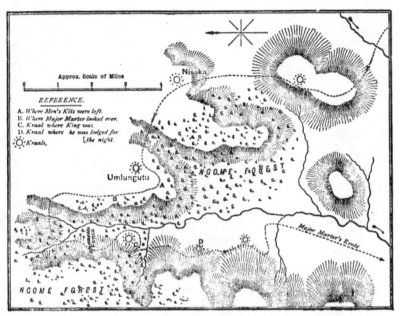

The troop of the King's Dragoon Guards had now been so long in the saddle—for the last ten miles under a fierce and burning sun, and over fearfully rough and broken ground—that the horses were almost done up. Barrow thus resolved to leave them at the empty *kraal*, and push on at three p.m. with the lighter portion of the mounted men, and he subsequently found he had been upon the king's track for two days nearly, as he reached another *kraal* wherein the former had slept the night before.

On Thursday, the next day, the party had a fatiguing journey, over ground which they described as "awful," in a most difficult and hilly country, till sundown, when another *kraal* was reached, where Barrow resolved to bivouac till the rising of the moon. This, however, occurred so late that he did not start till sunrise on the morning of the 15th, when the active Lord Gifford, who was scouting ahead with a few men, discovered and caught an old man in whom Vijn recognised a personal attendant of Cetewayo, about whose movements all his statements were studiously contradictory and improbable. However, he was induced on the 16th to guide the party to a spot where his master had passed the night of the 14th, and there all direct traces were lost

By this day's march. Major Barrow and his party were brought back to the left bank of the Black Umvolosi, but somewhat below the point where they had marked the tamarind tree after crossing, and there his men were divided. Only three days' provisions having been taken, he started on the 17th to return to Ulundi, while a small detachment under Lord Gifford advanced resolutely eastward, down the great valley of the Umvolosi, proceeding among wooded hills, where the thin blue smoke of many *kraals* could be seen ascending high in the pure air, showing that the district was populous, and often by treeless wastes and flats, where the jungles of bamboo and mimosa made the way all but impenetrable.

As it was asserted by some natives who were met, that it was the king's intention to seek shelter in the rugged country known as the Iconda Forest, which lies southward, and west of Kwamagwasa, Lord Gifford's detachment, on the 17th, moved across the White Umvolosi, and reached an elevation of 2,000 feet above the valley through which it flows. Near a *kraal* they met a stalwart Zulu warrior armed with a bundle of *assegais*, and carrying a long canvas bag like one for containing cricket-bats, and in it was found a handsome express rifle, some cartridges, and that which excited some surprise—a hand mirror! These, of course, were supposed to be the property of the king, on whose trail they believed they were certainly following closely.

Though it was now ascertained that the king himself was still near the Black Umvolosi, yet it appeared not improbable that he might essay an escape on the same path by which he had sent forward his property, and therefore, while Lord Gifford returned by the country northward of the Black Umvolosi, Sir Garnet Wolseley, on learning these facts, despatched a party of the 1st Dragoon Guards to patrol the district near Kwamagwasa.

Meantime, while encamped at Ulundi, Sir Garnet received the submission of many more important Zulu chiefs. Among these were Umnyamana, Cetewayo's prime minister, Usukane, and his sons or brothers, Umkihland, and Tshingwayo, the commander of the army at Isandhlwana. On the following day he telegraphed thus to the Secretary of State for War:—

Ulundi, Aug. 18th, 1879.
Troops have been in pursuit of Cetewayo since 13th inst, but have not yet succeeded in capturing him. He has only two or three following him. Umnyamana, the king's prime minister, Tshingwayo, and other important chiefs surrendered here on the 14th, bringing more than 600 of the king's cattle; 100 more

captured by the troops. Three of the king's brothers have surrendered here. Arms and cattle are coming in daily and to other
posts. I am in communication with Usibebu, next in importance to Umnyamana, and confidently expect him to surrender
here this week. Villiers advanced from Luneberg with his *burghers* and armed natives on the 12th, and expected to be opposed
on the *Assegai* River. I have sent orders to stop the advance of
the Swazies—the king is known not to be in that quarter. Remains of the Hon. W. Drummond were discovered near Ulundi
and buried. The health of the troops remains excellent Horses
and cattle much improved

The Hon. William Drummond, a son of Viscount Strathallan, had
been in the Intelligence Department

The reported movement of Cetewayo towards the Iconda Forest
led to the detaching on the 17th of August of a party of officers and
men to intercept him. They were under Captain Herbert Stewart, of
the 3rd Dragoon Guards (formerly of the 37th Foot), and moved
in a south-easterly direction, but failed to find him, and many other
expeditions that were sent out during the latter days of August were
equally unsuccessful.

Among the minor events of this week occurring elsewhere, may
be noted the mysterious robbery of £500 from the Pay Department
of Fort Pearson, and the burning of the records of the Buffs at Fort
Napier, Pietermaritzburg.

A writer say:

With regard to the first-named matter, it is only the beginning
of a very pretty story of departmental fiction and recrimina-
tion. . . . The recovery of a considerable portion of the money
has since been telegraphed. The supposition is that it has been
buried in the neighbourhood, and the reward of £50 has been
offered for the conviction of the offenders. In the meantime,
the whole men of the guard to which the possessor of the
suspected sovereigns belonged have been placed under arrest.

A soldier had been found with gold in his possession for which he
could not account

The burning of the records of the Buffs and other corps was an
instance of gross carelessness. It occurred in the so-called "barracks" of
Fort Napier, which were simply grass huts like those of a Zulu *kraal*.

In one place were the papers of the 17th Lancers, in another those of the King's Dragoon Guards; the documents of the 94th occupied a third hut, those of the 58th a fourth, while in a fifth were entrusted the records of the Buffs. A sergeant who slept in the last got drunk, and, it is said, upset a paraffin lamp with the result that in a very few minutes the whole place was in a blaze. Cash-books, ledgers, tabulated documents, together with a large amount of miscellaneous property, were hopelessly destroyed, the greater part of the documents being of a nature which rendered them difficult to replace. The heat of the fire may be judged of from the fact that a silver watch was picked up afterwards melted into a solid mass.

As Cetewayo was still at large, an infantry force, consisting of the 3rd battalion of the 60th Rifles and two companies of Barton's Natives, marched from Ulundi on the 23rd of August, and encamped on the bank of the Black Umvolosi, posting guards at the crossing places on the river.

Information was received by Lieutenant-Colonel Clarke, who was in command, from the chief of the staff, that during the night of the 26th Cetewayo was believed to be proceeding towards the Ngome Forest, and that Major Marter, of the King's Dragoon Guards, was ordered to proceed in that direction on the following morning. Accordingly, on the 27th of August, that officer set out with a force consisting of a squadron of his own regiment, a company of the Native Contingent, Lonsdale's Horse, and an officer with ten mounted infantry.

It is doubtful if Lord Gifford knew of the departure of this expedition. He knew, however, that the king was pursued by some of the native infantry, three companies of the 57th, and 150 of the 1st Dragoon Guards; but he felt it a point of honour that he should succeed in the capture of the fugitive, whose pursuit had been entrusted to him by Barrow; but with all their marching and countermarching on information alternately right and wrong, Cetewayo always contrived to be some thirty or forty miles ahead of them.

Proceeding by the 'Ndaza *kraal*, and from thence up the valley of the Ivuna River, Major Marter—who had three of his horses eaten by lions on this service—with his party reached the summit of the Nenge Mountain the same evening, and bivouacked near Umgojana's *kraal*. At ten a.m. on the following morning, when halted near a stream which there flows westward into the Ibululwana, a Zulu appeared

MAJOR MARTER.

who, after conversing on indifferent subjects with Mr. Oftebro, the interpreter, remarked somewhat suggestively, while pointing towards the Forest of Ngome, "I have heard that the wind blows from this side today; but you should take that path until you come to Nisaka's *kraal*."

It was well known that the Zulus were extremely averse to afford direct information as to the whereabouts of their king; but Major Marter resolved to act promptly on the hint conveyed in this speech, and consequently followed the track indicated as leading to the *kraal* of Nisaka.

While on their way there a native runner was met, carrying a note in a cleft slick. It was from Lord Gifford, and addressed to Captain Maurice, Royal Artillery, but being open, was, under the circumstances, read by Major Marter.

Lord Gifford, as has been shown, had never returned to camp since he had left it on the 13th, but had been indefatigably searching the wild country in every direction, and thus, on the morning of the 28th, the two parties commanded by himself and Major Marter respectively were at no great distance apart, but were acting independently, and by that time Gifford's men and his horses were tired, hungry, and incapable of much exertion, after the terrible work they had undergone during fifteen days and nights in the bush, and now they were actually within six miles of the *kraal* where he was told the king was lurking.

195

The note in the cleft stick contained no clue as to either the actual position of Lord Gifford or the hiding-place of the king; and the bearer of it was sent on that he might, if he could, deliver it to Captain Maurice, who had started from Ulundi on the 26th August with a third party to visit the *kraals* in the districts of Umgojana and Umnyamana, and whom the note never reached, as it was brought back to Lord Gifford

The latter, on the 27th, had obtained the distinct information as to where the king was concealed—the Kwa Dwasa *kraal*, which was described as being closely surrounded by dense and thorny bush on every side save one—and Lord Gifford resolved to wait till nightfall before attempting the capture.

Dark hours so passed in the South African bush were not without many grave perils and terrors, for often the yells of wild dogs and the barking of baboons announced the vicinity of some great beast of prey, and the crackling of fallen branches suggested the crawling of a poisonous snake.

Meanwhile, Major Marter moved up to Nisaka's *kraal*, and, on asking there for guides, without mentioning what his intentions were, he obtained two, who led his party to the summit of the mountain range, where the *kraal* of Umlungutu, Nisaka's brother, was situated. The mountains here, overlooking the Ngome Forest, are all flat-topped. The western side of that on which the major now found himself was most precipitous, and, after dismounting, he was asked by his guides to look over into the densely-wooded valley that lay more than 2,000 feet below.

Only two miles distant a small *kraal* could be seen by the side of a rocky stream, and therein it was concluded that Cetewayo would be discovered.

In fact, the place on which the major and his comrades now looked so eagerly was the Kwa Dwasa Kraal, which Lord Gifford had discovered about the same time to be the resting-place of the fallen king; and the major, ignorant of Gifford's intention and hope, decided on taking action at once.

As mounted men could not reach the bottom of the valley without making a tedious circuit. Major Marter desired his troopers to relinquish their steel scabbards and all accoutrements that were likely to rattle, and led his squadron northward three miles, till a less precipitous face of the hill was reached, while a small detachment was left on the mountain in charge of the discarded accoutrements and packhorses.

196

At the same time a company of the Native Contingent was ordered to make its descent down the steep hill-side towards the *kraal*, but to remain closely concealed in the forest till they saw the red-coated cavalry emerge from the head of the narrow valley.

At a quarter to two p.m. the King's Dragoon Guards began to lead their horses by the bridle down the steep and perilous slope, and by three o'clock they had reached the bottom of the valley, but with the greatest difficulty. They crossed the rocky bed of a stream and remounted in a hollow out of sight of the *kraal*. Next they had to circumvent the barrier of a snake fence, a marsh, some long grass and rocks, but after a two miles' gallop they succeeded in completely surrounding the place, while the Native Contingent dashed across from their hiding-place, and formed up on some open ground to the south of it.

In reality they were the first men on the ground, as they were on foot, and could move over natural obstacles more quickly than the horses. They rushed into the *kraal*, shouting to the startled followers of the king, "The white men are here—you are taken!"

Major Marter rode directly up to the entrance of the *kraal*, and called upon Cetewayo to yield. "Enter—I am your prisoner," Cetewayo was heard to reply. As he might have to encounter a snare or some madness born of savage desperation, the major prudently declined this invitation, and again summoned the king to come forth. Then the unfortunate Cetewayo, looking weak, weary, footsore, and very sick at heart, came out of the humble little *kraal*. With a certain amount of dignity, he repelled a dragoon guardsman who was about to seize him.

"White soldier," he exclaimed, "touch me not—I surrender to your chief!"

The few occupants of the *kraal* being taken completely by surprise, made no resistance, and were all captured. They consisted only of the king, a chief named Umkosana, nine men and a boy, five women and a girl. One of the men who was too infirm to travel was left behind. The rest were removed as prisoners of war. As they were all on foot their progress was necessarily slow, and thus it was dark when the party which left the scene of this important capture at four p.m. arrived at another *kraal*, five miles lower down the valley, and overlooking the Ngome Forest, where the king and his companions—strictly guarded—were placed for the night; and next morning the whole party again moved forward.

This was on the 29th of August

197

Major Marter met Lord Gifford and his men about eleven in the forenoon. The latter had heard at five o'clock on the preceding day, that the capture had been achieved, and consequently he had remained where he was in bivouac for the night; but now having obtained all requisite particulars from Major Marter, he departed for Ulundi, which be reached on the evening of the same day, and there made his report of the affair to Sir G. Wolseley.

Chapter 17
The Zulu War Concluded

It would appear from a relation of his movements given by himself, after the Battle of Ulundi, that the king was not present in that action, but that one of his brothers, Uziwetu, who had been mistaken for him—in company with Cornelius Vijn, or Viljoen, the Dutch trader, had witnessed the conflict from the summit of an adjacent hill. On tidings of the defeat being brought to him, Cetewayo retreated into the bush beyond the Ntabankulu Mountains, and ere long, to his surprise, he heard of the retreat of the British forces, and he lived for three weeks in a *kraal* belonging to his prime minister.

From this *kraal* and others, he had, as related, sent various messages concerning terms, but without definite proposals, as he had a fear of being killed out of hand by our patrols. After many wanderings to escape the white men's scouts, he travelled one evening as far as the bank of the Black Umvolosi and slept there. On the following day, tidings came that the white men were in the adjacent bush, on which he bade all the women, escape as best they could, and concealed himself among some long grass on the summit of an eminence, just above a ford of the river, where he could watch the movements of a patrol, and hear the soldiers talking and laughing.

As soon as they had passed, he and five or six followers, who were all the retainers that remained with him, journeyed farther up the Black Umvolosi, and lived for some days in various *kraals*. Remaining for three days in one *kraal* he was joined by one of his wives. Finding the troops still on the trail, he now struck across the country into the Ngome Forest, where news reached him, that Umnyamana had, instead of making terms for him, promised Sir Garnet Wolseley to use his best endeavours to capture and deliver him up, should he be found in any of the *kraals* in his, Umnyamana's, district Cetewayo was much grieved and exclaimed, 'Why does Umnyamana do this? Why does he act treacherously towards me? Why does he not send a message to me, to tell me to deliver myself up?'

He then moved to the *kraal* at Ngome, where he was taken by Major Marter, afterwards Colonel and A.D.C. to Her Majesty.

Major Marter having sent a message to Lieutenant-Colonel Clarke, desiring that a mule cart should be sent to meet him, moved forward to the 'Ndaza Kraal, which was reached before dusk on the evening of the 29th of August. Shortly before reaching it, three men and one woman (attendants of the king) attempted to escape in the bush, through which, from its density, the whole party had to proceed in Indian file. They had been warned that death would be the penalty of such an attempt, and the escort, acting in obedience to orders, fired promptly. Two men fell dead; the other man and the woman escaped.

On the following day two companies of the 60th, sent by Colonel Clarke, were met, with a mule cart, in which the king and some of the women were placed, and at ten on the morning of the 31st the whole came into Ulundi.

On beholding the ruins of his great *kraal*, Cetewayo for the first time showed symptoms of considerable mental distress; but otherwise his bearing and his fortitude were admirable. It was a singular coincidence, which very possibly weighed upon his mind, that the day on which he was marched a prisoner through his ruined capital to captivity, was the anniversary of his coronation.

At two p.m. on the same day, the king, with his attendants, under an escort commanded by Captain Poole, of the Royal Artillery, was despatched to the coast by the way of Kwamagwasa and St Paul's, to Port Durnford, where he embarked on the 4th of September for Cape Town, and on his arrival there was placed for a time in honourable captivity in the Castle.

With his capture the Zulu War ended; and it was frequently urged that Sir Garnet Wolseley, while insisting upon the delivery of all arms should have insisted upon the surrender, if possible, of the lost colours of the 2nd battalion of the 24th Regiment.

A writer says:

With regard to these, I believe it to be fact, that when the Zulu War first began the officers of the regiment, knowing the kind of fighting they were going to have, were very anxious to leave them in Pietermaritzburg, Sir Henry Bulwer offering to

MAJOR MARTER AND HIS MEN GUARDING CETEWAYO IN THE NATIVE KRAAL.

take charge of them; the wish was, however, overruled by Lord Chelmsford, with the result that the colours of one of the most distinguished line battalions are, in all probability, decorating some *kraal* in the heart of Zululand.

Nothing now remained but to make a political settlement of the country before it was evacuated by our troops. It had been decided by Sir Garnet Wolseley that Zululand should be divided into thirteen separate districts; and on the 1st of September, a number of the chief men of the country, including John Dunn, witnessed and put their marks to an agreement, the preamble of which ran thus:—

> I recognise the victory of the British arms over the Zulu nation, and the full right and title of Her Majesty Queen Victoria to deal as she may think fit with the Zulu chiefs and people, and with the Zulu country; and I agree and hereby sign my agreement, to accept from Sir Garnet Joseph Wolseley, G.C.M.G., K.CB., as the representative of Her Majesty Queen Victoria, the chieftainship of Zululand, &c. subject to the following terms, conditions, and limitations.

This document consisted of eleven clauses. By these each chief was to respect the boundaries of the territory assigned to him through the Resident of the division in which it was situated; the Zulu military system was renounced, and men were to marry when they chose. Arms and ammunition were not to be imported into Zululand. Life was not to be taken without a fair trial, and witchcraft or witch-doctors were not to be tolerated. Fugitives from justice were to be surrendered, and in all disputes the decision of the British Resident, Mr. W. D. Wheelwright, was to be accepted.

Mr. Wheelwright was entrusted with the general supervision of the different chiefs, and the details of the boundaries of their respective districts—work of an arduous and responsible character—were arranged by three officers, Lieutenant-Colonel the Hon. C Villiers, of the Grenadier Guards; Captains J. Alleyne, Royal Artillery, and H. Moore, of the 4th Regiment Captain Alleyne had served with Sir Garnet Wolseley on the Red River Expedition from Canada in 1870.

On the 2nd of September, the troops encamped at Ulundi were inspected by Sir Garnet Wolseley, and the evacuation of Zululand began forthwith. Lieutenant-Colonel Clarke, with the 57th, 3rd Battalion of the Rifles, the Gatling Battery, and the Natal Horse, started on that day for St Paul's, from whence he made his way into Natal by the route through Entumeni, and the central ford of the Tugela, while another column consisting of the 80th Foot, and two 9-pounder guns, marched about the same time for Utrecht by the Inhlazataye Mountain and Conference Hill.

Sir Garnet Wolseley and his staff remained in Ulundi till the 4th of September, when he proceeded to Utrecht, where he arrived on the 9th. Four days before that, Colonel Baker Russell and Colonel Villiers attacked the Manganobas in their caverns by the Intombe River, and killed eight of them. Two of our troops were wounded. These were about the last shots fired in the Zulu War, and the road to Derby was unsafe until this last handful of the enemy was dispersed.

Captain Macleod's 5,000 Swazies were sent back to their *kraals* full of dissatisfaction, because Cetewayo was left alive, and meanwhile, the bearing of the latter was deemed extraordinary; he seemed quite content to pass the rest of his life free from the cares of his savage kingdom.

The stores which had been collected at the various posts having been removed or consumed, all these points were abandoned, and by the end of September, 1879, the last detachment of Her Majesty's troops had left Zululand behind it

The total losses in action during this war were as follows:—

Killed—76 officers, 1,007 non-commissioned officers and privates, with 604 natives.

Wounded—37 officers, 206 non-commissioned officers and privates, with 57 natives; and in the period between 11th January and 15th of October, 1879, 17 officers and 330 men died of diseases consequent on the operations in Zululand; and 1,286 non-commissioned officers and men were sent home invalided.

The approximate cost of the war was £5,230,323.

In this war, great honour was due to those whose charitable labours led them, at the risk of their own lives, to visit Zululand to succour the sick and wounded. From the report of the South African Aid Committee, it would appear that Surgeon-General Ross accompanied by Dr. G. Stoker as assistant commissioner, and a number of ladies arrived at the seat of war, at a time when fever was at its worst among our troops at Helpmakaar, Rorke's Drift, and on the Lower Tugela, and when it was absolutely necessary that a vigorous effort should be made, if valuable lives were to be rescued from death.

This party dispersed over those parts of the country occupied by our troops, visiting the field hospitals, and wherever their services might be required, setting up movable ambulances, and bringing soldiers who were sick away from pest-stricken places. Later on, we find that Dr. Stoker accompanied Colonel Villiers' column, and under the direction of the latter went to several places succouring the wounded and ailing British, and Zulus as well. It is satisfactory to learn that these great results were achieved at a cost of less than seven thousand pounds in all, and that for this small sum, the best ambulance that ever left Britain, went for more than twenty thousand miles without losing one of its members, and came home with the warm commendations of every officer and official with whom it had to do.

Medals and clasps were freely given to the troops engaged, and medals even to those who were employed in Natal from January 11th to September 1st, 1879, but who never crossed the border. The latter were, of course, without clasps.

In closing our narrative of the Zulu War, it is impossible to omit some reference to those pilgrims of the heart, if we may term them so, who went as far as South Africa, to visit the graves of some who had fallen and were dear to them.

Among these were the young widow of Captain Ronald Campbell, who was slain on the Inhlobane Mountain (daughter of the Right Rev. the Bishop of Rochester). She accompanied the Empress Eugenie, and Sir George Scott-Douglas, Bart, of Springwood Park, Roxburghshire, whose son. Lieutenant J. Scott-Douglas, of the 2nd Battalion of the Royal Scots Fusiliers, serving in the Intelligence Department, was killed near Fort Evelyn on the 1st of July—a young lad of only four years' service. Guided by three soldiers, lent by General Clifford, he reached the Lower Tugela and proceeded to Kwamagwasa, where lay the solitary graves of his son, and the young Irish corporal of the 17th Lancers. They were found protected by an enclosure formed by Colonel Thynne, of the Cold stream Guards. Sir George erected memorial crosses of grey Aberdeen granite over them, and planted the spot with flowers, and on the graves of the corporal some seeds of the shamrock sent by his mother from Ireland.

The more important pilgrimage of the Empress Eugenie attracted, as her son's death had done, the attention of all Europe.

Travelling under the title of Countess of Pierrefonds, and with a suite including Sir Evelyn and Lady Wood, Mrs. Ronald Campbell, Dr. Scott, who had medical charge of the prince in Zululand, and Lieutenant Slade, R.A, her *aide-de-camp*, so to speak—an intimate artillery friend of her son—all clad in the deepest black, she reached

MEMORIAL STONE ON THE SPOT WHERE PRINCE LOUIS NAPOLEON WAS KILLED.

Durban, and occupied the room in the Government House which had been occupied by her son. Travelling by Cape carts, she was in time to reach Tortosa, where the prince was killed, strange to say, on the anniversary of the event

She expressed a wish to ascend where the ambulance stopped to take up the remains of her son. From there she proceeded on foot towards the stony *donga*, following precisely the track taken by Dundonald Cochrane and other officers, who went in search of the corpse. The way was rough and stony, but, in spite of all remonstrances, she persevered in her loving intentions to visit the spot, already marked since April, 1880, by the obelisk which Major Stubb of the Royal Engineers had placed there, by order of Queen Victoria.

The *Gaulois* says:

In the distance, gleamed the white monument, thrown into sharp relief by the dark background, but it only seemed to catch the eyes of the empress when she got to the bank of the *donga*. Then she lifted her hands as if in supplication towards heaven; the tears poured over her cheeks, already worn with sorrow and vigils; she spoke no word and uttered no cry, but sank slowly on her knees. A French priest repeated the prayers for the dead, and the servant Lomas, who had been an eyewitness, went through the sad story of what happened last year.

Round the spot where the two troopers who fell at the same time as the prince are buried, a wall had been built, within which some small trees and violets, the Napoleonic emblem, had been planted. Gebooda, the leader of the Zulus who attacked the prince, in presence of Major Stubb, had stood by these two lonely graves, and, with uplifted hands, had solemnly declared that they should never be violated, and, as Zulu superstition with regard to the dead is deeply founded, there is every prospect of the promise being faithfully kept. The tents of the empress were pitched in the valley, and there she remained two days.

On the 1st June, according to the *Natal Times*, those of the Catholic faith who accompanied her were invited to join in a solemn service, after which they retired, and during the night the empress prayed over the spot where her son had fallen. Funeral tapers, together with wreaths of *immortelles* sent by the queen, were placed on the spot, on the graves of the troopers, and even of the Basutos who fell with the prince. The *Gaulois* says:

On the following day, she went to Fort Napoleon, and thence

to Rorke's Drift, and on the fifth day she visited the field at Isandhlwana, and prayed with the Englishwomen who had come there to mourn their husbands and brothers.

So ends our story of the Zulu War.

One fine quality which the Zulus possess, says the author of *Through the Zulu Country*, is a readiness to forgive and forget:

They bear no malice, and considering that rightly, or wrongly, we invaded their country, slaughtered thousands of their best warriors, burnt their *kraals*, carried off their king, and reduced them—the most powerful nation in Southern Africa—to the condition of a conquered race, it is surprising how little resentment is entertained towards us. They say it is the fortune of war; it is past and there is an end of it; and they welcome the Englishman wherever he goes with the same cheerful and hearty greeting.

As one of their songs (which has happily been given in English by the editor of *The Cape and its People*) has it:—

My brethren, let our weapons,
Our warlike weapons all.
Be beaten into ploughshares.
Wherewith to till the soil.

Our shields—our shields of battle.
For garments be they sewed,
And peace both north and southward
Be shouted far abroad.

Northward, I say. and southward,
On every side afar;
Through Him who ever liveth.
The Lord of all that are.

CHAPTER 18

The Operations Against Sekukuni

We have already referred to the first part of these movements which were inaugurated against this powerful ally of Cetewayo, and which extended from February to October, 1878, and which were suspended after costing, according to the *Daily News* of June, 1879, half a million of money.

The reader may remember that Sekukuni was a powerful Basuto chief, who, from his almost inaccessible stronghold in the district called Lydenberg, had given the Cape Government much annoyance, had acknowledged the supremacy of Cetewayo, and had taken up arms against the Boers, when the Transvaal Republic attempted to wield authority over the "disputed territory" on the left bank of the Blood River, claimed by the Zulus as theirs.

Colonel Owen Lanyon had been ready to take the field against Sekukuni in June, but his advance was suspended by order of Sir Garnet Wolseley, on the arrival of the latter at Pietermaritzburg; and he was now reported to be in no way intimidated by the fate of his friend Cetewayo, or by the facts that other chiefs were also hostile, while the Boers, who were full of strange delusions as to the exhaustion of British resources by the Basuto and Zulu Wars, were thinking of nothing but a conflict

Colonel Baker Russell, who at this time was at Luneberg, was appointed to command the new expedition against Sekukuni, with a force consisting of the 52nd and 94th Regiments, with some cavalry. Irregular levies, and four pieces of cannon, though the season was deemed an unhealthy one for military operations.

Towards the end of August, 1879, Colonel Harrison, of the Royal Engineers, was ordered to make a careful survey of the military positions around the Lulu Mountains, wherein the territory of Sekukuni lay, and he reported that all the rich and once prosperous border farms were deserted, and the lands were waste, while cattle-lifting was greatly practised by the people of Sekukuni, who recklessly fired upon all comers, and murdered friendly *Kaffirs* close to our outposts.

> The chief, like one of the robber barons of the Middle Ages, was surrounded by all the warlike and lawless spirits of the country, whom he attracted by hopes of plunder. Occupying a mountain range of fifty miles long by fifteen wide, and a grand valley fitted for the pasturage of his flocks and herds, proud of his past successes and preparing for constant aggressions, Sekukuni sought, as he said, to become a great power, one of the three of which he spoke—'Let Cetewayo be King of the Zulus, Somsten (Shepstone) King of the Transvaal, and Sekukuni be King of the Basutos.'

It was the suggestion of Colonel Harrison that either he should be acknowledged as chief within certain boundaries, which would be guarded by a chain of posts sufficiently strong to overawe his armed bands, or that his power should be altogether broken, and himself be reduced to the grade of a tributary. The former plan would involve the admission of defeat which his fierce and proud spirit would resent, together with the serious cost of keeping many mounted men in an unhealthy district, with the risk of constant broils and trouble.

The latter plan could be achieved by a direct investment of his fastnesses by blockade, or by formidable expeditions against them from fortified posts; but this was deemed tedious. The third suggestion of Colonel Harrison was to establish a complete cordon of posts around Sekukuni's chief mountain, and to strengthen the volunteer garrisons of Fort Burgers on the Steelpoort River and at Jellalabad (or Fort Spekboom), which were five miles apart, and then to increase that at Fort Oliphant, near the junction of the Phiroo River with the Oliphant, on the other side of Sekukuni's stronghold, and make it a depot of supplies.

A column of 400 infantry, 150 cavalry, two 9-pounders and some rocket-tubes, a Royal Engineer detachment, and a Native Contingent, was to advance against Sekukuni's "Town," as it was named, and bombard it, while a similar column should advance from Fort Weeber (which stands equidistant nearly from Forts Spekboom and Oliphant), and seize a chosen point on the Lulu Mountain, so that by these combined operations the hostile chief should be reduced to flight or surrender.

Major Clarke, of the Royal Artillery, pending operations, was sent as Special Commissioner for the Lydenberg district, to negotiate with Sekukuni, and, as much was expected from his talent and influence on the obstinate and self-reliant chief, a few days passed before peace or war was decided on—but it was soon the latter; and meanwhile Baker Russell's column was gradually moving up the valley of the Intombe River towards Lydenberg.

A writer says:

The story of Sekukuni is one which may have to be told of other chiefs, till all South Africa be annexed up to—yes, up to the limits of European greed and native endurance, or the white man be forced back by the sheer weight and pressure of numbers, and the adverse conditions of his social existence as the *Kaffir* increases and multiplies.

When the Dutch emigrants under Potgieter penetrated into the north-eastern district of what is now termed the Transvaal, they found that powerful tribe, the Swazies, to which we have more than once referred, possessing, in addition to what they now occupy, a mountainous district near the present Lydenberg, in which a Basuto chief named Sitate was established, and whom the Swazies deemed a tributary, after having driven him into a part of the country which they claimed as their own, near the Crocodile River.

Potgieter received from the Swazies a district in which Sitate's "principality" stood; and he permitted the Basuto chief to remain, and then by skilful alliances with those who were retreating before the tide of Dutch emigration, he became in time powerful enough to assume a superiority over all the Boers near his borders; and when his son Sekukuni succeeded him, his Basutos, who had acquired firearms as the price of their labours in the Diamond Fields, asserted their independence, and drove the Dutch from their farms near his stronghold, though they were permitted to remain on paying blackmail to Sekukuni for his protection.

Forts Weeber and Burgers were built by the Dutch as barriers against him, and on our annexing the Transvaal we succeeded to the feud that existed between this Basuto chief and the Boers; and on the 22nd of October, 1879, Sir Garnet Wolseley left Pretoria with his staff to oversee the operations against the famous mountain stronghold. His efforts to secure a peaceful settlement with Sekukuni had failed, and he now announced his resolution to punish the haughty Basuto with the utmost severity, as he had totally failed or refused to pay the fine of cattle referred to in our twenty-eighth chapter.

The first instalment of the cattle had actually been sent, but was returned by Sir Theophilus Shepstone as not being the sufficient number, and Major Clarke had informed Sekukuni that the whole fine—about 2,000 head—must be paid, if he would live in peace.

On the 21st October, the major's messengers returned to Fort Weeber, with information that Sekukuni had ordered a cessation of hostilities, and summoned a council of his chiefs, after which his message to Major Clarke was somewhat to the following effect:—

You are my master, and I am a subject of the British Queen. I want to see you particularly, and feel sure that if we met, terms could be made. I am poor and needy. On a former occasion I paid you cattle, but they were returned, and now I have lost so heavily by the effects of long sickness and poverty that I am unable to pay any at all.

Major Clarke, who knew that the chief was as wily and false as any Afghan, replied, that:

If he—Sekukuni—wanted peace, he must pay the fine of cattle in full; that an army was coming up from Zululand, and the Great Chief, Sir Garnet Wolseley, was to lead it in person, so that there was no time for delay.

He was also told that Cetewayo was a prisoner, and that he would suffer the same fate if he resisted; but the chiefs replied, "that the English, though great in war and diplomacy, were the greatest liars in the world." They added that it was for the British to come to them, not them to go to the British; and that the mass meeting of the people which Sekukuni assembled was all for war—and war it was to be!

This was at a time when the weather was intensely hot for fighting, and the season in which the horse-sickness is fast developed, and some of the usual confusion, incident to the beginning of our greater wars, ensued. In some places, commissariat agents were selling off all kinds of transport and stores as fast as they could, the Zulu strife being just over; in others, they were purchasing both with equal energy. Volunteers who had just been disbanded and disarmed, were re-enrolled and equipped; and long trains of oxen and lumbering waggons began once more to traverse the grassy *veldt* towards Fort Weeber and Lydenberg; but, as usual, the commissariat was found faulty.

Sir Garnet Wolseley placed Colonel Harrison as officer in charge of his base at Pretoria (now the capital and seat of government of the Transvaal Republic), informing him, "that he relied on him altogether for supplies, and that if he failed, the whole campaign would be abandoned." The correspondent of the *Daily Telegraph* said:

This is a striking commentary on the *insouciance*, and, indeed, contempt, with which representations concerning these very supplies were received by certain officers a short time before. Whether it be wise for the general-in chief to proceed to the front before all is ready for the field or not, it is evident that he can, when there, form a better opinion of the situation than he could if he remained at the base; but it is contrary to the practice of the great masters—Lord Chelmsford is thought to have erred greatly, when he hurried to his advanced camp, and diminished the pressure his presence exercised on those who were organising the *matériel* in the rear.

Major Fitzgerald Creagh, of the 80th Regiment, who had served in the New Zealand wars with the 50th, at the storming and capture of various camps and *pahs*, and who had considerable knowledge of the Transvaal, was selected by Colonel Harrison to examine the depots at Middleberg, Lydenberg and elsewhere, and it was thought strange that no war-balloon was used to inspect the stronghold of Sekukuni, who, with his followers would have been stricken with terror, on beholding such an object hovering above them in the air.

By the 18th of November, the troops had closed up in some points to within sixteen miles of the stronghold.

At Fort Oliphant, a small irregular earthwork, having a square bastion at each corner, and a ditch and trench furnished with prickly thorn bushes, two companies of the 94th, under the ill-starred Major Anstruther, were encamped under canvas; near them were the huts of the Native Rustenberg Contingent, raised in that district which is named "the Garden" of the Transvaal, on the northern slope of the Magaliesbergen. In a gorge below the fort, flows the Oliphant, or Elephant River, ere it dips into a valley, between two spurs that jut out from the mountain range, then held by Sekukuni.

This fort was to be the base of the left attack, and from it was the approach to another post, Fort Albert Edward, held by the headquarters of the 94th, under Lieutenant-Colonel Murray, on the line

SEKUKUNI.

211

taken by the Commando of the Transvaal Republic in the former war.

Colonel Baker Russell came from Fort Weeber on the 16th, and reconnoitred the country along the left bank of the Oliphant for five miles beyond the out-posts, drawing fire more than once from Sekukuni's scouts, and no small abuse from his spies who hovered about

In the vicinity of these detached posts the officers found excellent sport for their guns, as antelopes, pheasants, pigeons, and hares abounded amid the long wavy grass of the *veldt*, thus contributing to the slender resources of the dinner table; but amid the same grass snakes lurked, several of them five feet in length, and of their bites some horses and mules died.

Captain Macgregor, of the Royal Engineers, achieved some good reconnaissances of the Lulu range held by Sekukuni; but its secrets were yet to be revealed Plunder, beyond the cattle, *karosses*, shields, and arms of his tribe, there was nothing to expect, though rumour, curiously enough, said that he had amassed treasure to the value of £40,000 in gold, as each of his subjects who visited the gold fields was obliged to deposit a sovereign at his feet on returning.

While the little force of Europeans and its large Native Contingent were preparing to attack the Lulu Mountain, much severe work had

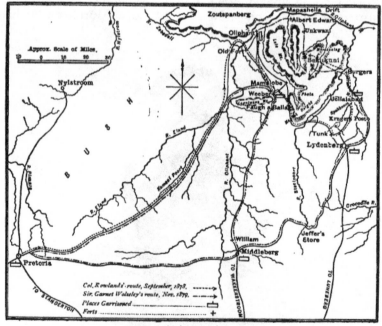

SKETCH MAP OF SEKUKUNI'S COUNTRY.

to be done at Fort Oliphant.

On the 20th of November, Captain Dahl came into camp at the head of his Native Levy, 1,450 strong. He was a Dane, who had been in the United States Navy at the outset of the war in 1861, and after being in Meade's Army Corps, served in the Chinese Army, and was present at the massacre in Tientsin, after which he became a settler in the Transvaal. The Swazies were now on the march to Fort Weeber, but 1,350 Knob-noses, after proceeding twenty miles, deserted.

Sekukuni's "Fighting *Koppie*," as it was appropriately named, was naturally enough deemed impregnable by the Basutos, and there can be little doubt that had it been held by well-armed and disciplined infantry, and adequately provisioned, it could have been taken only after a regular siege and the expenditure of much shot and shell.

At first view it seemed a mighty and conical heap of boulders rising from the green plain to the altitude of some hundred feet, with a base of the same length, and in outline it was like a ridge pole marquee. Grey boulders and vast slabs of rock piled over each other formed the sides, and upon these and at the foot grew trees of great size and masses of jungly brushwood.

Viewed externally, it seemed to be only one of the ordinary hills called by the Dutch "*koppies*"; but it was in reality one of the most singularly cavernous hills in the world. Its whole interior was honeycombed by nature, intersected by passages and galleries leading into great chambers, with chinks, clefts, and crannies forming natural loopholes for musketry, and in one place there yawned an appalling chasm, which had never been fathomed, and was believed to contain water at the bottom. When in the agonies of thirst on the third day of their blockade, some of Sekukuni's people went down by means of great leather thongs tied together, none of them ever came up again; no noise was heard from them.

Those in the cavern overhead shouted again and again but got no reply, so those who went down into the dark depths presumably from one cause or another, died. The *koppie* has been described as being like a vast tortoiseshell, with massive rocky partitions and galleries within it, and had the Basutos been well supplied with provisions and water they might, as we have said, have made a very prolonged resistance. Its atmosphere was pleasant and cool.

The garrison which manned it was about 14,000 strong, but of these, only 4,000 could be depended upon for defence. The rest were better suited for scouting, and predatory or cattle-lifting expeditions.

When all was ready, Sir Garnet Wolseley left his camp near Fort Weeber on the 21st of November, and the banks of the Ngoaritse (a tributary of the Oliphant) were made lively for a time by the presence and departure of convoys of ox and mule waggons, the ambulance train, the Scots Fusiliers, with pipes playing and drums beating, the artillery under Knox, the horse regiments of Ferreira and Carrington, the advance and commissariat trains, with more than one squad of donkeys from the Zoutspansberg.

The aspect of the volunteer cavalry was somewhat varied and even picturesque. Carrington's Horse comprised all sorts and conditions of men, even Japanese and Americans, who had scanty prospects in life before them when the war ended and with it their five shillings *per diem*; while so wild and mutinous was their spirit that he was obliged to flog thirty-five of them in one day; and all the Dutch under Ferreira and in the Rustenberg force openly declared that they would join the Boers the moment they revolted.

On the night of the 22nd there was a dreadful storm, when Wolseley's tent was blown down; and all night long, through the canvas of the tents, the pink lightning in the western sky could be seen flashing, while a storm of dust swept through the camp with a rushing sound.

On the 23rd November, Commandant Ferreira and Captain Dahl with his Zoutspansberg natives, attacked the *kraal* of Umgane, one of Sekukuni's most valued adherents, and on the firing being heard in a valley some miles away, Sir Garnet Wolseley, Colonel Baker Russell, Colonel Brackenbury, Major MacCalmont, and Captain Maurice McCreagh of the Royal Artillery, galloped off to see the result

Entering the valley through which the Oliphant flows, the scene of this encounter was amid huge rocks and boulders, from which the storms and waterspouts of ages had long since washed the soil away, and yet enough seemed to remain for the roots of the palm-like *euphorbias* and the more humble tribes of lilaceous plants, that served to impart a greenness to the place.

As Sir Garnet's staff came cantering up over ground strewed by withered stalks and great yellow pumpkins, the sound of shots was heard amid the rocks, and clouds of smoke rolled over the hills in front

The latter proceeded from the huts of Umgane's *kraal*, which was now in flames, within its boundary hedge of gigantic cacti. All along the hillside above the *kraal* rose puffs of smoke, as the men of the Zoutspansberg contingent kept firing their muskets at those of Umgane, and the contest seemed a very confused one. And there was seen

Captain Dahl in his shirt-sleeves, an eye-witness says:

> Hoarse with thirst and shouting, in the midst of his savage-
> looking warriors, who were streaming out of the *kraal*, laden
> with skins, carcases, spears, baskets, and articles of native manu-
> facture, in much excitement, and he told Colonel Russell how
> he had stormed the hills in front of us, while Ferreira had car-
> ried the farthest ridge and gained the valley between two lines
> of mountain.

He gained more, for already some of his men had retired from
the fight with 300 head of cattle and many sheep and goats. He had
despatched 700 men up the steep slope between two hills commanding the *kraal*, and then sent 400 to the right, while Ferreira, pushing
on from the left, took his way up some precipitous hillsides, fighting
and disputing every foot of the way. Yet the defence was weak, for 500
good men might have held the place against ten times their number.

The writer before quoted says:

> Dahl had not tasted water for six hours, and the heat was op-
> pressive. Never shall I forget his look as he drank the water
> which Colonel Russell gave him from his bottle. "Umgane was
> killed and many of his people.

He was the first chief whose voice, at the councils of Sekukuni,
was for immediate war

Some women and children were also killed in the confusion. Umgane would seem to have been in a cavern, from whence he fired
at Dahl as the latter came up. The ball ricocheted from a rock, and
wounded Dahl in the hand, as he summoned Umgane to surrender,
promising that his life should be spared. The chief fiercely and scorn-
fully refused to capitulate, and fell dead under a volley which was fired
into his cavern. Dahl had only seven casualties.

Only about 200 men defended the *kraal*; all the rest were gone to
join Sekukuni. Some 300 women and children were captured. Many
of the former carried the latter in their arms and wept as they were
marched off by Dahl's men from their blazing homes; but Sir Garnet
Wolseley gave orders that all should be kindly treated and set free in
a day or two.

As Captain Stuart was coming down the hill, with a number of
Ferreira's Horse in Indian file, the sergeant-major stooped to take a
kaross, or mantle, from the mouth of a cave, and at that instant fell, shot

through the heart, at a time when it was thought that all the fighting was over, or nearly so. His comrades rushed into the cave, and every man found there was shot or cut down. The correspondent of the *Daily Telegraph* wrote:

> It would be well, if Irish or Highland peasants, or English ar-
> tisans, had such clean, well-kept, and comfortable homes, as
> those from which volumes of flame were coming in front of
> us, and the widespread cultivation around spoke well for the
> industry of the people who were killed or ruined—their houses
> destroyed, their wives and children carried into captivity; but
> it was hoped that the ease with which the place was taken,
> and the severity of the lesson would have a proper effect upon
> Sekukuni and his councillors. After a halt of half an hour or so
> in front of the *kraal*, and a consultation with Colonel Russell,
> Sir Garnet Wolseley turned to ride back to camp, passing on
> his way groups of the Zoutspansberg natives, in front of whom
> warriors were capering with musket and *assegai* in hand, show-
> ing how they had killed the Mekatees of the mountain.

After a thirty miles' ride the staff came back to camp hot and weary. Ferreira and Dahl received orders from Colonel Baker Russell to hold the advanced ground they had taken, and at an early hour in the morning all the mounted men available were sent under Major Carrington to the vicinity of Umgane's *kraal*, prior to the seizure of a post named the Water Koppie, within a short distance of Sekukuni's stronghold. That night the heat in camp at Albert Edward was oppressive— the very tents seemed to crackle with electricity.

So thus, ended the attack on Umgane.

Chapter 19
The Operations Against Sekukuni (Continued)

On the night of the 24th, notwithstanding the overpowering heat, a force of 300 mounted men with some infantry, 200 Scots Fusiliers and 200 94th, in mule waggons, proceeded from Fort Alexandra, which is seven miles distant from Albert Edward Camp, and seized without op-position the Water Koppie, where the infantry entrenched themselves. Five miles distant 8,000 Swazies, under Macleod and Bushman, from Fort Burgers had taken post, and with Sir Garnet Wolseley there were now 11,000 natives and 1,400 European troops.

As he intended to make the most of the moonlight, and cover the ground to the Water Koppie, which he considered the key to his position against Sekukuni, the headquarter tents were struck at four p.m. on the 26th, and preceded by the Scots Fusiliers, with their pipes and bugles playing alternately, the march began through a difficult country, to which, ere long, a thunderstorm caused the troops additional trouble by harassing and impeding the progress of the column, which instead of reaching the ground fresh and with a prospect of rest early on the 27th, did not get to camp till the evening sun was low in the sky, and all were wet, sodden, and weary. The 21st had been under arms for twenty-four hours consecutively, and without food.

All animals and waggons were put in *laager* under a strong guard; the bugles sounded "lights out" early, as orders were issued that the tents would be again struck at two am. on the morrow, and all lay down in their boots and clothing, lest the Basutos from the mountain should try a night attack, which they might have done in front and rear, as the ground was favourable for such movements, but the short night was passed in perfect quietude.

Thus, the force of Colonel Russell lay in *laager* upon the plain, within a mile and a half of the point of attack.

At two a.m. the orders went round to strike the tents; the low hum of voices passed along the canvas lines as each in succession went down, and the pegs and mallets were bagged by the light of the stars and lanterns, and in less than an hour all were under arms and formed up in front of the camping ground, near a rugged ravine, through which flowed a rain-swollen stream, that separated the troops from the point of attack, and all moved off in profound silence at half-past three.

The Lulu Mountain is divided in two by a gorge named the Matlake. The south-eastern portion is well watered, and, like many African mountains, of tabular form, so flat that cavalry might act on its summit, and it is accessible from several points.

But the north-west range, where Sekukuni dwelt, is difficult of access, rocky, and rugged. His *kraal*, or city, as it was called, could be approached from the north by means of a valley, but neither by guns, waggons, or horses. Below the town is a *koppie*, or isolated hill, 150 feet high, with a base of 600 feet round, which formed the key of the position.

We have already described this famous and cavernous stronghold. Amid the cyclopean masses of which it is formed, the entrances of the caves were not visible from the valley, which was fertile in maize, and lies between the two ranges of hills, and contracts to little more than a mile at the distance of two from the town, which was divided into three great blocks or *kraals*—one occupied by Holoqua, a brother of Sekukuni, the second by a chief named Sowazi, and the third by Sekukuni himself.

Westward of where Sekukuni's *kraal* stood, is a detached and conical *koppie*, ridged by great masses of sandstone, its sides, like those of the greater hills, generally covered with trees and bush; but parts there are which are merely bare masses of rock, between which were the entrances to the caverns, and these entrances were covered by stone walls, which became formidable obstacles to an attack delivered in front, though perhaps weak if enfiladed.

Sir Garnet Wolseley's "General Orders," issued on the 27th, gave a succinct account of what he intended should be done. The concentration of the Transvaal Field Force was achieved, as we have described, amid storm and rain. It was arranged that the Swazies from Fort Burgers, under Major Bushman and Captain Macleod, should crown the ridge above Sekukuni's town at a quarter past four in the morning, and move upon it eastward down the mountain side, while the main column in three divisions should deliver an attack from the west

The right under Ferreira, consisting of his own Horse, and the contingents of Rustenberg and Mapoch, was to assail the southern portion of the town at a quarter past four a.m. The central attack was to be made under Colonel Murray, with a detachment of his own regiment, the 94th, six companies of the Royal Scots Fusiliers, and a detachment of the 80th; four guns of the Transvaal Artillery and two of the Rustenberg companies covering the train of reserve ammunition, were also to attack the Fighting Koppie.

The left attack was under Major Carrington, 24th Regiment, and was composed of all the mounted men (Ferreira's excepted), the Rustenbergers, and Dahl's Zoutspanbergers, and was to be delivered on the north side of the town, from a ravine leading up the hill that commanded the centre of it.

A slender detachment was left to guard the *laager*, with the cattle and stores, under Lieutenant O'Dell, 52nd Foot, while Captains E. J. Henry Spratt, of the 29th, Fraser, 60th Rifles, Walter Glyn Lawrell, of the 4th Hussars, and Christian, of Ferreira's Light Horse, were appointed to act as orderly officers to Colonel Russell.

No bugle calls were to be permitted in the action.

The ground had been thoroughly reconnoitred, but as the troops advanced from the *laager*, across the ravine and the stream in the starlight, there was a good deal of splashing, discomfort, and toil in getting through the water; then Colonel Russell, with Captains Stewart, Spratt, and Lawrell, dismounted, and after giving their horses to grooms to be kept out of the fire, went forward to superintend the disposition of the attacking force. Sir Garnet, with Major Hugh M'Calmont, of the 4th Hussars, and Lieutenant-Colonel H. Brackenbury, R. A., the military secretary, an officer of very varied and distinguished service, took post to the left of the guns.

A writer says:

> If you were to stand on the level ground outside Holyrood, and look towards the Calton Hill on a fine moonlight night, you would see something like the outline of the hills over Sekuku-ni's Stadt. There were two or three watch-fires visible at the base, but all the intervening space was void, and in our camp there was silence, broken only by the neighing of horses.

The dawn came in clearly and brilliantly, enhancing the great natural beauty of the scenery, and adding interest to a very exciting episode; but the Basutos in their rocky eyries were enabled thereby to get a clearer view from the *schanzes*, to acquire the range, and their balls began to whistle close, while the white smoke, streaked with fire, spirted out of the dark cavern mouths.

At a quarter past four, as there was at first just sufficient light to discern the form and outline of the mountain fortress, about 500 yards distant, the Transvaal Artillery guns, under Captains Knox and Reid, and Lieutenant Brackenbury, were taken off the mules, put together and placed in position, as well as two 6-pounder Krupps and two 7-pounders; while Ferreira moving off to the right with 80 dismount-ed men—Mapoch's 600 *Kaffirs* did not appear—and Carrington to the left with 700 natives, 161 Volunteers, and 34 Mounted Infantry, ascended the hills with their men.

A graphic correspondent says:

> There was only a faint flush of dawn in the east, as the flash of the first gun, followed by the report and the smacking noise of the shell against the stronghold, woke up the echoes of the hills, and, ere the reverberation had rolled away in the valley, a fierce yell and the blast of innumerable war-horns from *koppie* and mountain announced that the Basutos were ready for us. The light of the bursting shells was now answered by the sparkle of musketry; but the enemy fired wildly and wasted their powder. Scarcely had the guns opened when the Basutos in caves on the

chain of hills in rear of the camp, began to join in, and for a few moments it seemed as if Sekukuni had hit upon the device of a counter attack; but the camp guards replied, and the annoyance on that side was properly estimated and discounted.

This was by the activity of Lieutenant O'Dell.

The Scots Fusiliers and 94th forming the centre took their ground quietly, and did not deliver any fire, while the guns pounded away till the sun was well up, and all the features of the place could be seen distinctly.

About six o'clock, against the clear sky line, numerous black dots or points were seen moving and massing along the crests of the hills, and descending into the savage *dongas* and rugged fissures.

These were some of Major Bushman's Swazies pouring down in dark and naked masses—naked, save for their leopard skin kilts, head-

BOVANE, THE SWAZI COMMANDER-IN-CHIEF.

dresses of ostrich feathers, and fillets of fox and lynx tails—with their cowhide shields, spears and sheafs of glittering *assegais*, towards the now blazing *kraals* where Carrington was already engaged. But their weapons were useless against the rifles of the Basutos, lodged in caves and behind rocks and stone walls; and they were compelled to retire in shattered masses under a dreadful fire, and seek shelter behind the crests, over which they had come, with their lofty feather head-dresses waving in the breeze.

Before this took place, it would seem that one column, 500 strong, had descended a gorge to the left of that which it should have taken, and became exposed to a dreadful fire from the Basutos perched on some near rocks. Unable to reply by a shot, with savage courage and rage, they made a furious rush up these cliffs, and caught the Basutos with their backs to one precipice, and their feet to another, and an eye-witness describes the scene that followed as a fearful one.

> Before the Basutos could re-load, the Swazies had fairly got among them, and hurled them down the cliff, not without great loss to themselves, for the Basutos clung to their enemies, met *assegai* with *assegai* and musket stock, and dragged their opponents over with them into the ravine, the edges of which were hemmed with vultures that evening. The column of Swazies on the right of the ledge of rocks, nearly 4,000 strong, began meantime to drive the Basutos down from crag to crag towards their left point
>
> As they advanced at 6.25, Ferreira pushed on from below, and the flames of the *kraals* of the king's town, and the rush of captured cattle into the plain, marked the line of his progress. Equally, on the left, the volumes of smoke from the northern town told where Carrington was, and his men could be seen all the morning working their way through the difficult bush and ravines filled with rocks, now halting to open concentrated fire on a *schanze*, now scrambling like goats along the ledges, till they joined hands with the Swazies in the centre, over the middle town.

Meanwhile Major Carrington, with the force already detailed, had worked his way round to the left, and had speedily become engaged with the Basutos on the hills above it. The Transvaal Mounted Rifles, and Border Horse quitting their saddles, charged up the hill on foot, and soon stormed the first line of *schanzes*, ably supported as they were

STORMING OF SEKUKUNI'S STRONGHOLD: SIR GARNET WOLSELEY CHEERING ON THE SWAZIES.

by the Mounted Infantry, under Lieutenant De Courcy O'Grady, of the 94th Regiment; and then the whole, rushing with cheers up the steep and rugged ground, drove the Basutos out of the second line of defences higher up, and won a ridge of sombre-looking rocks, though under a plunging downward fire, which ultimately drove back the Native Contingent; on this the men of Sekukuni made a rush upon Carrington's men and their horses below, but were compelled to retire under the withering fire that bowled them over in heaps.

About half-past six, the left wing of the Swazies appeared over the hill tops in this quarter, and came down towards the dark ridge just mentioned, and within an hour the united divisions had cleared out the caverns and defences of all but the dying and the dead, and then Major Carrington descended towards the central town, the huts of which he left sheeted with flame, as he worked his way downward to the plain. In the early part of this conflict. Captain Maurice, of the Artillery, had a dangerous wound in the shoulder, and Sergeant-Major Constable was conspicuous for his bravery.

During all this fighting the centre had been chiefly in observation; but a little after six a.m. the Scots Fusiliers deployed in front and on the left of the guns, towards the *koppie*, at a time when the Zoutspanbergers and Rustenbergers on the right refused to go on, though horsewhipped by Baker Russell and his *aide-de-camp*, though cursed by Dahl, and though they had roasted and eaten the right hand of the gallant Umgane (who had been killed shortly before) to inspire them with courage.

Ere the Scots Fusiliers deployed in skirmishing order, along their front poured a horde of Swazies, their *assegais* all bloody, laden with plunder from the burning *kraals*, and leading boys and girls by the hand—their own children they asserted them to be, who had gone up the mountain to see the fight; though it was strongly suspected they were little Basutos who were to become slaves in Swaziland.

The centre attack under Lieutenant-Colonel John Murray, of the 94th, was directed chiefly against the stronghold alone. A portion of the Scots Fusiliers, in skirmishing order, kept up a fire on what was called "the tower," from which the enemy had exchanged shots with them before the advance. The 94th, under Major Anstruther, on the right of the Transvaal Artillery, had been similarly engaged from an early hour till a quarter to ten. For four consecutive hours the *koppie* had been shelled, doing no great physical damage to the enemy, till two of the guns were sent round to the left to take it in flank, and it was to this manoeuvre the Scots Fusiliers conformed.

From the cavernous recesses of the *koppie* various kinds of bullets came pinging, whistling or whirring, for some were fragments of stone lapped in lead, and others were big charges from elephant guns. A man of the 80th had his spine traversed by one, as he lay on the ground taking "pot shots;" a snider ball killed Colonel Russell's horse under him. The Fusiliers and 94th never permitted a puff of smoke to appear without paying close attention to the spot from which it issued.

The chief attack of the centre column was made by the Scots Fusiliers and two companies of the 94th, under Captain George Froom, on their left, with one company of the same regiment on their right, while a third was in reserve; and in the advance, the fusiliers had two men killed, two officers and eleven men wounded, and the 94th seven, thus proving how bad was the general firing of Sekukuni's thousands.

The correspondent with the staff says:

> At eight o'clock, the scene was a mere spectacle, but one of extraordinary animation and beauty. There were still puffs of smoke cropping out on the hillsides, where some of the Swazies were hunting the Basutos to death in their caves; but the gross tumult of the musketry was restricted to the plain. The *kraals* vomiting out smoke and tongues of fire formed the chord of an arc of nearly one and a half mile long. From the centre town on the left, all round the Fighting Koppie to the right, the plain was seamed by the regular red lines of the British infantry firing on the fortress, with shifting clouds of Swazies, Zoutspanbergers, Mapoch's Kaffirs, and Rustenbergers looking on, enjoying the fusillade, and especially interested in the practice of two guns which had now been moved round to the north side of the *koppie*. Several changes of position were made occasionally, and from eight to half-past eight the skirmishers were pushed nearer and nearer.

Every man in the detachment of the 80th—save one who was ill—volunteered to join in the assault when it was to be delivered; and by nine, when the cannonade ceased, and the crisis was approaching, there was a silence over all the place, excepting an occasional shot or so, the blowing of war-horns and the crackle of the burning *kraals* that shrouded the hills and ravines in smoke.

Anon the guns opened more briskly than ever, and the orders were issued for "a general advance to carry the *koppie* by storm." This was about a quarter to ten o'clock. When the signal was given by two rockets from the left—one to "prepare," the second to "advance," with ringing cheers the Scots Fusiliers and 94th made a rush at the stronghold in splendid order. In ten minutes, the rocks seemed alive with red-coats and Swazies, half seen, half hidden in eddies of smoke. Sword in hand Baker Russell led them on from his point of the position. Ferreira rushed on from the right, and the leading companies of the 94th had a regular race to be first at the *koppie* with the 21st, whose pipers were soon at the foot of it:

> Beating the ground with their feet and filling the air with the breath of battle, while playing with infernal energy, sending out skirls which sounded far above the fusillade, the screams and yells of the combatants.

So rapid was the advance, so furious the rush, that scarcely a man dropped till the troops were inside the place. Fire and smoke still spouted from cave and cranny, and every Basuto who failed to win cover perished on the spot; but many a Swazi, with feathers, shield, and *assegai*, came crashing down the rocks, which perhaps his bare feet had failed to surmount; and wild and picturesque was the intermingling of tattered uniforms, with native war-gear in the *mêlée*, while the Europeans strove to wriggle through the narrow entrances of the well manned caverns, and to close hand to hand with those who were within.

The three towns were all in flames below, but by eleven o'clock the *koppie* was solidly held by British troops—the 21st and 94th—who crowned its summit; below them the whole hillsides seemed alive with Swazies—led by Bushman, Campbell, and Macleod—with volunteers and men of the Native Contingents, all closing in and upward to join in the conflict.

Colonels Murray, of the 94th, and Hazlerigg, of the 21st, large men, on large horses, though conspicuous objects, escaped the enemy's fire; and Colonel Russell, steaming with perspiration, for the day was one of intense heat, hurried on foot—as his horse had been shot—to congratulate Sir Garnet on the successful attack, though the fighting was not yet over. The *Daily Telegraph's* correspondent says:

> At 10.30, the Fighting Koppie, in which Sekukuni enshrined his faith, belonged practically to Queen Victoria; but inside its stony bowels was still hidden a band of desperate and resolute men, of women and children, of wounded and dead—a

fearful combination. When next day the resources of science were brought to bear on the hard rocks, and gun-cotton or dynamite—perhaps both—in the skilful hands of Captain M'Gregor, tore open the caves or filled them with a rain of broken boulders, and the madness of thirst and hunger, and the stench of corpses came upon the survivors, in that dreadful charnel-house, there must have been an accumulation of horrors not easy to match in the records of human misery and endurance. . . .

No Highlander of bygone days—no follower of the ancient Lochiels, of the Farquharsons of old, or the Forbeses of Newe—could display more devotion to their chief than these black fellows to Sekukuni They died in the *koppie*; when all was over, they sought death almost certain in attempts to break through our lines, driven desperate as they were by thirst and starvation, because he told them not to surrender, and they guarded the secret of his hiding-place most tenaciously, coming out of their caves and giving themselves up to their mortal enemies in the hope of deceiving the pursuers by the assurance that the king was not there.

The explosions when the caves were blown up by gun-cotton on the 29th reverberated among the mountains loud as tropical thunder.

The 1st of December found the chief Mapeshla, a fat and stout man, with others still holding out among the remaining caverns, and though two companies of the Scots Fusiliers, under Captain Daniel Auchinleck, were detailed to watch the caves and prevent their defenders from coming out to the springs, on that day many wretched creatures came out screaming—

"Water—water! give us water!"

The fusiliers did not fire on them, but an interpreter informed them that if they surrendered, they should receive both food and water.

These gallant Basutos had been lords of the land for three centuries and more, and had never before been conquered. There is a tradition among them, says the graphic writer last quoted, that long years ago, an expedition of white men clad in steel came out of the sea, and all perished among the mountains, where up to this day, old wheellock muskets are found in the caverns. These men are supposed to have been Portuguese musketeers from Delagoa Bay, who called their settlement Lorenzo Marques, after its first discoverer in 1544.

On the 1st of December, Sekukuni was still holding out, and the most of our troops, with their coats thrown off, unable to wear them in the heat, were watching the caverns, rifle in hand, clad only in their trousers and shirts.

The Victoria Cross was bestowed on Privates Flawn and Fitzpatrick, two Irishmen of the 94th, for bravery here on the 28th of November, in carrying out of action. Lieutenant Cumming Dewar, of the 1st Dragoon Guards, who had a thigh shattered by a bullet. At the time he fell, he had with him only these two soldiers and six of the Native Contingent. Being incapable of moving without assistance, the latter proceeded to carry him down the hill, but deserted him, when some thirty of the enemy appeared in pursuit, about forty yards distant; and he must have been killed, but for the humanity and valour of Privates Flawn and Fitzpatrick, who carried him alternately, one covering the retreat and firing on the enemy.

On the evening of the 28th November, when McGregor began to blow up the caverns, and enormous masses of rock were tossed upwards, a party was seen to escape from one—and among those composing it was Sekukuni, who was recognised. A strong detachment of the Scots Fusiliers was sent up to cut off all access to water from the new cave in which he had taken shelter—called the Marine Cavern, twelve miles up the mountain, and there he surrendered at six a.m. on the morning of the 2nd December, to Major Clarke and Commandant Ferreira. He and his immediate followers were without food, and there he made his last desperate stand. There was some firing without any casualty on our side, and after an attempt had been made to light a fire at the cavern's mouth and smoke him out, he surrendered, and was borne out on a stretcher, and conveyed to the camp in a waggon, surrounded by crowds of men, women and children.

He proved to be a thin elderly man, bent with rheumatism, with a face of that type belonging to his race the Mekatees, as the Dutch name them, though we term them Basutos. His wife, a pleasant-looking young woman, with a babe in her arms, and a boy at her knee, accompanied him into the bell-tent that was assigned him, under a guard.

Our losses amid all this, fighting were not severe—some twelve Europeans killed and fifty-six wounded, yet the Swazies lost at least 300—some say 500—killed. But they never counted their dead, nor cared for them, and scarcely ever carried off their wounded

Captain Macaulay, of the Transvaal Mounted Rifles (late of H.M. Lancers), and Captain Walter Glyn Lawrell, of the 4th Hussars, were killed—the latter as he was leading Captains Brackenbury and Spratt, both heavier men, up the rocks. He was shot through the head by a Basuto, whom his servant, an old hussar, shot immediately afterwards. Captains Maurice McCreagh, R.A., MacCorbie of Baker's Horse, and Beeton of the Native Contingent, with Lieutenants O'Grady, 94th, and Dewar, K.D.G., were among the wounded

Among those who fell leading the Swazies was a Scottish soldier of fortune, popularly known as "Shipka" Campbell, whose loss was greatly regretted, and who there closed a career so varied and adventurous that we are tempted to notice it briefly.

A. H. Campbell had come to South Africa in 1878, on a tour of exploration, after having served at the storming of several *pahs* in the New Zealand War, and after serving as major, under Suleiman Pasha, at the Shipka Pass. He became the idol of the Turkish troops, and in the intervals of military duty acted as correspondent for a leading London paper. He led the forlorn hope at the storming of the Russian Fort St Nicholas at the head of a few hundred men, with remarkable bravery. He fought in the Kamarli Pass, and when the Ottoman Army fell back across the snow-clad wastes of Roumelia, the last officer to embark on board the fleet was Shipka Campbell.

He intended to explore Africa up to Timbuctoo, but the Zulu War caused him to change his mind He proceeded to Swaziland, seeking there to enlist the sympathies of the natives in the British cause. He was a man of robust and powerful frame, and hardships that would have killed other men had no effect on him. As a soldier of fortune, he was ever ready to go anywhere and do anything. He came with Macleod and the Swazies against Sekukuni. During the engagement on the 28th November, he was warned not to go near a certain cave as it was full of Basutos; but heedless of the advice, he stooped down to enter, and rolled over dead under a volley from its recesses, and we believe his body was never found, though minute searches were made in the caves, into one of which the Basutos are supposed to have dragged it. He had a presentiment he was to fall, of which he spoke many times before the action, and he rashly seemed to do his best to bring his fate about.

Captains Lawrell and Macaulay, with six European privates, were buried in a row outside the camp, at six in the morning.

Sekukuni was sent in a mule waggon to Pretoria, together with his wife, two daughters, his brother, and two attendants. He was not without fear of being killed by the Swazies *en route*. He was sick, and now laid the blame of the war on his chiefs and people, who would not consent to pay taxes or tribute to the British.

To Major Clarke was assigned the charge of his "country," as it is named.

Sekukuni arrived with Sir Garnet Wolseley at Pretoria on the 9th of December. His reported treasure of gold coin and diamonds, we need scarcely say, was not discovered, though Commandant Ferreira prosecuted an active search for it. Many women who had been captured by the Swazies were taken from them by order of Sir Garnet Wolseley and set at liberty; but many more with their children perished in the exploded caverns of the Fighting Koppie.

A series of military posts was established throughout the acquired district, under Colonel Murray of the 94th, who was placed in command of a Flying Column, to dominate the Lulu Mountain. On its southern slope, Fort Victoria was to be held by two companies of the 94th, some of the Native Contingent, and twenty Transvaal Mounted Riflemen, under Captain James Browne of the 94th.

Fort Albert, with a little garrison, held the other slope; while Forts Albert Edward, Oliphant, Weeber, and Burgers, were all to be similarly maintained, and it was confidently hoped that, in a short time, Sekukuni being hopelessly a captive, all his mountaineers would submit

The headquarters now marched for Pretoria by the bush *veldt* road and crossed the Oliphant—a difficult process as the stream had become swollen; the heat was great and supplies were scanty.

The troops brought away with them all the captured arms. In most cases these were of very inferior quality—old Tower muskets, that probably had done service under Wellington, as many of them had flint locks, or were early percussion old rifles and double-barrelled guns. The pouches were full of substitutes for bullets, and there was plenty of powder in large buffalo horns.

The march back to the recently annexed Transvaal was very arduous. A correspondent says:

> It was usual to have the tents struck at three a.m., and to start at half-past three, for there was moonlight, and how the lions, leopards, and wolves put up with such irruption in their hunting time, I do not know; but I can answer for its effect on my own temper, when aggravated by sun, dust, and slow riding for thirty miles a day through the stifling bush. Sometimes, by way of a change, the tents were struck at half-past two; in fact we only went to sleep in order to be roused again, and when a halt

came, every man sought out a bush and took a short repose, the men who were carried in the waggons having by far the best time of it, for the officers had to ride, and the jog, jog, day after day, made one hate the sight of a saddle.

This was a common experience.

The arrival of the fallen Sekukuni at Pretoria afforded the inhabitants an opportunity for great rejoicings; and there was a review and field day, which—though the troops were rather tattered and patched in costume—was deemed the finest military spectacle ever witnessed, as yet, in the Transvaal. On this remarkable occasion there went past in marching order, Curling's Battery of 9-pounders, the 1st Dragoon Guards, the 4th or King's, the 58th Rutlandshire, and the 80th Staffordshire, under Colonel Harrison; and it was on this occasion also that Sir Garnet Wolseley bestowed the Victoria Cross upon Commandant D'Arcy in presence of all the troops and people.

LEONAUR

ALSO FROM LEONAUR

AVAILABLE IN SOFTCOVER OR HARDCOVER WITH DUST JACKET

THE FALL OF THE MOGHUL EMPIRE OF HINDUSTAN *by H. G. Keene*—By the beginning of the nineteenth century, as British and Indian armies under Lake and Wellesley dominated the scene, a little over half a century of conflict brought the Moghul Empire to its knees.

LADY SALE'S AFGHANISTAN *by Florentia Sale*—An Indomitable Victorian Lady's Account of the Retreat from Kabul During the First Afghan War.

THE CAMPAIGN OF MAGENTA AND SOLFERINO 1859 *by Harold Carmichael Wylly*—The Decisive Conflict for the Unification of Italy.

FRENCH'S CAVALRY CAMPAIGN *by J. G. Maydon*—A Special Correspondent's View of British Army Mounted Troops During the Boer War.

CAVALRY AT WATERLOO *by Sir Evelyn Wood*—British Mounted Troops During the Campaign of 1815.

THE SUBALTERN *by George Robert Gleig*—The Experiences of an Officer of the 85th Light Infantry During the Peninsular War.

NAPOLEON AT BAY, 1814 *by F. Loraine Petre*—The Campaigns to the Fall of the First Empire.

NAPOLEON AND THE CAMPAIGN OF 1806 *by Colonel Vachée*—The Napoleonic Method of Organisation and Command to the Battles of Jena & Auerstädt.

THE COMPLETE ADVENTURES IN THE CONNAUGHT RANGERS *by William Grattan*—The 88th Regiment during the Napoleonic Wars by a Serving Officer.

BUGLER AND OFFICER OF THE RIFLES *by William Green & Harry Smith*—With the 95th (Rifles) during the Peninsular & Waterloo Campaigns of the Napoleonic Wars.

NAPOLEONIC WAR STORIES *by Sir Arthur Quiller-Couch*—Tales of soldiers, spies, battles & sieges from the Peninsular & Waterloo campaingns.

CAPTAIN OF THE 95TH (RIFLES) *by Jonathan Leach*—An officer of Wellington's sharpshooters during the Peninsular, South of France and Waterloo campaigns of the Napoleonic wars.

RIFLEMAN COSTELLO *by Edward Costello*—The adventures of a soldier of the 95th (Rifles) in the Peninsular & Waterloo Campaigns of the Napoleonic wars.

LEONAUR

ALSO FROM LEONAUR

LEONAUR

ALSO FROM LEONAUR
AVAILABLE IN SOFTCOVER OR HARDCOVER WITH DUST JACKET

ZULU:1879 by D.C.F. Moodie & the Leonaur Editors—The Anglo-Zulu War of 1879 from contemporary sources: First Hand Accounts, Interviews, Dispatches, Official Documents & Newspaper Reports.

THE RED DRAGOON by W.J. Adams—With the 7th Dragoon Guards in the Cape of Good Hope against the Boers & the Kaffir tribes during the 'war of the axe' 1843-48'.

THE RECOLLECTIONS OF SKINNER OF SKINNER'S HORSE by James Skinner—James Skinner and his 'Yellow Boys' Irregular cavalry in the wars of India between the British, Mahratta, Rajput, Mogul, Sikh & Pindarree Forces.

A CAVALRY OFFICER DURING THE SEPOY REVOLT by A. R. D. Mackenzie—Experiences with the 3rd Bengal Light Cavalry, the Guides and Sikh Irregular Cavalry from the outbreak to Delhi and Lucknow.

A NORFOLK SOLDIER IN THE FIRST SIKH WAR by J W Baldwin—Experiences of a private of H.M. 9th Regiment of Foot in the battles for the Punjab, India 1845-6.

TOMMY ATKINS' WAR STORIES: 14 FIRST HAND ACCOUNTS—Fourteen first hand accounts from the ranks of the British Army during Queen Victoria's Empire.

THE WATERLOO LETTERS by H. T. Siborne—Accounts of the Battle by British Officers for its Foremost Historian.

NEY: GENERAL OF CAVALRY VOLUME 1—1769-1799 by Antoine Bulos—The Early Career of a Marshal of the First Empire.

NEY: MARSHAL OF FRANCE VOLUME 2—1799-1805 by Antoine Bulos—The Early Career of a Marshal of the First Empire.

AIDE-DE-CAMP TO NAPOLEON by Philippe-Paul de Ségur—For anyone interested in the Napoleonic Wars this book, written by one who was intimate with the strategies and machinations of the Emperor, will be essential reading.

TWILIGHT OF EMPIRE by Sir Thomas Ussher & Sir George Cockburn—Two accounts of Napoleon's Journeys in Exile to Elba and St. Helena: Narrative of Events by Sir Thomas Ussher & Napoleon's Last Voyage: Extract of a diary by Sir George Cockburn.

PRIVATE WHEELER by William Wheeler—The letters of a soldier of the 51st Light Infantry during the Peninsular War & at Waterloo.